BURN
THE PAGE

BURN THE PAGE

A TRUE STORY OF
TORCHING DOUBTS,
BLAZING TRAILS,
AND IGNITING CHANGE

Danica Roem

VIKING

VIKING
An imprint of Penguin Random House LLC
penguinrandomhouse.com

LIBRARY OF CONGRESS CATALOGING-IN-PUBLICATION DATA
Names: Roem, Danica, author.
Title: Burn the Page : A True Story of Torching Doubts,
Blazing Trails, and Igniting Change / Danica Roem.
Description: [New York, New York] : Viking, [2022]
Identifiers: LCCN 2021050737 (print) | LCCN 2021050738 (ebook) |
ISBN 9780593296554 (hardcover) | ISBN 9780593296561 (ebook)
Subjects: LCSH: Roem, Danica. | Virginia. General Assembly. House of Delegates—
Biography. | Transgender legislators—Virgina—Biography. | Transgender journalists—
United States—Biography. | Virginia—Politics and government—1951–
Classification: LCC F231.3.R64 A3 2022 (print) | LCC F231.3.R64 (ebook) |
DDC 975.5044092 [B]—dc23/eng/20220119
LC record available at https://lccn.loc.gov/2021050737
LC ebook record available at https://lccn.loc.gov/2021050738

Printed in the United States of America
1st Printing

BOOK DESIGN BY LUCIA BERNARD

Some names and identifying characteristics have been changed
to protect the privacy of the individuals involved.

To Tal and Ellu

To quote the great philosopher Little Kitten . . . ::*ahem*::

"Maow!"

Contents

INTRODUCTION

This is a book about both the importance of the stories we tell one another and the power in setting fire to the stories you don't want to be in anymore, whether written by you or written about you by someone else. I'm writing it for the person I was in 2016 when I lived in a much different story than the one I'm in now.

Picture it: a five-foot-eleven, long-haired brunette metalhead trans lady reporter wearing a rainbow bandanna, an A-line skirt, and a black hoodie—okay, got that visual? Now she's screaming obscenities behind the wheel of her four-door '92 Dodge Shadow America (. . . in 2016). She's just shy of her thirty-second birthday; she's 1.5 years into her first-ever long-term relationship and she has a negative net worth of tens of thousands of dollars *after* paying off her college loans. As usual, she's half an hour late to her weekend job at a kebab shop, thanks to an insane commute in her $324 rust bucket, which has been painted primer blue—as in, primer and blue.

Her job involves delivering food, plus some washing of trays, the occasional cutting of baklava, the placing of drinks in the slide-door fridge, and the ladling of tzatziki sauce into tiny to-go cups. The only thing going right in her life at the moment is the state of her calves, which look amazing after sprinting up and down every apartment staircase in Arlington.

This woman is lonely as hell. As she shuffles into the kebab shop kitchen, she mumbles "Hi, hi, hi" to all of her coworkers, then barely speaks to anyone again for ten or eleven hours, instead staring at the walls between tasks—she can't afford a smartphone to distract her, let alone health insurance, and the weight of those facts keeps her mind busy in the silence. Her coworkers would be shocked to learn that she's an extrovert. In fact, they would be surprised to learn that she even likes people at all. She doesn't mean to be a predictably ironic lady dick to anyone; she just has no idea how the $5 hourly pre-tip wage she's ended up making at thirty-one is somehow lower than the $5.15 an hour she pulled in at fifteen.

By this point in her life, this woman has also logged ten years of experience and thousands of bylines as a local reporter. She has interviewed the last six governors of Virginia multiple times each. She's on a first-name basis with U.S. senator Tim Kaine, who at the time was running for vice president. But she's been laid off twice in two years—first from covering state and federal political campaigns for *The Hotline* (often referred to as the "Bible of American politics," which aggregates news clips about candidates running for office and features original reporting in the morning, afternoon, and evening news releases) and then from Yoga Alliance (a nonprofit dedicated to credentialing registered yoga teachers). By mid-2016, she has been on hormone replacement therapy (HRT) for 2.5 years, and while her physical appearance is aligning more with where she wants to be, it seems employers may think otherwise—she has sent out application after application for a real job with benefits, but no one is biting.

She's tried the entrepreneur thing by opening a mobile yoga studio that plays heavy metal. It went belly-up within months of her selling out the first two classes, though the sight of a bunch of people in black hoodies stretching out into downward-facing dog to the soundtrack of *The Pursuit of Vikings* by the Swedish metal band Amon Amarth made those months so worth it. It turns out she has a lot to learn. Even a nonprofit transgender-rights organization in need of a storyteller recently passed her over—a transgender storyteller—for another transgender storyteller with flashier credentials. That's a pretty special level of fail, if you think about it.

So the Afghan Kabob House it is: a job where she spends more money than she makes, thanks to the endless car repairs, but one where the boss hired her after two interview questions—"You speak fluent English? That's good. Can you start Monday?" She's got this gig and one other: a part-time reporting job for a local paper in Rockville, Maryland, offered by an editor who told her during the interview, "Why the fuck would you want to work here? This job pays for shit." She works seven days a week and has missed out on five months worth of weekends with her partner and stepdaughter, because that's what happens when you're a "lazy millennial" with a B.A. working two jobs without benefits.

This woman has dreamed of ditching it all to become a full-time touring musician—but that dream is on its last legs, too. She's been a fixture on the local metal scene for a long time, but transitioning as a live musician hasn't just been scary—it has involved her trying to figure out on-the-fly who *she* is onstage. Usually, metal chicks work that out as goth teenagers, but when you're in your early thirties, you can only slather on so much fake-tortured eyeliner before it creeps its way into your crow's-feet.

Her friends have all been cool with her transition, but now that her voice isn't holding up live—in fact, it's become more and more timid—she finds herself losing confidence. Meanwhile, her band hasn't been practicing much, and the gigs are few and far between since both Jaxx and Ball's Bluff Tavern—two staples of the Northern Virginia metal scene—closed. The dream isn't just slipping; it's on a glide path out the door.

On top of it all, this woman happens to live in a country where Donald Trump is about to accept the Republican presidential nomination, and forty-nine LGBTQ people and their allies have just been shot to death at Pulse nightclub in Orlando. The morning after the Pulse shooting, she drove, completely dazed, around Arlington and Georgetown, sobbing her way through deliveries as NPR reported a seemingly endless increasing body count, fighting to maintain a stoic face every time she handed a plastic bag of lamb and lentils to someone whose rent for their two-bedroom apartment cost far more than she would make that month.

This poor woman is crying—a lot. And not just because the terrible shift in the political climate feels unstoppable. She lives in Virginia, where at the start of the 2016 Virginia General Assembly session, a few months before she started the kebab job, Republican state delegates filed nine anti-LGBTQ bills—the most in any state legislature in the country. She's been trying to assume a more activist role in her community, carving out a few mornings a week to go down to Richmond and talk to legislators about voting against these awful bills. Despite her efforts, she's feeling pretty pessimistic.

While in Richmond, she doesn't even bother talking with her own state legislator. He's a right-wing fixture as permanent as the Lost Cause Confederate statues in her hometown. This man, Bob Marshall, was first elected to office in 1991, when she was seven years old. During her first year as a working journalist in 2006, he proudly declared to *The Washington Post* that he was Virginia's "chief homophobe." That same year, he authored a state constitutional amendment to ban all legal recognition of same-sex couples, and Virginia voters approved it, passing it by 13 percentage points.

Ten years later, the man hasn't shifted course at all. He's authored two of the nine anti-LGBTQ bills she's protesting. Every January, as Marshall and the rest of the state legislature converge on Richmond for the opening session, she asks herself, "Which of my civil rights am I going to lose this year?"

What this sad-ass woman doesn't realize, though, is that today, August 4, 2016, when she gets home from work, she's going to get an email. This email will impart a lesson she'll never forget: Life can change in an instant, even if said instant involves no material transformation, no births or deaths or sudden financial windfalls.

Instead, what it does is shift this woman's self-perception—the way she's been connecting the dots of her life into a bigger story. A new picture emerges in her mind: She's no longer Danica the inadequate failure, Danica the dead end. Instead, she's standing at a turning point: the moment when her story becomes the origin story *I now recognize as my own.*

The email is from Don Shaw, the Democratic nominee who ran against Bob Marshall in 2015 and abandoned a plan to run a second time in 2017. By that point, we had met many times over the course of my recent activism work. His email is short and poses a quick question: "You live in the 13th—have you given any thought to running against Marshall? You'd make a fantastic candidate! ;-)"

My inner Ralph Wiggum is the first to react: "Me run for office?

That's unpossible!" I stare blankly at the screen for a bit, say "Huh!" and walk away from my laptop and the open email.

That little "huh" follows me around the rest of that Thursday night, floating about me like an ember. When I climb into bed and try to go to sleep, the ember drifts down and sets my sheets on fire. The following afternoon, when I get a follow-up call from Rip Sullivan, recruiting chairman of the House Democratic Caucus, I grin around the big bags under my eyes. I'll need a couple of months to wind down my work at the newspaper and the restaurant and I'll need to get trained, but if everything works out by December, then I'll do it. I'll take on Bob Marshall. I'll find a way to win.

Go figure: On November 5, 2019, a little more than three years from my dark nights at the kebab house, I was reelected to Virginia's House of Delegates, proving that my 2017 victory over Bob Marshall was more than a fluke. Since I took office, I've helped bring health insurance to 600,000 Virginians—and counting—who didn't have it before. I helped the Democratic Party take back not just the House of Delegates but total control of the Virginia government for the first time since 1993. My colleagues and I, in our first year in the majority, voted for Virginia to ratify the Equal Rights Amendment to the Constitution of the United States after a nearly one-hundred-year fight—one win of many during our two-year majority.

On top of that—because every thirtysomething kebab delivery girl knows how this goes—in the past five years I've sung onstage with Arcade Fire's Will Butler, received a congratulatory phone call from Joe Biden, promoted anti-bullying efforts with Demi Lovato at the American Music Awards, spoken at the 2020 Democratic National Convention, and starred in a *Vice* news documentary about winning grassroots elections. Oh, and the Westboro Baptist Church (WBC), of "God hates fags!" fame, protested my existence as a trans woman in the legislature in Richmond, which led Randy Blythe, vocalist of the quite appropriately named metal band Lamb of God, to lead a two-hundred-person-strong counterparty that drowned out WBC's worst for half an hour with . . . kazoos.

Governor Ralph Northam signed twenty-three of my bills into law during my first two terms; we passed the largest transportation funding bill since 1986 and raised teacher pay; and my 2017 victory inspired trans folks across the country to run for office, increasing our number of out-and-seated transgender state legislators from one in 2018 to four in 2019 to eight in 2021, including the first trans state senator, Sarah McBride of Delaware. I even earned a third term!

Life can change in an instant. It can change *in an instant*. I am living proof of what can happen when you discover that your story doesn't have to be what you thought it was. Reality doesn't have to follow the pacing and predictability of fiction, and neither do you.

Of course, my own story continues to unfold within a bigger national one, and the latter is far from complete. None of us knows exactly where all of this is headed or what to do. On a national level, we've spent two years fighting a global pandemic that's killed millions of people around the world while also battling something much more visible: racism, bigotry, and hate. On the local level, however, we're identifying the diamonds in the rough who are willing to channel their frustrations into activism, not giving in to the politics of defeatism but choosing instead to look at the challenges as obstacles to be overcome.

That's why I felt called to write this book: to encourage more of those diamonds in the rough to unearth themselves from mind-sets and lives that they don't need to be in anymore. When I think about it, each of the most important developments in my own life has involved a moment in which I rejected a narrative that no longer worked for me: a moment in which I realized that I could tell other people *myself* what my story was going to be instead of accepting their interpretation of a life they'd never lived.

Each of the chapters that follows is about one of these moments in my life. Fundamentally, this is a book about politics (also: *Simpsons* jokes, awkward hookup stories, flaming beer bongs). In part, it was inspired by the opposition research I hired a team to do on me during my first two elections, as well as some of the narratives that ended up as news headlines. My team's job was to dig up every potentially embarrassing thing that's out there (they got . . . some of it) and give me a bulleted list of anything anybody could ever use to shame me so that I had time to think through my responses and figure out which body pillow made for the most comfortable fetal-position accessory.

Some of what they found was accurate, some of it was not, and some of it was just so outlandish that it seemed like a prank. They were definitely right about one thing, though: My challengers found and used a lot of the same information. (There's nothing like watching a television ad portraying me as a conceited whore when I knew it was a total absolute lie: I am *not* conceited!) But it's become clear to me that the stories we tell ourselves and the stories other people tell about us have tremendous political power. True power never comes from trying to fit yourself into someone else's story. When people tell you to look and act a certain way to be powerful, they're telling you this to keep you *out* of their power, not to share it. To have power, you have to generate it for yourself. You have to show other people who it is you are and how it is you can help them to achieve their own dreams.

As more and more women enter politics, we hear people frequently use the word "electable" when talking about candidates for office. That word keeps so many people who have been historically unrepresented in our politics—LGBTQ+ people, women, Black and Brown people, non-Black or Brown people of color—out of power. That word "electable" has weight and power. It is a story in itself. It matters.

Nothing about my life screams "electable" (or even "hygienic") on paper. I've woken up in more than sixty parking lots across the country (and ranked my top forty!) due to years of road trips, long commutes, and *deep breath* *heavy fuckin' metal*. But you know what? I couldn't be prouder of (most of) the shit that's out there on me. I embraced who I was and authentically showed up on the campaign trail—talking to people about all of the things to vote *for*, all of the things we could accomplish together.

The facts of your life are what they are. The question is: Are you going to tell your own story about them, or are you going to let other people do that for you? I wrestled with that premise when setting out to write this book. Why would people across the country care what I have to say as a thirtysomething white trans lady state rep who spends her days trying to fix roads, feed hungry kids, and do all the basics of legislating in the western burbs of Northern Virginia?

Well, the fact that I didn't come from central casting and that I put my warts and flaws on full display for the public at large to see might be the sort of story that resonates with people. You don't have to have the text of the Equal Rights Amendment tattooed on your left arm, take six milligrams of estradiol a day, or grow your hair out long enough to serve as a stunt double for Cousin Itt of *The Addams Family* to relate to being different, to being the only person like you in the room. (But it helps.)

A lot of people—especially women—worry that if they run for office, not only will they be attacked with negative ads (spoiler alert: they will) but that every screw-up in their lives will be laid bare as a carcass of sadness on a roadside buffet, left to the political vultures who are paid to follow the tire treads to their feast. They don't want to be judged for their faults, even though the very scavengers picking at what's left of their emotional flesh have probably done far worse than they ever will. (Those bastards!)

There's just one catch, though: What happens if there is nothing left to pick at because you've already mounted it on a wall?

What if you could go from flattened roadkill to finely coiffed taxidermy?

Behold, the modern campaign: Be the taxidermist! Own your narrative. Put your shit out there. Let everyone gaze into the plastic eyes of your severed head affixed to a pike coming out of a board attached to a wall and think, "She's got my vote!"

So that's what I decided to do: stuff the hell out of what was supposed to be my political corpse by putting my whole self out there for others to see before my opposition could tear me apart. When they tried, it backfired and failed so miserably that the weekend after the 2017 election, Michael Che of *Saturday Night Live* remarked about my predecessor, Bob Marshall, the self-described "chief homophobe" of Virginia, "In fact, he's so homophobic, he refused to get within eight points of her."

Doing research on yourself is a must for any high-stakes campaign, but what I learned was about more than any single campaign or even just about politics. Striving to embrace my flaws and mistakes was also an effort to claim every part of my story as my own and, in doing so, demonstrate actual power. The day Don Shaw asked me to run for office, knowing exactly who I was, he showed me how to have power. I hope I'm doing that same thing today for every little closeted kid in America, showing that it's possible to live a big and honest life and be successful *because* of who you are, not despite it.

I hope the stories that follow will inspire you to thrive because of who you are, too, no matter what you look like, where you come from, how you worship (if you do), or who you love. If you've got good ideas, bring them to the table—because this is *your* America, too, and it's time for you to run it.

BURN
THE PAGE

CHAPTER 1

LOSER

Danica Roem was born September 30, 1984. She received an undergraduate degree from St. Bonaventure in 2006. . . . She either lives with her mother or does not live where she claims to live, which would be potentially illegal.

—Friends of Danica Roem self-opposition research for 2019, conducted by Reger Research

O n the night of November 5, 2019, I looked to my right and saw my partner standing over my right shoulder. I reached up for a kiss, and with the sultry, passionate exhale of a young Sassenach whose dream of seduction has finally been realized, I whispered, "I get to keep my health insurance."

At thirty-five, I achieved the fantasy of every progressive suburban woman in Trump's America: two more years of little to no co-pays to make up for my $17,640 salary. I had also just been reelected to the state legislature in Virginia. That was also a thing.

Having lived uninsured from August 27, 2015, until February 1, 2018, the allure of two more years of health insurance, which came with my new role as a state delegate, certainly captured my attention. In case you haven't had the experience, living uninsured in your early thirties can be . . . demoralizing. (But, ladies, remember what those same asshole powerbrokers who make it so that we're living uninsured say to us in the first place: "You should smile more!") You get to a point where you start wondering about the choices you've made that have led you to this point (for me, mainly choosing newspaper journalism as a career in the age of the internet).

Earning reelection also came with a side benefit: it would continue to drive transphobic bigots mad over accusations like "Transgender Delegate Gets Transgender Prescriptions Paid by Transgender Taxpayers!" or some shit like that. ("I think the transgender taxpayers would be quite happy about that," says my transgender* partner upon reading that sentence.)

On a much more macro level, though, winning reelection also punctured that last lingering bit of resentment left over from 2017: that I was a flash in the pan, that 12,077 people wouldn't be so dumb as to reelect a transgender metalhead reporter stepmom in 2019 after they'd see what a disgraceful heathen she'd be with power—heathen, perhaps, but certainly not a disgraceful one. Well, I guess there was some validity to that: only 12,066 people voted for me the second time (I knew I should have knocked on doors in Mulder Court and Scully Court in Manassas one more time . . .) for a voter retention rate of 99.9 percent—and that was without any statewide candidates at the top of the ticket to drive up turnout. That's 'cause your girl ran a reelection campaign that roughly boiled down to "Danica 2019: I did a good job. Please vote for me to keep doing a good job."

The reason I ran for office in the first place is because . . . well . . . I was asked. A couple of times. Data from Emerge America—an organization that trains Democratic women to run for office across the country (and one of the organizations I trained with to prepare for my run)—shows that women are more likely to run for office after being recruited to run, while men are more likely to take

---

*For those playing the Danica drinking game at home, grab your Lulus and your yoga mat: that's five kombucha shots—one for each "transgender" in two sentences. Go!

the initiative to run. While that's certainly not universal, it just so happened to pan out in my case, if for no other reason than to make the heads of transphobic bigots explode.

There were a lot of reasons that ultimately led me to declare my candidacy, but suffice it to say that my "Oh, hell no" dismissiveness toward the idea took some time to thaw. The first person to ask me to think about running was James Parrish, who led the LGBTQ rights organization Equality Virginia (EV) in Richmond. He asked me about it in February 2016, when I drove down to the General Assembly four times in just over a month to advocate against anti-LGBTQ bills.

I had never been involved with activism before this point. Getting involved to actually advocate for an issue instead of just covering other people doing it for the newspaper made me feel uncomfortable as hell in that I never wanted my neutrality as a reporter questioned. At the same time, I also felt like I was in a unique position to actually connect with some of the Republican legislators and win their votes because I knew them after covering them as a reporter for years. Yet to throw another curveball into the wind . . . most of those legislators hadn't seen me in person since I changed my name, corrected the gender marker on my legal documents, and left the *Gainesville Times* half a year earlier. After almost a decade of the neutrality I'd held as a journalist, I knew I wanted to get involved at this level and I had some hope that I could convince a few legislators not to fuck over my life and the lives of their trans constituents. Yet by the time I would leave the capitol, I would just collapse in my car, usually with a pulsating headache and an occasional vomit on the side of Ninth Street. That, as you'll find out later, became a recurring theme for how my body processes anxiety: via explosive and—well, let's go with messy—catharsis.

Anyway, I had stopped by James's office on one of my trips down to talk and coordinate because I didn't want to step on Equality Virginia's toes and duplicate efforts. We knew then-governor Terry McAuliffe would veto any of these anti-LGBTQ bills and we just barely had the votes to sustain any veto in the state house. Still, we both had a larger mission: kill the bills before they even reached the House floor, which we managed to do with seven out of nine of them, leading us to run out the clock on one bill and Governor McAuliffe to veto the remaining one live on the radio during WTOP's "Ask the Governor" segment. We considered it a win-win: the bill didn't go through, and it functioned as a warning to the other anti-LGBTQ bills not to enter the governor's office. When James and I started talking about Bob Marshall's anti-LGBTQ bills, that led to a conversation about the 2017 election.

"Why don't you run?" James asked me.

It was the first time anyone had asked me to run for office, that day in February 2016—and I ruled it out because the 2015 Democratic nominee for the same seat, Don Shaw, was preparing to run again.

But still, the question sat there. I don't know how to describe it exactly other than to say that someone asking me to run for office felt like a giant steel gate had materialized in the middle of my life path. It suddenly loomed over everything I was doing and over why I was doing it. I could say no and the gate would lift; I would go on with my life as it was. Saying no is easy in that way. No is comfortable; it delivers you right back to where you were. You know what you're getting when you say no; life is predictable, knowable. It's like never making it past your freshman year's "Iron Man," "Crazy Train," and "Enter Sandman" mixed tape because God forbid you might find out Black Sabbath, Ozzy Osbourne, and Metallica wrote songs you don't hear on FM radio.

But what was that predictable, knowable life, exactly?

I'd just taken a job as a reporter at the *Montgomery County Sentinel*, a newspaper in Maryland, mostly so I could be closer to my partner and stepdaughter who both lived in that county. After all, nothing says commitment and love like a forty-eight-mile commute from Manassas in D.C.-region traffic. This at least gave me the option of occasionally spending the night up there when I didn't have band practice or other obligations back home. After the first eight or so months of that job, in which I had a brief refreshed feeling after a few investigative pieces, I started to stagnate again. By June 2016, I had been building my career as a journalist for ten years and was burning out. My enthusiasm was dipping, and along with it, my mood and my self-esteem. I had loved this career, but it quite simply wasn't panning out. It's hard to be excited about a career that's left you wondering how you're going to afford your bills after a decade of doing it. You don't have to be a financial wizard to know a career in local journalism won't make you rich, but it was *bad*—I just wasn't able to support myself or my family, or even properly take care of myself, without working two full-time jobs.

As a result, I caught myself citing the minimum number of sources I needed to get the story through editing while also being flippant in defending my writing. My boss, however, could see right through my bullshit and would call me into his office to tell me in no uncertain terms that my story sucked and I needed to write it over again. That's what happened with a front-page investigative story about water infrastructure, which quite literally brought me to tears when I saw all my shortcomings unfold before my eyes while we were on deadline. My half-assed work was jeopardizing the production of that week's paper and I had to fix it fast. In the end, I got my shit together and, despite my moping and insufferable self-pity, it was a great piece, complete with a memorable headline from a local mayor about why voters and politicians alike often don't prioritize water infrastructure repairs: "It's not sexy."

By the time that water infrastructure series was published in September 2016, my activism in Virginia had expanded beyond Richmond and into my home community of Prince William County, all while I considered a run for office. Of course, I had to make sure my activism in Virginia didn't conflict with my reporting and editing work in Maryland, so I had to at least stay issue-based instead of partisan. Still, my focus at this point in my life was drifting much more into my goals as an activist. I had become intent on plotting how to get the Prince William County School Board to revise their nondiscrimination policy to include sexual orientation and gender identity. We had the representation—we had five Democratic-endorsed members on the school board out of the eight elected members, so we had a pro-equality majority in theory—but we hadn't locked down their votes yet. The Democratic Party that I knew from growing up wasn't a shoe-in for LGBTQ issues. In previous decades they had been, at best, somewhat less awful on these issues, but present-day levels of progress were unthinkable even just a few years ago. So I knew that I couldn't take for granted their support of the policy change.

I spent every shift at the Afghan Kabob House, washing trays and filling tzatziki containers, plotting how to earn those five votes. At that point I wasn't really thinking about what this policy change would mean to me personally as an adult or what it would have meant to me as a kid or even whether it would have made my own childhood easier. As a thirty-two-year-old journalist and food delivery driver, the policy wasn't for me, so I never applied any special meaning to it beyond wanting it to be easier for LGBTQ school staffers and students to be themselves and come out without getting hurt emotionally or physically. For the kids in Prince William County schools, I knew it would be a big deal as a statement of affirmation that they belong. That's something LGBTQ kids in the '90s just didn't have any expectation of whatsoever in Virginia schools. Whatever energy I might have put toward really digging in on my reporting for the *Sentinel* beyond the basics was being high-beamed at this issue as I obsessively crafted rebuttals toward opposition arguments, dismantling them one by one.

I spent my lunch breaks at my kebab job sitting near the window, phone in hand, notepad on the table, furiously planning and making calls between bites of falafel and jasmine rice dotted with carrots and raisins. While that focus made those lonely kebab shifts less soul-sucking, every loss or possible setback felt all the more damning in my life, especially as my activism coupled with my two jobs and my band meant I was barely seeing my family at all. So in some sense, that big question—running for office—causing total disruption to my life was coming at the exact right time. Earlier that year in Richmond when James asked me about running, I didn't think Prince William County voters would be ready to elect a trans woman for at least a few more years. After all, Bob Marshall and a number of social conservatives in the House of Delegates and on the Board of County Supervisors still represented Prince William County. No one had seemed willing to hire me for more than a part-time gig, so how was winning an election going to go?

Also: I was poor! Poor people didn't run for office, or at least not successfully, I thought. How the hell is someone who's uninsured, driving a rusty-as-junk (yet super effin' sweet) '92 Dodge

Shadow going to be able to afford to run for office, let alone against a thirteen-term incumbent who just got reelected by 12 percentage points a year prior?

Then things started to change. I'd been advocating all spring and summer for the school board's nondiscrimination policy when the Pulse nightclub shooting happened. I was a blubbering mess. I couldn't face customers at the kebab restaurant, but I also didn't want to be alone. I ducked out of a shift to be part of the Pride festival in D.C., where an otherwise festive atmosphere had a cloud of mourning hanging over it, as evidenced by one man I saw holding a Pride flag with a black ribbon drawn on it making a lot of new acquaintances as people approached him to express a sense of solidarity. Personally, I needed that moment just to know someone else—or, in that case, a lot of someone elses—got it. My grief at least then felt more communal instead of lonely, which made it easier to process.

Well, little did I know the school board chairman I had been working with all year on the policy change, Ryan Sawyers, declared immediately after the massacre that the school board would be voting in a few months on the nondiscrimination policy change. I remember thinking, "Well, shit . . . here we go," as I quickly realized we were moving ahead without having the votes locked down. That meant I needed to accelerate my timeline for ensuring my whip count tallied five members. So, being as bluntly direct as you'd expect from an extroverted reporter with Sicilian blood, I showed up at a school-renaming ceremony and approached every Democratic-endorsed member of the school board, asking them for their vote. All four of my swing votes said yes, with Potomac District member Justin Wilk telling me to make sure advocates for it would "pack the house" at the first hearing. Giddy with glee, I reported to Ryan Sawyers that we had the votes so, here we go, let's get it done. I was elated, suddenly full of purpose and/or caffeine. We had all five! Could I get a Republican on board maybe? I could see one or two coming around to it and I ended up talking to two of the three of them for a good while, though neither would commit. While I knew I was personally making a difference in terms of my aggressive pursuit of the policy change after months of working behind the scenes with both Ryan Sawyers and Don Shaw—the former being the school board chairman and the latter being the father of an out gay son as well as my aspiring political mentor—I really didn't care about that aspect. I just wanted to get the job done. It was the single most important thing I had in my life outside of family at that point because it would mean a holistic change in how my lifelong home county actually treated LGBTQ people.

Working with Don on the policy change throughout the early stages and him asking me to run for office that August, a month before we started defending it in front of the school board together, meant that the person asking me to win the 13th District seat after he couldn't pull it off in 2015 had faith in my abilities to organize people, strategy, and policy alike—all of which would be early tests for running a campaign. It meant he had confidence in me, and when I sometimes lacked that myself, it was definitely affirming. I knew I wasn't doing all of this alone. I would have help, both from the inside with Ryan and from the outside with Don.

All the while, I started to imagine what would happen if I said yes to running for office. Sure, I could punt that August on a decision, saying I wanted to win the school board fight first, get my newsroom through the 2016 election second, and then, third, get trained to run as a candidate with the LGBTQ Victory Institute after the election, but I couldn't really envision much beyond what my actual day-to-day might be like other than the health care (sweet) and the shitty salary (nothing new there). That said, it seemed possible that my life was already beginning to change forever.

Once Delegate Rip Sullivan, the recruiting chairman of the House Democratic Caucus, called me on August 5, 2016—the day after Don sent his email asking me to run—making the same request as Don, I knew I could be a plausible candidate; I knew Bob Marshall was wildly out of step with a district that voted Democratic in higher-turnout federal elections; and I knew from my time as a newspaper reporter during five of his campaigns that Democrats chronically underfunded and underorganized almost all of their campaigns against him.

I figured Hillary Clinton would win the White House later that year, which would make Virginia U.S. senator Tim Kaine her vice president. Governor McAuliffe would then pick longtime Democratic U.S. representative Bobby Scott to fill that Senate seat, and then we would have a special election in November 2017 to complete the final year of his term. With Scott at the top of the ticket in 2017, I figured that would excite Democrats into turning out to elect Virginia's first Black senator, which would help out the down-ballot candidates, too. In the last statewide gubernatorial election year, Bob Marshall only won by 498 votes out of the more than 17,000 votes cast, when he ran against middle-school teacher and Marine Corps veteran Atif Qarni, who happened to be a Muslim immigrant. In short: I had rationalized all this shit in only the way that dwelling on it for eleven hours a day while scrubbing trays, filling sauce containers, and dropping off kebabs between Northwest D.C. and Arlington could provide.

I also thought that, given the district had grown by more than two thousand registered voters since Marshall narrowly won in 2013, and

I had covered the district for more than nine years as a newspaper reporter, it wasn't exactly much of a stretch for a white woman who's a lifelong Prince William County resident from Manassas to win, with the sole caveat being "OMG, trans!" There was also, admittedly, some small piece of me that mentally war-gamed what could happen in the extremely unlikely event that Donald Trump somehow won.

As long as I could raise the money to pay for a full campaign team and a full ad campaign—direct mail, television, digital, and even a little on radio—and get enough volunteers knocking on doors to talk with voters every day, then I could out-organize Bob Marshall and his volunteers. As a reporter-turned-candidate, I also knew that developing good relationships with reporters and getting adequate coverage wasn't going to be a problem, especially given my status as a trans woman and Marshall's as the self-described "chief homophobe" of Virginia. I knew the issues, knew the community, and knew I could learn how to run a winning campaign fairly quickly—just as long as my three decades of ye-olde-personal-effups wouldn't actually be much of an issue. I mean, after all, do voters *really* care that much that, in my twenties, during my band's after-show parties, my Jägermeister-to-blood ratio was roughly 3 to 1? Probably not. Probably.

That fall, the Prince William County School Board finally held the hearing for their nondiscrimination policy. During the first hearing, the room was basically divided evenly, with strong but predictable support on both sides. But the second time it came up, it was a different atmosphere. Republicans had started busing in church groups wearing red shirts (which, if *Star Trek* taught us anything, isn't exactly a precursor for victory). The groups—many of whom didn't even have kids in public schools—spent their time at the microphone during citizens' time often expressing genuine concern, sometimes mixed with just the most hateful, vile shit you can imagine toward LGBTQ kids as a whole and trans kids specifically.

It would be pretty generous to say they'd be first in line to bake cakes for a gay wedding, but their homophobia had been at least transmuted into—let's call it—*polite* homophobia. On trans people, though, it was open season. It was the kind of pure vitriol and villainization that was normal and legitimized even more then than it is now—it was the time when bathroom bills were all the rage. One speaker referred to these *children* as "perverse sexual sinners" who were "damnable" and "damned by God." I don't know what trans kid pissed in his Wheaties, but the fact that he got applauded for it makes you realize in that moment that these parents were setting the example for their own kids to follow on how to treat their LGBTQ classmates. The school board ultimately punted the vote on the issue until the end of the school year in June 2016, which was deeply disappointing to me—but, in some strange sense, it was motivating, too. I saw how having a position of political power would impact others—both in what legislation I could pass and in how viable trans people might be as candidates. Naturally, it was terrifying to imagine everything that could be used against me and would be—and if I lost, it would set the whole trans movement back. I wrestled with the fact that all the dumb shit I'd ever said and done would be dredged up and put on full display as a reason for my unworthiness to represent eighty-three thousand people in western Prince William County and the City of Manassas Park.

But on the flip side, I could see the power in the stories others had shared. During the early part of 2016 in Richmond, I saw the difference a trans high school student named Andrew Wilson made when he testified against a bathroom bill that would have restricted his ability to use the same locker room as the other boys on his soccer team, and watched that ripple out from him. One teen, who just wanted to play soccer—and use the appropriate locker room—by showing up and sharing his story, impacted the lives of other trans kids across the commonwealth that he'd never even met as the subcommittee he spoke in front of eventually killed that bill. Even though I couldn't possibly ask trans kids in Prince William County to take the microphone that fall and subject themselves to hundreds of people gathering in a room to oppose their civil rights, I knew that I, as a fully grown adult, could share parts of my story and the story of the trans community at large to help make inclusive change. And if I could do that in front of one of our local school boards, imagine what I could do in Richmond as a state lawmaker.

That's the magic of storytelling, of course—but it's also the magic of political action. That possibility was what fueled my activism, which sometimes could become a grind, so many miles and so much time and effort, spending sixteen months to fight for adding four words—"sexual orientation" and "gender identity"—to a single school board's nondiscrimination policy. But those efforts could ultimately bring meaningful change to someone else's life. That someone could have a childhood a little easier than mine, be comfortable coming into themselves a little earlier than I did. If I won in front of the school board and then won in front of the voters, then I knew my story could inspire others, allow others to run or take charge of making policy changes and take positions of power throughout the country. We'd still face this kind of bullshit rhetoric in state General Assembly meetings (and . . . everywhere else), sure—but we'd be considered electable as candidates and effective as policy gurus.

In retrospect, one of the things I'm proudest of was challenging the notion of what makes an "electable" candidate: recognizing both my shortcomings as well as qualifications and deciding to run for office just as I am, and then earning reelection all while embracing the fact that I can do well in office while still being myself. If you, my dear reader, have read anything about me at all before picking up this book, you likely know about my obsessive focus on local issues like Route 28, personal visits to constituents' houses, and a genuine enjoyment of all things Manassas (I even attend high school drama productions—voluntarily!), all of which led voters to either overlook or fully embrace the whole transgender/heavy-metal/lewd-drunkenness-of-the-past thing.

When I won my first election in 2017, people were still reeling from the 2016 election—people who cared about getting out of the darkness and were so giddy about the promise that maybe, just maybe, imperfect progressives could win. It became clear to me pretty quickly that, at a time when so many people were scared for our collective future, there was a winning strategy: Meet voters openly where *they* are, be honest and direct about who *you* are, listen and learn about what matters to them, and you'll be surprised at how much they'll accept. With voters—with all people—it's not about trying to be who you *think* they want you to be, it's about being real with them about who you are and what results you can deliver for them. Because people care more about being able to trust you, and they can't trust you if you're hiding parts of yourself.

And yet, of course, the years since 2017 have . . . complicated that understanding. We screamed our way through the Brett Kavanaugh hearings (clearly his woe-is-me fake tears and anger were much more meaningful to the United States Senate than the millions of women screaming—no disrespect to his homeboy Squee, of course), and not long after that watched all that shit go down with Rep. Katie Hill. It seems some people's pasts *are* too much for the public, while others whose pasts are way, way worse get to stay in power. (Hint: The ones who get to stay often have some key characteristics in common.) When cisgender, straight white men have been the ones holding power since forever, it turns out they can get away with a lot more—and rely on protection from other men in power who are like them—than women, LGBTQ+ people, and people of color. It's one of the reasons we need more diversity in elected office, why it's so important that we run authentically as who we are when we do run for office, and why it's so much harder for us to do that.

Alas, millennials haven't killed patriarchy and inequality the way we're (thankfully) killing the diamond industry and (less thankfully) Macy's. But we're beginning to realize that being able to control and maintain the normalcy in our lives depends on us grabbing ahold of our narrative and telling our own stories before the charlatans get the chance to do it for us. Victory is about telling a better story— embracing the inevitable scrutiny of your past and telling your story first, while remembering that the higher profile your job, the more likely people will talk about you and try to dig up and exploit the details of your past, regardless of whether or not it's flattering.

In 2017, people knew they were electing a transgender thrash-metal vocalist *who dedicated a decade of her life to writing the news about their community.* So no one in 2018, during my first year in office, was surprised that January when I introduced a piece of legislation to fix

Route 28. And no one was surprised to see me on the side of the stage that summer at Jiffy Lube Live, an outdoor amphitheater in Bristow, rocking out to "Raining Blood" during Slayer's farewell tour.

It's so much easier to find a reason *not* to do something challenging than it is to find a reason *to* do it, whether it's work-life balance, financial commitment, or intense dissatisfaction with office doughnuts (so many doughnuts). Yet I promise you, what keeps more people (maybe not straight white men, but everyone else) from running for office more than anything else is the fear of rejection—specifically, if people knew about all of your "whoops" moments, then you would be screwed. "Oh my God, that time in high school/college/my early twenties/late twenties/midthirties/first marriage/the bar/first marriage at the bar/first marriage with the bar. Like, the whole bar. Stools and everything. The divorce was a mess." The same goes for why women disproportionately don't apply for jobs when they don't meet 100 percent of the prequalifications, whereas men will apply for those same jobs when they are less qualified. We're often incredibly hard on ourselves, and our fear of failure can be real enough to prevent us from trying to live our dreams, pursue our goals, or emotionally invest ourselves in something that might not pan out, especially when we have a giant audience—or even a super intimate one—wanting to pick apart our every move. After all, people love slowing down to watch a car-b-cue smoking up a storm on the side of the highway, but have considerably less love for wanting to be the driver of said roadside pyre.

For those of us who grew up in the age of social media, it can be an exercise in demented self-loathing to figure out just how much of your history the public can truly stomach, given how thoroughly our lives are embedded on the internet. A lot of photos, videos, and your sharpest "George W. Bush is a war criminal!" hot takes from 2004 are lodged behind a privacy filter that you control, which makes cleaning up your shit a lot easier—though, trust me, even if you think it's private, it ain't if it's anywhere on the internet. (Pull. That. Shit. Down.) Yet we know that every time we stuck our tongue out at the camera, it wasn't necessarily *our* camera. Every time our middle finger channeled our not-so-inner "I don't care, maaan! Fuck the system, brah!" rebel, our Aristotle-like insight into the world likely ended up on someone else's Facebook, Myspace, AIM, or message board. Yeah. All of that. AIM doesn't even exist anymore (*bless**) and Myspace deleted its blogs (*BLESS**). Yet your photos are still out there, and the dumbass shit you wrote at age twenty-two publicly explaining how you lit your beer bong on fire from the outside using Stroh 80 (160-proof alcohol I'd charitably compare to gasoline) as substitute lighter fluid while you briskly inhaled the contents inside the funnel and tube just might be, too.*

So what are you to do now that you've reached the age at which you've (supposedly) gotten your shit together?† Not run for office because someone might find that picture of two of your (fully clothed) guy friends fake–Eiffel Tower–ing your (fully clothed) dumbass self after a gig at some dive bar in West Springfield . . . which is totally hypothetical and not at all a memory of you feigning hilarity amid trying to scream your queerness without actually coming out . . . *rapidly darts eyes left and right*

Here's the thing: People did stupid stuff like that before the dawn of the internet, too, and some of them won elections. Some were just

---

*It most certainly is.
†Results may vary.

better at hiding it than others. I reconciled my years of chicanery with the idea that by the time I was thirty-two years old, I genuinely believed I could honorably serve my lifelong home community without embarrassing my constituents.

I seriously considered—prior to hiring a campaign manager who would have absolutely nixed the idea—having a section of my campaign website be titled "The Dirt." I thought about just posting in that section all potentially damaging information about myself so that everything that my opponent may have used against me was just out there, compared to the worst of President Trump or Delegate Marshall. I was quite confident that me acting like a jackass in my twenties wasn't even in the same league as locking up children in cages (Trump) and earning a 2010 CBS News headline that stated "Va. Lawmaker: Disabled Kids Are God's Punishment for Abortion" (Marshall).

What changed my mind, though, was some advice from a mentor named Donald, my former editor from a newspaper in Pennsylvania where I interned in college. He told me, "Make 'em earn it. And if they find something on you and ask why you didn't put it out there yourself, just be honest about it: 'I wasn't going to make it easy for you. I wanted you to have to work for it.'"

Throwing all of your shit at the wall and seeing what sticks isn't necessarily a winning strategy in politics—or in life. There are some societal norms that keep us from a Big Brother level of transparency where all actions, thoughts, and dirt are out there in the public. If your entire life is just "Look what a tragic figure I am!" then it's hard not only for other people to move past that roadside wreckage that is your life but also for you to get into the tow truck to haul that bullshit away, get a new ride, and start fresh again. Drama queens belong in exactly one place and it's called *RuPaul's Drag Race*.

However, you also don't want other people to suddenly find out something unflattering about you that you didn't prepare a response for or, even worse, find out something about you that takes away your ability to control the narrative of who you are—or, more often, were. If that happens, you lose people's trust.

That's where the balancing act comes in handy. For me, that meant being up-front about my most obvious liabilities: My band, which I was still in at the time, though we were winding down. My party drinking, which I was done with but clearly had a long history promoting. My shitty grades in my first semester of college, which I could actually portray as a positive learning experience, so long as I set the narrative. And, of course, my gender.

So I did what came naturally: I put it all out there, bit by bit, in as tasteful a way as possible and with the intention of demonstrating that not only had I learned from my past but I was actually much more confident and comfortable in my own skin at thirty-two than I had been at twenty-two, and because of that, I was ready to lead. My goal was to actually take the eccentricities of my life and turn them into a relatable story arc, tying in the lessons I learned with public policy initiatives that would help the community. I didn't have to be ashamed of living for 2.5 years in my early thirties without health insurance. Instead, that made me relatable. I had gone through hard times and came out the other end, still uninsured for a couple more months, sure, but also still having something to say and something to do about making change in our communities.

This is what I hope people get out of my story: that reflecting on what it's like to be you, for all of its quirks and twists, allows you to be transparent and authentic without it turning into a sideshow of tabloid-style stupidity. It's something I took from my yoga practice— during savasana (otherwise known as the "corpse pose," when you're lying on your back, hands at your sides, palms facing up, your eyes closed), one of my instructors would tell her students not to ignore the thoughts in our minds as we meditated but rather to acknowledge their existence. Then, like clouds, we should let them drift away. So that's what I would do. Instead of ignoring the things that many might say were liabilities, I would acknowledge their existence and then pivot to what people really cared about: how I was going to improve their lives.

Beyond politics, being genuine about your life's story also means that you don't have to act like one person in front of one set of people and someone else in front of a different audience. I did that so much in my life that it was hard to keep track of who I was supposed to be at all by 2014, the first full calendar year of my physical and social transition into expressed womanhood. There gets to be a point where you get tired of that duality; where you just want to look and talk the same in the evening as you do in the morning, without fear of judgment or reprisal. Where you don't want to spend so much energy worrying about if you wiped enough of your black eyeliner off before stepping foot in your ma's house. I finally discovered that life during the summer of 2015, when I legally changed my name as well as my gender marker on my driver's license, which allowed me to change my byline in the newspaper. But I get that not everyone reading this is trans or a newspaper reporter (though to all you trans newspaper reporters: I pray for only the finest spiked beverages to serve your livers), so maybe that declaration of authenticity might not be so dramatic or obvious. But it's still real no matter what kind of stories, and selves, you're juggling.

When you do have that moment of confronting your fears and

putting yourself out there just as you are, that means acknowledging all the warts, flaws, and foibles of your past as well as the cool, kick-ass things about yourself—and being that same person no matter who you're around.

For me, my audience is now the tens of thousands of people in the district I represent and the thousands of people who walk the halls of the Virginia State Capitol during our sessions. But it used to just be twentysomething people at my morning job, whoever I was covering or interviewing during my evening job, and whatever audience came out to see my band or practice yoga with me at night or during the weekend.

My mind is no longer weighed down by the burden of secrets. The person I was when I ran for office in 2017 didn't exist in that same mental capacity in 2013 when I started transitioning with hormone replacement therapy. When I started that December, I was a nervous wreck. I was nervous to be onstage, nervous to come out to my ma, nervous to present as myself to friends. Fast-forward four years, and there I was, on the cover of *Time* magazine. That's not to say my panic and never-ending stress disappeared—it definitely still has a permanent place in my mind.

But at least I can wear eyeliner now whenever I feel like it, crow's-feet be damned.

LIFER

WHO DOES DANICA ROEM REALLY WORK FOR . . .
<u>US</u> OR AN OUT-OF-STATE MILLIONAIRE?

—*Mail advertisement, paid for by the Republican Party of
Virginia, authorized by Kelly McGinn, candidate for
Delegate, 2019*

'm just a grown-up burbs kid from Manassas. The Republicans I beat in 2017, 2019, and 2021 all lived less than three miles from me. The first two came from the same Roman Catholic church in Manassas as me. Surprisingly, holy water doesn't burn trans harlot flesh as much as you'd think.

In that way, some chunks of western Prince William County are still the same as when I was a kid. Yeah, we elected Transgender Candidate to be our Transgender State Delegate, but keep in mind: this isn't a super blue, progressive beacon of humanity.

Manassas is Manassas. This is Manasty. Our Cracker Barrel to Whole Foods ratio is 1:0.

The 13th District part of Manassas that I represent is where a police officer in 1993 found John Bobbitt's dismembered member in the grass next to a 7-Eleven in Yorkshire, ran inside, picked up a (questionably sized) Big Bite hot dog box and ice, and placed said phallus in the container to await transport to—presumably—Dick Tailors 'R' Us.

Our history in Manassas is checkered. In fact, it was only in re-sponse to a now-former police officer kneeling on the neck of George

Floyd—an unarmed Black man in Minneapolis who was suffocated and died in 2020, leading to a murder conviction for the officer—that the Prince William County School Board voted to rename two of our minority-majority schools in the county part of Manassas to something other than a tribute to Confederate General Thomas "Stonewall" Jackson.

Prior to the summer of 2020, it was possible in Manassas for you to live at Stonewall Acres, head past Stonewall Court along your commute down Stonewall Road, to get to your job at Stonewall Dental Associates next to Stonewall Square. You might remind your oldest child at Stonewall Jackson High School to pick up your middle child at Stonewall Middle School, so they could swim laps together at Stonewall Park Pool.

On the weekend, your family might pay your respects to loved ones at Stonewall Memory Gardens, then take your dog to get shots at Stonewall Veterinary Clinic, before picking up groceries at The Shops at Stonewall and playing the back nine at Stonewall Golf Club.

So . . . when you've had more things in your area named after a Confederate general who enslaved people than you have, y'know, Starbucks coffeeshops, that should be a hint it isn't exactly Greenwich Village or West Hollywood. There is one place in the town of Haymarket that does vegan wraps and brews a mean kombucha (if kombucha can actually be mean), but yeah, that's about as close to SoHo as you're going to get around here.

We don't have Pride parades down Sudley Road or Route 28, but we do have two Confederate cemeteries in Manassas (one in the city and one in the county at the battlefield) and two firing ranges (one indoor and one outdoor). That's not to say that we don't have parades, though. I've marched in the ones for Christmas and St. Patrick's Day—and there is actually a small contingent of out LGBTQ service members who've recently started marching in the Veterans Day Parade, which is really cool in that they've all heard far worse than anyone's going to shout at them from lawn chairs along Center Street.

In fact, they're emblematic of the recent changes we've experienced here. However, aside from the blatant bigotry you'll see here and there, political debates these days in western Prince William generally center on land use, transportation, education, economic development, and real estate tax rates, compared to, say, which restroom people like me can frickin' use.

Those are the hot topics: where to build more roads, multimodal projects with pathways, or mass transit; competing for talent with the rest of Northern Virginia when we have the lowest teacher pay in our region; whether to allow giant transmission lines to hook up to data centers that consume a ton of energy; and how to pay for all the services provided by the county government. If you really want a good old-fashioned political blood sport the way Ma used to make it, then sit in on the school-boundary-line-adjustment fights and arguments about whether to build new schools or renovate the ones we already have in Prince William County.

Can't you just feel the excitement?!

The thing is, most of these issues aren't really Republican versus Democrat. When we have steel water pipes buried in Manassas Park dating back to the 1950s that haven't been replaced with more modern and durable material, and stormwater management systems that need to be upgraded, you don't have Democratic or Republican counterpoints. You just have infrastructure that needs to be fixed. These are the fundamentals of just living in a growing area that's becoming more diverse.

While there are certainly issues unique to Prince William County, it's really reflective of America at large. It's why there are Republican governors in deep blue Vermont, Massachusetts, and Maryland working with Democratic legislatures, and Democratic governors in bloodred Kansas and Louisiana working with Republican legislatures. Whether the country's run by George W. Bush, Barack Obama, Donald Trump, or—thank our lucky aviators—Joe Biden, traffic still sucks. Parents want to be able to pick up their kids at a reasonable hour, not punch their steering wheel into submission while working out their road rage from sitting in traffic from dusk till dark on Route 28 until they make it home from work.

BORN SEPTEMBER 30, 1984, at Prince William Hospital in Manassas, I lived with my mom, dad, and older sister for 2.5 years in a brick townhouse along Brandon Way in the northern part of Manassas before moving out to the woods on Montyville Drive in May of 1987. I have one distinct memory from that time of looking through the front window on the drive over to the new house from my seat in the back of the car.

A few months after that move, I learned quickly about death, separation, and disattachment: my father, at age thirty-seven,* intentionally immolated himself in the backyard two days after Christmas in 1987, when I was just three. I still remember running across the grassy plateau from our home to my neighbor's house as my mother stood at the top of the driveway yelling, "Johnny! Johnny!" as the firefighters arrived on the scene. I remember being in my neighbor's house playing foosball later, and then, a few days later, coloring at someone else's

---

*Which was my age as of publication of this book. Oh, joy.

house while my mom was somewhere—at what I found out many years later was my father's wake—but not much else.

At the time, my mom told me and my sister, who's two and a half years older than me, that the refrigerator in the basement caught on fire and our father died trying to put it out. It was easier for little kids to blame the fridge than wrap their minds around "Your father was severely clinically depressed for years with multiple failed suicide attempts to his name before he finally got what he wanted in the worst way possible, leaving your mother alone to raise two little kids while working her ass off to pay the brand-new mortgage he left her with."

I didn't learn the truth until middle school, when I brought up the "fire" to my mother while sitting in the back seat of her Subaru on Signal Hill Road. That's when she told me that he killed himself. I didn't have to ask why my mom had held off explaining to two little kids how Daddy poured out the fuel from a gas canister over his head and lit himself on fire. She didn't provide the context for the second part at the time—for good reason. Likewise, I didn't find out the full details until much later—that it wasn't his first attempt; that he had been institutionalized in D.C. not long before he died.

When I was a kid and then as a teenager, I didn't talk a lot about my dad or even really think about him. I didn't have any reason to; he wasn't a part of my life. When I did ask my family about him, I usually just wanted to know about the funny stuff. He would make cassette tape recordings making fun of all sorts of people when he was twenty years old as a U.S. Navy sailor stationed in Vietnam. At home, he would tell a police officer when he was pulled over for not having both hands on the steering wheel, "Haven't you ever picked your nose while driving?" On another occasion, when he got stopped for speeding, he said he was just trying to keep up with traffic. When informed by the officer that there was no one near him, he replied, "That's why I've got a lot of catching up to do!"

Nearly thirty-two years later, when I was knocking on doors in my home precinct of Yates Ford during my 2019 reelection campaign, I met a firefighter from the Buckhall Volunteer Fire Department. We got to talking—as you do with voters when you knock on their doors—and I mentioned that it was his department that had responded to the call when my dad killed himself. He told me he remembered the call coming in that day, more than three decades before. I guess calls so gruesome that they lead to closed-casket funerals are hard to forget.

T he year following my dad's death, my grandfather and grandmother on my ma's side of the family moved in with us. They weren't there to help raise my older sister and me but because they needed the help—my grandmother had developed symptoms of Parkinson's disease and moved in a wheelchair by the late 1980s, which meant my mother needed to install a lift in our house so that my grandma could get around. It sort of just worked out logistically that my mom would help take care of her parents—they lived the closest to us compared to my ma's three siblings, and even though my father had just died, Ma became their primary caretaker. So there was my ma, recently widowed and still grieving, taking care of two kids and her own parents, with a new mortgage and a full-time job that was twenty-plus miles away with a horrendous commute, and just trying to get by. She worked her way through her feelings, and it seemed like she never had a moment to herself. Yet she still made the time to take my sister and me on vacation all over the place: Scotland, Canada, Arizona, Hawaii; she really mixed it up.

Unlike a *lot* of overachieving and/or broke-ass millennials in my age bracket, my Boomer mother insisted on taking a couple of weeks off each year. I respect the hell out of that.

At home, my grandfather was a gentle giant, a steady calm presence in the house and to me as a kid. He was deliberate in everything he did—he ate slowly and was always the last one to finish dinner. He was a voracious reader, and my most salient visual memories of him all have him settled into a recliner with a book in our front room, which he had taken over as his own personal living room. He'd brought his own couch, bookshelf, and record player, and hung photos both of New York Yankees slugger Roger Maris crossing home plate when he hit his record-breaking 61st home run in 1961 and of the greatest Italian American to play the game, Joe DiMaggio, his favorite baseball player. ("Joe D!" he'd say.) We called it Grandpa's Room, and it had just the slightest feel of a time warp when you stepped into it from the rest of the house.

Though he'd taken a parental role in my life, he felt like a connection to an entirely different era. Grandpa was born in Harlem in 1915 and later moved with his family to an Italian neighborhood in the Bronx; he came up in an intense kind of poverty that I never did, even with all of us under one roof being supported by just my ma. His mother died when he was twelve and he had to drop out of ninth grade to help his dad support his two younger brothers before all three of them ended up serving in the Pacific Theater during World War II. His brother Jim was a genuine war hero, earning a Silver Star for saving the lives of injured Gurkha soldiers under a hail of gunfire. His brother Salvatore—aka "Uncle Babe," as we called him—came home from the Philippines with a purple heart from shrapnel that stayed in his body the rest of his life.

One of the most endearing things to me about my grandfather

was that he spoke bits of Italian here and there in a low, halting voice usually coupled with a laugh, like when I'd take him to Tony's NY Pizza along Mathis Avenue in Manassas and he'd talk to the Italian immigrants Vinnie and Tony who ran the restaurant, while they stood behind the counter. And he would tell me stories about being a kid: breaking his nose while playing football (and another sports injury that left one pinkie finger always bent inward), playing hockey and stickball with the guys on his block, and competing in Golden Gloves boxing during the 1930s. I mean, you didn't have to have a lot of money to hit a ball with a stick or a face with a (glove-wrapped) fist, so during the Great Depression that wasn't a bad way to pass the time for a bunch of Italian guys in their teens and twenties.

My grandfather put his muscular six-foot-three frame, which earned him the nickname "Legs," to work, hauling fifty-pound bags of coal up New York City stairs during the winter and giant blocks of ice during the summer. Along his route, he met a Jewish family who would offer him free shoes and books, which sparked his love of reading. At home, he also read the New York *Daily News* every day, telling me that reading the newspaper served as the basis for his knowledge, something important for a Bronx guy who never got to graduate from high school.

After a rather eventful life that culminated with raising four kids, he wasn't the enforcer of the rules of the house that his second daughter ran: that role was unquestionably held by my ma, who let no one speculate about whether she was in charge at all times. While she would—and usually did—sacrifice everything for her family, she still had no intention of ever, ever letting a single one of us off easy. It was impossible to win an argument with her if you talked back to her and didn't have your shit together. By the time I had my political awakening during the 2004 presidential campaign as a nineteen- and twenty-year-old college student, I was clearly headed down the left-wing path, while she hadn't voted for a Democrat for president since 1976—"And that was a mistake!" So you can imagine that during George W. Bush's presidency, with two wars waging overseas and a huge fight over marriage equality domestically, we had a lot to talk about, *especially* labor unions in New York City, the one thing my customs-broker mother, who's now retired, loves to hate the most. ("Oh, c'mon, Ma! Grandpa put a roof over your head with a union salary!" "Yeah, they had a time and place. Now? They hold up *everything* at the airports! And who do you think runs the unions? The mob!") There was only one topic that I dared not broach: abortion. Literally everything else was in bounds, but I learned *very* quickly that for my practicing Catholic, conservative Republican mother, there wasn't going to be an educational opportunity or a demonstration of verbal athletics on that topic. Debating politics is, if nothing else, engaging and interesting (if not insanely frustrating) when you've met your match—but when religious conviction enters the mix about good versus evil, it's a whole different vibe that's not the same as, say, marriage equality. On that topic, even in 2004—ten years before I officially came out to her—I would get super animated during our debates, but she wouldn't get heated over it. She supported civil unions instead of full-on marriage rights (at the time). That was an issue where I actually felt like my arguments were impervious, in part because the chief opposition argument, "every child needs a mom and a dad," just wasn't based on reality in our house.

When I was growing up, our arguments were rarely about politics, though; they were much more likely to be about my relationship with homework, which would have been best summed up with a Bronx cheer: *pffffffft*. By my sophomore year of college, when my missing homework days were behind me and we needed something else to debate, that's when I started to engage with her about politics, knowing full well that even before Fox News existed, a not-insignificant part of my childhood was spent riding in her Subaru, listening to conservative commentator G. Gordon Liddy, the late Watergate felon who had a radio show after he got out of prison. What I learned from debating politics with my ma, though, was that some issues just rev you up and others may be interesting to you but you're more dispassionate about them. Through her example, she taught me how to read the room and identify when someone really cared about something and would be intractable; when they cared but were persuadable; and when they were just generally indifferent—though, as she's a Sicilian-Italian Bronxite extrovert, trust me: the latter hasn't exactly been my ma's forte (or, well, mine).

FOR ALL OF OUR differences, I would never bad-talk my mom. Ever. Even as a little kid who didn't understand the word "burdened," I knew that she was, every single day. It could seem like she had a short fuse, but some part of me recognized even then that she was working so hard and carrying so much weight to provide for her family. When my friends would say that they hated their parents or made fun of them, I just didn't get it and wouldn't do it. Arguing with your family is one thing; for us, it's communication. But disrespecting them in public? Absolutely not. And when your dad dies so young, you know that when you're fortunate to have family in your life who love you, you appreciate them.

Just a couple of years after my grandparents moved in with us, my grandmother's Parkinson's got worse. My mom moved her into a nursing home and she died by the time I was six. So before I was even out of first grade, two immediate family members who I lived with had died. Naturally, I did what any good Roman Catholic Italian would do: bury the shit out of it into the deepest crevasses of my mind.

My coping mechanism for death is dismissal—acknowledging that it happened while subsequently avoiding any thoughts about it. On the few occasions I would wonder about my dad, I grabbed my mental remote and pressed whatever button changed the channel to anything else. It took about twenty-seven years before I ever truly confronted his death beyond looking at his tombstone with a "Yup. That's a thing that exists. Okay. Moving on," which I did while sitting on the grass at Stonewall Memory Gardens. I finally forced myself to say out loud, "This is all I've ever known you as—a lump in the ground."

It took a couple years after my dad died for my mom to start dating again. Once she did, the guy who moved into the house as her boyfriend and our new stepdad didn't work out, though it took six years. Let's make up a name and call him "Jack." When I waited at my babysitter's house after school from first through third grades, I could hear the diesel engine of Jack's maroon Ford F-350 (the one with six tires) before I even saw the truck coming. He'd smoke Benson and Hedges cigarettes constantly, cracking the window only slightly to let out the smoke with my sister or me in the truck.

During one hunting trip to Winchester, he described a tall, muscular Black man as a "buck" n-word, dehumanizing him not just with a racial slur but comparing him to the very sort of animal he saw as a sport. Even I knew as a little white kid that the n-word was wrong, but I wasn't in a position to tell him, "Now, now, mind your racism." At one restaurant near Winchester that Jack took me to, I saw a white man playing pool, wearing a shirt with the Trix cereal rabbit on it . . . except instead of it saying "Silly rabbit; Trix are for kids," the words spelled out "Silly faggot; dicks are for chicks." This kind of thing clearly made an imprint on my kid brain, even if I didn't realize it at the time. The reality of the situation, though, was that at a redneck dive bar in 1990s Appalachia, you sure as hell weren't going to find rainbow flags celebrating Pride month hanging over the heads of dead deer mounted on the wall. I didn't know any out LGBTQ people whatsoever at that age beyond the occasional guest I'd see on a daytime talk show or a ridiculed villain in a movie like *Ace Ventura*. Even if I knew I wasn't a cis-het straight kid by the time I was in fifth grade, I saw exactly zero positive representation of LGBTQ people in my life . . . and I stayed firmly, deeply in the closet because of it.

When I was about ten years old, I absolutely hated waking up in the middle of the night to put on a one-piece warm suit and grab my break-action .410 shotgun to go hunting with Jack. Knowing he was a heavy sleeper, I would wake up when his alarm clock blared and turn it off before he woke up, so it would be daylight by the time he came to and it would be slightly less cold.

I never killed any deer while hunting. I fired off a single shot at a doe that I missed. I also missed while aiming at a squirrel (yes, eating squirrel was a staple of our trips), so he shot and wounded it, then made me finish it off. I still remember its warm, fuzzy, lifeless little body being balled up in my front right pocket. (Guess who grew up to be a vegetarian . . . surprise!)

The only animal I killed unassisted was a blackbird or a robin from at least fifty yards out with my .22 bolt-action rifle. I did it in front of one of Jack's friends to impress him and, well, I did. The bird, which moments earlier was minding its own business on top of a mountain near a lone, solitary trailer, bounced around on the leaves after my shot spun it to the ground. I hated to see it suffer and I just thought, "Aww, shit . . ." as I prepared to bludgeon it with the butt of the rifle. Thankfully, the poor little thing died before I got to it.

That said, one of the rules we lived by on the mountain was that you had to eat your kill, so that bird turned into all of two bites of breast meat, which made for a nice contrast to the savory delight of, um, squirrel. (I didn't like venison at all, so no Donner or Blitzen for me.)

Alas, killing things with guns was a cold-weather activity. During the summer, we impaled bleeding insects on hooks attached to the end of a line so that we could use their corpses to catch something else we could kill: fish. Once, when I didn't have any worms, I scooped up a cricket and a grasshopper in the yard, brought them down to this little pier, used the grasshopper as bait, and, bam, snagged a twelve-inch catfish.

There was only one problem with this scene: my adolescent brain forgot to bring a bucket with me. So, like a total jackass, I waddled past line after line of trailers with this gray fish violently flipping its tail fin but unable to free itself. The fish absolutely refused to die, even after our neighbor skinned it alive in front of me, which is when "oh, God, no, never again" ran through my mind. This probably marks the first—and last—time I've counted a decapitation as a form of mercy. So if you're surprised that I've voted in the General Assembly against just about every bill that makes it easier for people to kill animals, I'll be happy to refer you to my childhood of living things dying—human and animal alike.

As much as I didn't enjoy hunting and fishing, each weekend on the mountain or the campground came with a defined terminus point: We would normally leave within a day or two. At home, there wasn't an escape.

At one point in the first half of the 1990s, my mom had just come home from being admitted to the hospital for having high blood pressure and was lying down on the couch when Jack picked me up by the neck and pinned me against the wall for talking at the dinner table, something he strictly forbade the kids from doing. Nothing says "Welcome home" quite like watching your kid turn into a human tapestry display. So my ma got off the couch and she and my grandfather yelled at him until he put me down.

I would retreat to the cigarette-smoke-stenched basement and either play a kid-size acoustic guitar or video games on an old television "until the yelling stops" upstairs, as I thought about it at the time. (This was so routine that it felt legitimately strange when I spent the night at my best friend's house and didn't hear a battle royale between his mom and stepdad.) I vivdly remember one night when my mom and her boyfriend went out for a night and my sister and I stayed up late . . . playing Monopoly (I know, adventurous). For doing just that, we were put "on restriction" for one month when he came home and saw the lights on and my sister and me running to clean up everything and get into bed.

There is at least a happy ending to that saga. A few years after those two (finally) broke up in 1996, my mom started dating someone in the late '90s who she's been with ever since. He's been great.

They're even retired together now, which is all I could ever ask for my mom since he's made her happy.

Despite the turbulence in my childhood, I never got into fist-fights or anything like that with other kids. Instead, by the time I was in sixth grade, I was more familiar with loss than other kids my age, given that two immediate members of my family who I lived with died (my dad and grandmother) and another (Jack) got kicked out of the house. Even my babysitter ended up getting divorced and moving away when I was in the third grade. Likewise, that marked my last year of public school and the end to my four years at Loch Lomond Elementary School. Aside from the losses, I wasn't socializing well in public school. My pre-kindergarten teacher even recommended that I repeat the grade because I wouldn't (couldn't?) pay attention, to which my mom called bullshit because, *Are you serious?!* Give it a couple of years.

After that, my ma sent me to All Saints Catholic School for fourth grade, taking me away from the school and people I knew, but where I had few friends, and starting my thirteen-year journey of Catholic schools, including Paul VI Catholic High School in Fairfax and St. Bonaventure University in western New York.

After school I would sometimes be stuck at Extended Day—day care after the school day ended at All Saints—where a room full of kids would stay until someone came to pick us up. Before I had a carpool to take me home, I'd be there some nights until 7:00 P.M., waiting for my mom, who was battling soul-sucking, bumper-to-bumper traffic on Route 28. Typically, she would be there by 6:00 P.M., but every now and then she had to work late and/or traffic would just be a nightmare. Go figure that twenty-one years later, I'd win a campaign with the slogan "Fix Route 28 Now!" As it turned out, her commute wasn't uncommon.

Extended Day is also where I learned how to play chess, which led to me thinking strategically about my opposition, another handy benefit for Mommy's little politician. My best friend, Charlie, and I basically ran the table against most kids (with two exceptions) when we weren't raising hell with the Extended Day instructor, including sending one of the younger kids up to her to ask, "What was it like when the dinosaurs died?"

She immediately glared at the boy asking and then over toward my best friend and me.

"You can tell them it was very sad," she said.

Sincerely: Well-played, Mrs. Anderson. Game recognizes game.

BY THE TIME I hit puberty, my mind had two things playing on a loop—being trans and how to not let anyone know I was trans. *I wish I could look like her . . .* was the lamenting, driving thought in my head all day, every day, as I saw my classmates in skirts and wearing their hair long. I desperately wanted to have long brown hair like one of the girls in my class. On one themed dress-up day in high school, another girl in my class wore a solid blue princess gown with her hair curled and everything. Sitting behind her in geometry class, all I could think about was how badly I wanted that dress, to the point that I had to scrunch up my face and squeeze my eyelids shut for a moment so as to not just yell, "Gaaahhh, why can't that be me?!" Of course, this longing to be me was also in constant battle with not wanting to get my ass kicked, to be taunted more than I already was, and of course, to disappoint my family. My transness as a kid manifested itself in internalized angst, which slowly made itself evident and then scared the shit out of me.

I had already had years of encounters with homophobia, starting around second grade, which is the first time I can remember ever having such an experience in school. My best friend at the time and I ran with our arms over each other's shoulders during a P.E. class after running on the track and someone asked my sister if my friend and I were gay. I have no idea what happened after that and can't say it was the defining moment that sent me on my way to wearing a rainbow bandanna twenty-six years later. But it might have planted a seed somewhere deep in my lizard brain for never wanting to be perceived as "gay" when horseplaying with my guy friends, which in turn kept me closeted to my guy friends for much, much longer than with my girl friends.

My story doesn't have an activist childhood or an assertion of my transness like "I am wee woman, hear me roar!" Rather, it has this actual thought pattern I had while holed up in the bathroom up-stairs at home during middle school: "If I wear nude tights under my uniform pants and I get tackled playing football,* will my pants leg run up and everyone see that I'm wearing pantyhose? Shit . . . I really, really, really want to . . . but . . . ummm . . . no, can't risk it . . . What if I wore a pad instead? I mean, they stick, right? And it's what women have to do, so I should, too . . ."

Some kids know they're trans right away, and they assert it from the time they're toddlers, like actress Nicole Maines. For me, it took a lot of figuring out, from being fascinated in kindergarten that this

---

*We were supposed to play two-hand touch football during middle-school recess and often did, but if the adults weren't paying attention, you could quickly get leveled. Just because the teachers couldn't legally inflict corporal punishment anymore didn't mean your Catholic school classmates wouldn't take it upon themselves.

one boy sat with the girls all the time during lunch and seeing him as a curiosity; to constantly staring at one boy with long hair in third grade, amazed that his parents let him have a dirty blond ponytail instead of—unfortunately common for the early '90s in the South— a rat tail; to being excited to play former president John Adams during a fifth-grade play because I thought it was an excuse to wear white stockings to school; to answering the question from one of my seventh-grade girl classmates, "Are you wearing lipstick?" by tearing off pieces of my bottom lip to prove beyond a shadow of a doubt that I was wearing Chapstick because my lips were so chapped (you see!) instead of the cherry lipstick that I wished to God I could have worn.

I don't get to have that moment-of-defiance story. I get to have the my-mom-caught-me-with-my-sister's-clothes-under-my-bed-the-morning-after-Halloween-when-I-was-thirteen-or-fourteen story. I'd dressed up as a goth girl for Halloween night, which raised some eyebrows but gave me a cover we could both use to avoid any conversation about it. When the clothes were still there the next day, including a black slip you'd wear under a skirt, the kind my ma considered underwear (though I didn't think of it like that at all), well. . . . let's say she's a lot cooler with it now than she was then. Suffice it to say that I decided that day that I wouldn't come out to my ma unless I was marrying someone, or turning thirty, whichever came first.

As I grew up, my identity became more and more clear to myself, even if I was too scared to show it to other people. One rainy day in high school, I was walking through the parking lot to get to my sister's car and I saw a lavender hair tie on the ground. I didn't have any hair ties at home, and oh, did I want one. A guy from one of my classes who I rode to school with glanced at me through the window. I didn't want him to see me pick up the hair tie, but I also *needed* it. Carrying my blue duffel-bag backpack, I knelt down, let the bag slide down my shoulder, and used it to block my hand picking up the hair tie. I was so nervous. I got home and washed it off, then even though my hair was not that long, I pulled up my hair with it as best I could. When I was a kid, the whole thing about dismissal and burying shit in the back of my mind turned out to be quite a utility. It's how I dealt with being a closet case. I chose the path of least resistance, which was to do typical "boy" stuff—play sports, watch sports, collect sports cards, and go to sporting events. Despite my profile as a heavy metal vocalist, my intense interest in music didn't develop until high school. Baseball was my first true passion, which I also used as a means to connect with my grandfather.

Music was, and is, my sister's domain; she's the human encyclopedia for 1960s to 1980s rock. When we were kids, she drew, painted, and listened to music while, being the older one, still managing to make more friends on our block than I did. So I spent hours at a time, year in and year out, throwing a baseball up in the air and catching it, throwing a football at trees in the front lawn without ever figuring out how to make the nose of the ball dip like the pros, and shooting a basketball into a makeshift hoop, a rim without a backboard on top of a wooden pole that my mom's ex-boyfriend had planted in the ground. When the snow packed in real high one day, I climbed to the top of a snow mound for my first and only attempt at dunking and bent the rim so it snapped out of place and tilted up.

With the Wiffle ball, I'd play home-run derby by myself on the driveway, throwing the ball up and trying to hit it over the garage roof. When it'd get stuck in a corner near a gutter, that's when the game was over. The acre-plus of woods in the backyard probably has a number of golf balls still back there from when I tried out my grandpa's primary driver club. All of that is to say that I didn't have a bunch of kids to play with on my street. And when I did play, I had sports. The idea of even being introduced to dolls and dresses wasn't an option (my sister wasn't into them either), so I made do with Cal Ripken Jr. and Troy Aikman like a lot of kids growing up in the early to mid-1990s. I spent years of my early life wondering if liking sports really made me a boy even when I felt like a girl, until I had this strange, sudden epiphany: *Girls play sports, too.* The reason you see few cisgender girls play the popular ball-based sports at recess is because the boys discourage the hell out of them: refusing to pass to them, picking them last, and either taunting them or refusing to be physical. Boys can be outright terrible toward girls when it comes to sports, and girls often either put up with it and work even harder to just be respected or say some version of "That's it, I'm out," and find something else to do.

For about eight years, I played Manassas Park–Yorkshire Little League (MPYLL) baseball at Costello Park in Manassas Park. After two years of playing Pee Wee, I tried out on the Majors field to determine whether I'd move up to the next level (Minors) or skip that and go directly to Majors. Having loved the Los Angeles Dodgers for as long as I could remember, I wore my beige and beat-up used Tommy John fake-signature glove from the long-since-closed Play It Again Sports to tryouts. Tommy John's storied twenty-six-year big-league career included six years pitching as a Dodgers left-hander during the 1970s on a squad that lost the World Series three times before he lost one more with the New York Yankees against—surprise!—the Dodgers in 1981. (To Tommy's credit, the Yankees actually won the one game he pitched.)

Buuuut most people don't remember his All-Star career or that he was the runner-up for a Cy Young award in 1977. They remember that a ligament in his elbow dissolved so badly in 1974 that the 1975 surgery to replace it is named after him—Tommy John surgery—

and that thirteen years later, he committed three fielding errors while on defense in one single at-bat.

So that's the legacy I decided to bring onto the ball field with me that day in 1994: hurt yourself so badly, people remember your pain.

Standing in the second-base position on the infield dirt, one of the coaches hit a line drive toward right field. I thought I had no chance of catching it whatsoever, so I just stuck my gloved left hand out *Daria*-style without moving more than a step.

plop

I looked left and tried to control my eyes from bulging out of my head. The damn thing stuck right in the webbing of my glove.

The coaches behind home plate furiously scribbled notes.

I can't remember the rest of the tryouts. Later that evening, I got a call from the voice of a thousand cigarettes, Mr. Miller, congratulating me for making a spot on the White Sox roster.

Majors. As in, I skipped a level. That would be my first and, not so coincidentally, last memorable moment of my four-year stint in Majors—I was a bench player.

I wore a T-shirt jersey with the last name of the Dodgers' Japanese pitching phenom Hideo Nomo, the 1995 Rookie of the Year, two-time All-Star, and two-time strikeout leader with an unforgettably elaborate windup delivery. When you're a kid, wearing the jersey of a professional player is meant to be aspirational, sort of like wearing all black to mimic Johnny Cash, or resupplying all your blood to mimic Keith Richards. (That's normal, right?) However, having a mop of brown hair, no friends on your teams after years of playing, and being the worst player, all while being surrounded by tween and teenage boys, led to an alternate interpretation of the name on the jersey: "Nomo the Homo."

I never talked about my sexual orientation, let alone my gender identity, to anyone back then at all, which maybe was a clue. When my teammates would ogle one of the players' "hot" sister—a teenager with shoulder-length hair wearing a tank top to the game—I wondered where she shopped. When a cisgender girl joined my team, and the guys would talk behind her back (and sometimes to her face) about her looks, I just fixated on her pink scrunchie, wishing I could grow my hair out long enough to wear one. She was actually a hell of a good player. Girls playing baseball had to fight so hard to earn respect among the boys and she had a great swing that no doubt came from constant practice. (Which is not unlike how hard women have to fight to serve in elected office, often making them great lawmakers, might I add . . .)

But that's the thing about being a childhood closet case: You said nothing to anyone lest you stand out. If someone asked you what you thought of fill-in-the-blank girl's looks, you either agreed that she was hot or you put her down. You didn't describe how her French braids looked or even remark on her personality, unless it was "She's a bitch" or "Yeah, she's cool, I guess . . ."

Doing that neither helped nor hurt me. It just kept me from outing myself, insofar as a child internalizing toxic masculinity to achieve that objective allowed. It wasn't just relegated to the girls either; when you were making fun of guys, the first thing you did was call them "gay" or "fag" or whatever other homophobic slur that was objectively terrible and yet utterly commonplace, without any pushback beyond "I know you are, but what am I?" Not to put too fine a point on it, but it's been more than twenty years since I played baseball as a kid, and a player from one of my teams whom I had long, long since forgotten about *still* writes transphobic comments about me on social media, even though we haven't spoken in more than two decades. (Incidentally, someone who knew you as a kid insisting that you've always been queer as if that was a bad thing is oddly affirming as an adult making the case that you were born this way. Thanks, buddy!)

When you're ten years old, you don't even know what "internalize" means, let alone sexism and homophobia. What you can put together is that being a "boy" who "wants to be a girl" means you would be a social pariah, 100 percent unable to attend your Catholic school, and 100 percent likely to cause trouble in your Catholic household. So you shut your mouth about it and act like a boy until you're at home, by yourself, and can daydream about being a flight attendant—which is exactly what I did. On more than one occasion, when I was home and my sister and Ma were out, I'd wear a pleated black skirt I found in my sister's closet with black tights, a little white dress shirt with black trim, and a Delta Air Lines hat while staring into the mirror and visualizing myself in the aisle of a plane somewhere high above and far, far away, being asked for drinks or food by passengers who called me "Miss."

I had to learn about trans people from daytime talk shows, not from actually talking to anyone—and it wasn't like I even knew the phrase "transgender" when I was a kid. If I didn't know anyone who was openly gay in my life, I sure as hell wasn't going to know anyone who was trans. I just knew that when I saw girls, I wanted to be like them—I had a Cindy Crawford poster on the back side of my closet door of her looking over her shoulder, a pose I mimicked many, many times in private while still giving the outward impression that I thought she was hot—but knew that was absolutely out of bounds. "Boys" didn't hang with the girls. The girls would have kicked you out, anyway, for intruding on their space.

So sports it was. Back on the baseball diamond, when I aged into playing on the big field for Juniors and Seniors (as in, teenagers), the experience went about as well as expected: starting out as a bench player, ducking toward the dirt in the batter's box as quickly as I could, thinking the baseball was headed right toward my head when I finally did have a chance at bat, only for the ball to curve toward the catcher's mitt for a called strike.

In eight years, I had an extra-base hit exactly once in my career on a liner to left-center field. That, however, was the exception. The boys on my team knew I admired a long-since-retired former Dodger-turned-Washington Senator, Frank "Hondo" Howard, as he was a close friend of my former neighbors who were D.C. sports buffs.

With runners in scoring position, they told me to hit one for Frank . . . and when I struck out to end the inning, and despite my well-trained, well-honed repression skills, tears escaped my eyes. The physical aspect of the game just wasn't for me, no matter which bat I tried or which glove I wore. When I made the starting lineup as the ninth hitter and the right fielder during my final season in 1999, it was only because the coach wanted to reward the fact that I never complained, always hustled, and tried to do what the coaches said without back talk. Likewise, the people skills I completely lacked with the players I made up for with my coaches, to the point that they sometimes let me pencil in the lineup for the games during my last two seasons.

Socially, I was a nerd about baseball: I was the player who knew who won, who lost, and how many games it took for every World Series since 1903; what Cal Ripken Jr.'s season batting average was that morning; or who won the 1960 National League Rookie of the Year. (Answer: Frank Howard. He wrote it on a baseball he gave to me.)

It's not like I was a mature adult-in-waiting by any stretch (I once used my jockstrap cup to simulate a gas mask while bored in the dugout in Pee Wee league, trying to make my teammates laugh). I just sucked at making friends. The easiest way to earn respect on a team is to be good at playing your sport, and as previously established, I wasn't. I was a bench player who didn't talk back to the coaches, so I spent plenty of time seated near them.

While I played baseball in the spring and early summer, the fall and winter from fifth through eighth grade was for my Catholic school's boys basketball team. Like with baseball, I didn't have any physical talent. And like with baseball, I kept a real good warm seat until my five minutes to sort of but not really shine during the second or third quarter—or the fourth quarter when we were winning in a blowout.

I had some legit friends who all had in common a basketball coach who'd shout until he was red-faced during practice. Then, during games, he'd do his best Bobby Knight you've-got-to-be-f'n-kidding-me impression until he was (repeatedly) ejected. Our assistant coach once told us in a huddle as we were getting clobbered, "Okay, guys, let's make this respectable."

I saw the difference between public school baseball and Catholic school basketball—in how kids would act with their coaches and vice versa. With the exception of corporal punishment now being a relic of my mom's generation, all the stereotypes about enforced discipline in Catholic school were completely true. Some players would talk back to the coach, but usually at their own peril. In Little League, kids talking back was just a bit more common and with fewer consequences.

The public school Little League parents would also ask my mom about why my father or stepfather wasn't present, which wasn't their business, but they wanted to know anyway. She didn't feel like having to explain the whole chronic depression leading to suicide by gas canister thing, so she just said he died in a fire. Jack, her then-boyfriend during the early- to mid-1990s, had no interest in ball sports—he much preferred killing animals along with his other hobbies of blatant racism and misspelled homophobia—so there was no way he was showing up at my games at any regular interval.

T he thing about playing youth sports as a closet-case trans kid is that you get used to wearing a uniform. Add to that going to Catholic school, where having your uniform shirttail untucked can—and very much did—lead to a Saturday detention. I also learned to curse the name of Flynn O'Hara, maker of the yellow golf shirt and yellow button-down shirt with striped tie we had to wear every single day, paired with our blue trousers. The uniform wouldn't get any better in high school, with blue button-down shirts, a different color plaid tie, and tan trousers. It wasn't until college that I could have a Catholic education in the comfort and flattery of heavy metal T-shirts with skulls on them. After all, nothing quite screams, "I'm a delicate, feminine flower!" like a spiked mallet crushing bones under a Metallica logo on a T-shirt.

Here's the thing, though: I don't do victimhood well and it's not like my day-to-day existence as a kid was a constant carousel of trauma. It's just that when I came to realize I was trans, it sucked, and it's something I had to learn to manage from the time I was ten years old, just like I had to learn to deal with death from the time I was three. By that point, as puberty set in, I had a lovely introduction to closet-case Catholicism by crying myself to sleep after I had my first sexual thought, fantasizing about being under a nondescript guy. See, the problem wasn't a sudden reckoning of my sexuality or thoughts about how I could make it go away. Oh, no, no, no; it was "Oh, no, I'm going to hell!" Thanks, Catholic school.

At least at the time, priests during Friday mass would talk about homosexuality rather than gender identity, which wasn't even a concept brought up at the time. Catholic school morality in the 1990s basically boiled down to "don't be gay"—no joke, in tenth grade, my religion teacher actually taught the "God made Adam and Eve, not Adam and Steve" crap—and definitely "don't have an abortion." Abortions were a big no-no under any circumstance, including rape, because "it's not the baby's fault!"

We weren't even presented with "Here are reasons why someone may even consider an abortion," "Here's why it's legal in the first place," or "Here's what happened when some people were so desperate to end their unwanted pregnancies that they unraveled coat hangers and risked infections, heavy bleeding, and even death because they didn't want or simply couldn't go through a pregnancy for a variety of circumstances you couldn't even possibly begin to understand as a kid in Catholic school whose survival is facilitated by other people instead of being entirely on your own in a world that views you as an object of the street and considers you a leech to the dole." Knowing that none of that's changed in the twenty years since I graduated from high school, I shudder to even begin to think what closet-case trans kids hear these days at the lectern now that being trans is part of the national dialogue.

One day during the tenth grade, one of my friends and I sat in the bleachers at the end of P.E., just talking about music until the bell rang. The gym was filled with the murmurings of students talking to one another, knowing we were all about to leave.

That's when one of the girls walked up in front of the bleachers, looked up, and loudly asked me, "Are you gay?"

It seemed like the whole world shut up at once. I could hear conversations instantly end and see eyes turn toward me. My eyes bugged out. I had no interest whatsoever in revealing my truth, so I simply said, ". . . No!" while justifying this bullshit in my mind by telling myself, "I'm bi!"

High school sports kept getting the worst of me. During P.E., I'd dive for a dig during volleyball, only to hear comments about me being on my "hands and knees" when I looked up. That became typical. I took wrestling after school as an extracurricular activity my sophomore year. I figured I needed one of those to put down on my eventual college application, and it would also do me well to take something similar to a self-defense course. My teammates quite literally poked and prodded, trying to determine my sexuality. A ho-hum example came in the locker room when one of the boys asked, "Aside from wanting to roll around on mats with a bunch of guys, why else do you take wrestling?" A more messed-up example of it—which at the time didn't register as sexual assault, but which as an adult I have come to realize definitely was—came when I was in referee's position (on hands and knees) during practice. My sparring partner put his left hand on my left elbow per usual, but then took his index finger and poked it directly into my ass as he laughed himself red in the face, leading me to jump up and yell whatever threat at him that he and everyone else knew I had no means of carrying out. I was just humiliated.

For being a closet case, I don't know what I did at the time to be so obvious, but time and time again people just seemed to assume I was gay, and they were dead set on either informing me about this or asking me about it, as if to confirm this information for themselves.

The irony, of course, being that at the time, the person I thought the most about was actually a girl I met online when she was four-teen and I was fifteen. But more on that later.

Being scared to show people who I really was also meant that the people I was most afraid to disappoint in my family by coming out never actually met me as the woman I am, just the guy I dressed up as every day. Getting to the point where I could experience the hills and valleys of transitioning with family took a long, long time. Gender dysphoria is like a hand that clutches your throat and closes over time. For some people, it's rapid; for others, it's gradual. I fell into the latter category and lived in this choke hold until I was twenty-eight.

Even though playing sports didn't exactly contribute to my social life, it at least provided family time. My grandfather would, every now and then, play catch with me in the yard, well into his eighties. I even remember on New Year's Day in 2006, just weeks after his ninetieth birthday, it was nice enough outside for us to throw the ball around, which ended up being the last time we would do so before he moved into assisted living, then a nursing home, and then the same hospital where I was born, where he died in 2008.

Though it was becoming increasingly fraught for me at school, navigating the challenges of being a closet-case trans girl also taught me resiliency. That's a trait I saw on display every single day from my mother, the most resilient person I've ever witnessed. She could be tough on my sister and me—and even on Grandpa from time to time—but it was always crystal clear to me that she was full of the steel resolve not to let my father's suicide take everything from her that she had worked so hard for. She ran a tight ship and we learned that a person had to earn what they had. Yet she still managed to take care of us in such a way that we never felt poor or any sense of real lacking. Seeing my mom's perseverance play out in real time and learning about my grandfather's struggle through poverty and the death of his mother when he was a kid taught me early that you don't get through life by playing the victim (unless, I guess, you're a billionaire former president of the United States, at which point grievance is all you know). You tough it out and figure out a way to make it work. Seeing this high school dropout, widower, World War II veteran in his seventies and eighties sitting in his recliner, smiling while watching a baseball game in the living room each day, served as that day-to-day reminder that there wasn't a person in the house who didn't know struggle. We've all experienced it at some point, just to different degrees. In hindsight, I suppose that's one of the reasons I looked up to my grandfather without even realizing it. After my grandmother died in the early 1990s, when he was seventy-six years old, he said he thought he would only have a year left in his own life. Yet he endured, through the 1990s and into the 2000s.

When I came home from college during winter break for my grandfather's ninetieth birthday in December 2005, I brought a black binder with me to a restaurant where our extended family joined him for lunch. In twenty-four pages of single-space text, I had written a biography about my grandfather for my senior capstone project. Knowing this milestone birthday was coming, I thought that dedicating my senior capstone to him seemed like the perfect time and way to honor his life and all he meant to me. At that point, my grandfather's health was deteriorating—he was having memory lapses, leaving his false teeth around, flushing things down the toilet that shouldn't be, etc. In those moments you realize that time is short, so you should do something meaningful while you still can.

At that birthday lunch, I told my grandfather what the book was about, but he didn't fully understand what I presented to him. A few weeks later, I saw the binder in his lap in his living room—Grandpa's Room—as he sat in his recliner with the television on.

"Hey, this sounds like me," he said, reading a passage about an Italian guy from New York City stationed at Fort Bliss, Texas, during World War II.

"Grandpa, it *is* you," I replied.

He smiled, but again, it didn't quite sink in. At least not yet.

Another few days passed. I was twenty-one years old, days away from leaving home again to complete my eighth and final semester at St. Bonaventure before graduating that May. As I walked down the stairs from my room, I passed the white drywall on my left and peeked over the railing into Grandpa's Room, where he was sitting in his recliner as usual.

The binder was open in his lap again, but something was different this time. I walked over to him and, without saying a word, he extended his right hand out toward me. I sat on the couch behind him, clutched his hand, and could see the tears welling in his eyes behind his glasses.

I don't know what page it was or what passage he had read. I don't know what memory the book jogged or why it was on that particular day the book finally clicked for him.

But it did. And we didn't say a word.

I just pursed my lips in a repressed smile and sat there holding his hand—without a word needed, we said everything we wanted.

CHAPTER 3

METALHEAD

Roem has spent "over a decade" fronting the thrash metal band Cab Ride Home, whose biggest hit is a party anthem "about getting wasted."

Danica in her own words discussing the band: "The entire premise of my band is the party, drinking band, right? Our big song is called 'Drunk on Arrival.'"

—Friends of Danica Roem self-opposition research for 2017, conducted by Grindstone Research

D o you have a particular album that just unleashes a flood of memories for you? For me, that album is *Comalies*, the 2002 follow-up to the Italian gothic metal band Lacuna Coil's 2001 album, *Unleashed Memories*. Funny how that works out.

It's been twenty years now since Lacuna Coil's third full-length album dropped during my first semester of college, but every time I listen to it, it's like saying hello to an old friend after a long absence. The kind of friend you don't make many new memories with, but when you do see each other, you find the ones you did make were so vast and so good that they've etched a smile on your soul.

That's the power and beauty of heavy metal for me and many, many metalheads around the world. I embraced heavy metal as a teenager because it was audio rebellion and somehow also a healthy channel for fear, alienation, and the terror of mortality, all of which I carry with me to this day. Seeing badass cis women fronting metal bands also gave me hope that maybe there was a place for a woman like me onstage, albeit one who happens to be trans.

My final two years warming the bench at baseball overlapped with my first two years of high school, which is when I got into heavy metal. My journey into heavy metal started with listening to the classic rock radio station in my mom's car. Led Zeppelin was her favorite and I can't remember a time that I didn't know "Paranoid" by Black Sabbath. While my music tastes at that point were centered on whatever was on the radio—the first cassette tape my grandparents on my dad's side of the family bought for me was *Quadrophenia* by The Who and my first CD was a George Thorogood live album recorded in 1986, because what middle-schooler doesn't want "One Bourbon, One Scotch, One Beer" in their life?—I dabbled in other genres that just didn't stay. I had cassette tapes ranging from MC Hammer's "2 Legit 2 Quit" to "The Sign" by Ace of Base in elementary school, with some mainstream, radio-friendly, definitely-not-outlaw country and a couple Neil Diamond albums mixed in there, too. Still, though, you were most likely to find me during long road trips with cassette tapes by Dire Straits and The Who in my Walkman with the over-the-ears, felt-covered headphones that, no matter how hard I wished it into existence, just didn't quite resemble a headband.

My sister was often my way into new music. When Nirvana frontman Kurt Cobain died in 1994, I was only nine and wasn't familiar with his music, but my sister got into Nirvana and the whole grunge scene within the next couple of years. By the time I was in eighth grade, I had picked it up from her and was drawing the Nirvana logo on my marble notebooks, along with the logos from alternative bands like Sublime and Live.

When I got to high school in 1998, I found out very quickly that while it was cool to wear a Nirvana *From the Muddy Banks of the Wishkah* live album T-shirt in the eighth grade during a band field trip to Hershey Park in Pennsylvania, wearing that same shirt—of someone who killed himself—made for easy bullying fodder in the ninth grade. I wore my Nirvana shirt exactly one time for a dress-down day (when we didn't have to wear uniforms) and just heard a parade of shitty suicide jokes—someone even wrote "What's got more brains than Einstein? Kurt Cobain's ceiling fan!" in my yearbook—which was just delightful for a kid whose dad killed himself.

So, as egregious as the prompt had been, trying not to get picked on for liking one band oddly led me to embracing an entire genre of music seemingly engineered to alienate as many people as possible: *heavy fuckin' metal.*

I had heard Black Sabbath on the radio from the time I was a little kid, so liking them and Ozzy Osbourne was a natural fit for me. I at least had them going for me when I entered my social studies class as a freshman. In the back row sat one guy who, at his fifteenth birthday party, covered "Enter Sandman" by Metallica as a lead guitarist. Two of the other guys in class were drummers, including one who had a wicked sense of humor and actual underground bands like Snot written on his backpack. He listened to the one band my mom forbade in her house—Marilyn Manson—so when he and the others talked about music, I listened like a rookie apprentice.

I laid a stake early during my freshman year into proclaiming Black Sabbath as my new favorite band, followed by Ozzy and Metallica, because I wanted to fit in, and, frankly, I really did like Black Sabbath a lot. That led me to the Spencer's store at Manassas Mall to buy a black shirt with BLACK SABBATH printed in neon blue and white on each side, a picture of the band printed in the same color on the front, and a giant crucifix—resembling the one guitarist Tony Iommi wears onstage—above the words on the back. Perfect for (freaking out kids at) Catholic school.

When I wore that shirt to school on the next dress-down day,

"Are you satanic?" or "Do you worship the devil?" came up four times. Now I was getting to be the rebel—and that's something I liked because that meant I was different in an antiauthoritarian way, that I wasn't going to follow whatever fashion sense and attitude were trendy and popular but instead let the logos of my favorite bands speak up for me. It seemed the jocks—the people who gave me shit on my baseball team—liked rap. They didn't like metal. This was something I could use to separate myself from them. Freaks versus jocks! Yeah! Also, the thing about metal is—cue closet-case trans girl— long hair on guys is totally normal! In fact, Metallica ate loads of shit for cutting their hair in the run-up to releasing *Load* in 1996. I knew I only had four years left of having to wear a uniform. As soon as I graduated, I could grow out my hair and everyone would just assume that's because I liked metal. Sure . . . That, too . . .

During my 1999 spring baseball season, I brought my newfound love of heavy metal with me to the field. One of the coaches—who had a dark sense of humor—would wear a gray 1912 TITANIC SWIM CREW T-shirt to practice and, as I found out, liked metal. Before I attended my first concert—Ozzfest '99, with Black Sabbath headlining and Rob Zombie in direct support, and the legendary thrash band Slayer fourth from last main stage for some reason—I told him I wanted to go into the Slayer mosh pit.

He arched his chin down toward his chest as he looked at me. "*I'm* too small for a Slayer mosh pit," he said.

Noted.

Not that it mattered—I got to my first ever live show just after Slayer finished playing on the main stage at the Nissan Pavilion and caught the super-intense industrial metal band Fear Factory headlining the side stage at the bottom of the grassy hill. Walking the concrete steps up the hill, my ninth-grade Catholic school eyes saw a Cradle of Filth T-shirt with JESUS IS A [EXPLETIVE] written on the back—my first of several culture shocks to come that day on the grass.

On the one hand, I was a bit scared seeing something *that* sacrilegious. That was someone I was certain I did not want to get to know. One of the kids in my band class had introduced me to Cradle of Filth's *Cruelty and the Beast* album earlier in the school year and it was too much for a fourteen-year-old underground metal virgin. Little ol' Black Sabbath–listening me, who was just starting to learn that Metallica, the biggest metal band in the world, had a 1980s catalog that was heavier and thrashier than their radio-friendly 1990s catalog, wasn't at shrieking, vampiric black metal with blast beats yet—even though black metal fans today would laugh you out of the venue if you thought a band like Cradle of Filth meant anything beyond Baby's First Black Metal ornament.

Hell, I wasn't even at its album cover yet: a naked, gothic woman with a jet-black Bettie Page haircut looking up from a blood-filled tub as streaks of blood ran down her face and legs along her scrunched-up body. I mean, the *Paranoid* album cover just had three identical versions of a guy with a sword and a shield. Seeing the back of that Cradle of Filth shirt at Ozzfest served as a quick reminder that I wasn't as badass as I thought I was, and even though I wanted to be there, I was still very much a fish out of water during that part of my first concert.

The second culture shock came at the sight of this puffy little cloud that made my lungs itch. It was exactly what you think it was: my first encounter with the smell of pot. Nope. All I had heard in my life up to that point was, "Drugs are bad. You shouldn't do drugs. Mmm, 'kay?" I wasn't even curious to start. (Fun fact: To this day, I've only ever drunk alcohol and taken my prescriptions. That's it. Not even a cigarette.)

Then came my first encounter with aggressive antiauthoritarian-ism, as I saw the singer of Fear Factory, Burton C. Bell, tell the audi-ence that he wanted to see us flipping cop cars over in the parking lot. Not that any of us did it, but as a relatively sheltered private-school kid, hearing someone actually yell that into the mic and re-ceive a roaring ovation of approval served as another "whoa, holy shit" moment.

Finally, looking down from the hill into the crowd and seeing a crowd-surfer amid a dust cloud appear to be bent into a backward V as the heels of his shoes seemed about ready to hit the base of his skull ended whatever mosh-pit fantasy I had concocted pre-show. It informed me that staying at the top of the hill as a fourteen-year-old wearing a black shirt of the band I was there to see—Black Sabbath—was enough of an introduction for one day.

I didn't have the money for a T-shirt, so I bought a program and took it to my next baseball practice, giving my coach—who often wore a Metallica "Pushead"-designed shirt (skulls, lots of skulls)—something to flip through and, hopefully, think better of me.

There were other metalheads in my high school, but I hadn't grown up around them—I commuted forty-five minutes to school in Fairfax from my home in Manassas. So I didn't have that to fall back on in terms of relationship-building. At the same time, being some-one who drifted from niche to niche, I wasn't wholly rejected or wholly embraced by any one group. In a weird way, being a social misfit can breed its own sense of conformity and I found myself try-ing, and failing, to fit in.

You might think we'd all bond over our shared tastes, but the thing that will separate metalheads is the people who play in bands and are good at it versus the people who like the music but either don't play it or struggle to learn how to play it themselves. While I was just trying to put two notes of a Jimi Hendrix song together without losing the grip of one of my fingers on the fretboard at age sixteen, some of my metalhead classmates were already covering Metallica and Swedish melodic death metal pioneers In Flames in their bands. There's just no catching up there. While it was a different setting than sports, I still had to wrestle with the same feelings of inadequacy that my lack of athletic prowess brought to the surface, only now for music. Sure, I played trumpet. But even with that, I was constantly second or third trumpet. I just didn't have the chops and had to learn to accept that reality, one drop of spit leaking out from the release valve and onto my lap at a time.

When you're a malleable teenager seeking the approval of others, you can find yourself conforming to what you think other people's tastes and interests are instead of figuring out what works for you. That brings with it a special degree of contradiction for many young metalheads: reveling in an anti-conformity attitude of rejecting popular culture while also figuring out how to conform within social circles based on the expectations, styles, and tastes of those setting the tone for what's *really* cool. Just because you reject mainstream groupthink doesn't mean you're not susceptible to *underground* groupthink in your own bubbles, circles, and bullshit.

And while rejecting mainstream groupthink to assert individualism was a goal, seeing Metallica, Black Sabbath, Pantera, and Ozzy Osbourne (solo) live as a fourteen- and fifteen-year-old was a lesson in being part of a whole: Individually, our voices wouldn't be able to compete with their amplified guitars, drums, and booming vocals over the PA. But together, twenty thousand or even seventy thousand people strong, we could be the fifth instrument. There's nothing like it—and it gave me bragging rights at school: I was seeing the cool bands while most of my friends weren't at *those* shows.

Guess they just weren't cool enough to have their moms drive them in a station wagon and agree to find the "meeting spot" in the parking lot after the show—"just remember to call from the pay phone first so I can come and get you!"

The underground metal scene, however, is much, much more intimate and personal than what you see at big festivals and concerts, and the one thing I did have going for me, more so than any of my friends, was that I was going to *a lot* of underground shows. Like, a ton of club gigs, starting during my junior year and into my senior year of high school, because I was working after school as a courier for a land-surveying company and saving my money. That's something I kept up, and even accelerated, in college, going to places many hours away just to enjoy a couple of hours of music. I could then turn to an internet community where I wasn't inherently less cool than anyone else; I was driving the conversation about new bands and sharing experiences with other people doing the same. If control issues were currency, heavy metal message boards could really give Bitcoin a run for its money. (Dogecoin, however . . .)

That's the thing about the internet: it's so vast that if you're a metalhead with a specific taste and lots of time on your hands, it's quite possible to find a community of peers who share your interests—or at least it was in 2002.

GOING TO COLLEGE in New York and meeting other people from other cities and states meant that I finally didn't feel like a reject outsider because meeting new people was inherently part of freshman year—and if you wanted free beer as a seventeen-year-old, you had best be meeting someone who could provide it. I could count on

two hands how many other Virginians went to St. Bonaventure—
and that made me feel unique. Part of the appeal of going out of state
for college was that I didn't feel like I was going to live in anyone else's
shadow. I could establish myself on my own grounds—but only as it
related to metal. And, well, Jägermeister consumption. But mostly
metal. Since one person I went to high school with was at my college
with me and the two of us didn't get along particularly well at the
time, I felt that if I came out, word would get out at home and I just
couldn't have that—I feared being outed was a fate far more punish-
ing than being labeled with the most typical metalhead insult: poser.
(Or poseur, depending on your brand of Euroness.)

Instead, I felt like that just meant I needed to live up the metal
part of my identity, which I did all through college. I went all in.
Lacuna Coil became the first band I got super into after high school,
and because they were new to touring the United States, I could treat
them as *my* band, an extension of my identity, because no one else I
knew in real life away from the internet knew them. That meant I
could be the person introducing my friends to something I loved and
see them enjoy it, too, when they would hear it, kind of like watching someone eat your cooking . . . only you bought it premade and
the only prep work you did was unwrapping the damn thing. (Hey,
Paul Hollywood had to start somewhere, too . . .)

Still, that felt good, and I kept branching off from that, spending
hours on heavy metal forums and news sites or driving 1.5 hours
to Erie, Pennsylvania, to sit in the Borders magazine section for
three hours reading *Metal Maniacs, Decibel, Metal Hammer, Metal
Edge,* and whoever else published pictures of obscure Scandinavian
metal musicians frowning in black-and-white corpse paint like a
bunch of tr00 kvlt Nordic panda bears. This was, of course, how you

learned about bands before Myspace, Twitter, YouTube, Bandcamp, and Facebook existed, and then you went to see them live. Each of the new bands I found, either on my own or from internet friends, made me feel like I was etching out my own identity within the underground community.

And nothing compared to when I started writing for a heavy metal site called Sin's Metal News, thanks to an English friend I nicknamed Hos who I met on a message board and who invited me to write and edit for him. It gave me a sense of real authority I'd never experienced before; a sense of belonging around these musicians who were now guest-listing me for shows, inviting me on their tour buses, and drinking/partying with me after shows: chief among them, Lacuna Coil. I felt like Queen Shit internally in the best way possible. I had a role to play in the community and I loved it.

The underground is also where you can form personal connections with bands playing venues that range from the size of walk-in closets to a capacity of a few thousand people. I've played the former and have raged at the latter. Trust me, both have their time and place. The only black eye I ever got was from performing in front of a super-packed audience of about fifteen people in a basement room in Annandale, Virginia. As I put my wireless microphone behind my back and went down to headbang, my friend Annie, who was in the front row right in front of me, was on her way back up and, sure enough: *pow!* The back of her head collided with my face. But, alas, the show must go on! When there's an injury in the pit, you help someone get back up to their feet, hug it out, and rock out— together.

Without question, though, one of the best parts about being in the underground is the camaraderie that comes with sharing a space that few other people could appreciate as much as you and the people around you. The people who are so into heavy metal and heavy music that they're willing to see bands that aren't getting mainstream attention and are hoping to collect enough gas money to get from venue to venue on their American tour. With that, you can form a bond, not only with the other fans in the room, but with the bands, too, getting to know them before and after the shows. Underground musicians are generally much, much more accessible than the millionaire giants you see setting off fireworks at the end of their stadium-headliners because, well, they have to be. More times than not, they're the ones who are personally selling you their merch after the show, and the best way to someone's heart in the underground when you're a musician is to just be cool and hang out. That means you get to connect with a band in person when they're just starting out or haven't quite hit their peak yet.

That was Lacuna Coil for me. I first saw a photo on an online metal forum during the summer of 2002 of their band, whose singer, Cristina Scabbia, was wearing an ITALIANS DO IT BETTER T-shirt. Being of Italian descent and desperately wanting to see myself represented onstage, but without any real trans representation in metal that I knew of, I wanted to like Lacuna Coil before I even heard them. It just so happened that they changed my perspective on music when the first single from their upcoming album *Comalies* dropped.

That. Voice. OHMYGOD. It was just butter.

I had never heard anything in the genre so simultaneously haunting and beautiful—it was everything I wanted, along with the catchy yet well-constructed melodic doom tracks from my family's ancestral homeland. Cristina was also someone who I could admire as a positive role model, with her dark, heavy metal aesthetic, the contrast to the band's male vocalist Andrea Ferro, whose range of harsh vocals to clean singing made it super fun to go forehead to forehead with him in the front row. While I wanted nothing more in the world than to start presenting with a feminine gender expression, I instead wore black size-XL metal band shirts that hung over me like loose garbage bags every day or a button-down gray worker's shirt with the Nevermore band logo etched on the left breast pocket. Within the month I started college, I would be walking through the mall with my best friend, Lauren, as a newly minted college freshman wearing a shirt of the gray, dark, and bleak *Blackwater Park* album cover from the Swedish progressive death-metal band Opeth, when we passed the Regis hair salon. There, I saw this true gothic woman, Patti: like a seventeen-year-old Morticia Addams, she immediately caught my attention, given that I was also a seventeen-year-old metalhead growing out her hair (albeit while still wearing metal guy clothes).

Patti complimented my shirt when I walked in and we struck up a quick conversation. She was surprised; not a lot of metalheads went to St. Bonaventure. I was surprised there was a genuinely gothic hairstylist in the middle of "Bumfuck, New York," as one of my professors called it. I had an inkling that I could come out to her, correctly guessing that someone willing to be so eccentric and all-around metallic would likely be okay with "different." Indeed, the hint I gave her was that I wanted my hair to look like Cristina Scabbia's from Lacuna Coil—and it turned out, she was a fan. Coming out to her from that point was so easy and she was (and is) such an amazing stylist, I would drive three hundred twenty–plus miles each year after college for the better part of a decade so that she could still be the one who cut my hair. While she wasn't the first person I had come out to, she was one of the very few women I actually did talk to about being a closet-case trans woman instead of telling her I was bi first as a stepping-stone to get to gender. So she and I did what seventeen-year-old gothic metal chicks do: talk about super-hot metal dudes and the sultriness of gothic metal vocalists Peter Steele from Type O Negative and Fernando Ribeiro from Moonspell. I felt like I could melt into the chair, actually being talked to and treated like a young woman by a peer without any pretense. As I would come to find out throughout my teens, twenties, and thirties, my safest, happiest place where I can just open up and talk about anything is in the chairs of the hairstylists who are some of my dearest friends.

As it also turned out, my newfound love of Lacuna Coil ended up being how I would make a bunch of other friends across the Northeast. From 2003 to 2004, I saw the band at least twenty-five times in nine different states because, apparently, I hate having money as much as I love being on the road. It started out on May 15, 2003, at Birch Hill in Old Bridge, New Jersey, one of three times I saw them *just at that one venue* several hours from home or campus. After the show, I saw them in the parking lot talking to other fans. When it was my turn, I just meekly asked for a hug. It was hard to explain in the moment—how I saw in Cristina who I wanted to be and in the band's music a sound I loved so much.

At one point in September of that first year, I drove five hours out to Albany to see them play at this tiny place called Valentine's in front of 110 people. I had dinner with them on the bus afterward, something that made me feel accepted and welcomed by a group of people who I not only respected but genuinely looked up to and admired so much. When you're in your late teens and you're being validated by hanging around people you consider more important than you, then hot-diggity-damn, you're in! You've got a story and you are, objectively, cool as shit. So that's how I felt leaving a little before 3 A.M. to make it back to campus by 8:00 A.M. in order to catch my 8:30 A.M. class that Friday morning. Fun side note—I hallucinated like mad-hell (despite being completely sober), which is a terrible idea for driving but, for what it's worth, really funny. Like, at one point, I thought I saw a twenty-foot-tall, slow-running cowboy—completely with a ten-gallon hat—along the side of the road and, not long afterward, a herd of buffalo scampering across the interstate. "Ohhh myyyyyy Godddddd!" I muttered to myself out loud under my breath, eyes bulging. Both times, of course, turned out to be just trees on the side of the road, but there's something about sleep deprivation that turns rational thought patterns into *splat*.

I powered through my day, slept for two hours, and drove with my friend John six or so hours back out to Birch Hill for a second night so that I could restock on good tunes and validation. We then headed up to his parents' home in Long Island after the show, then left in the morning for another five-hour drive to Syracuse for a third show in three nights.

The following year, I quite literally bled for that band, catching an elbow to the nose while moshing to "Tight Rope." I spun around and hit the floor, lying stunned as someone flashed a light in my face and people yelled "Get up!" to me before I felt the rush of warm liquid pour out from my right nostril, over my lips, and down in streaks along my chin. Before I got patched up on the tailgate of an ambulance that happened to be parked outside the venue, I asked the medics to take a photo for me with my disposable camera. I crossed my arms into an X-shape, threw the horns (index finger and little finger up, other fingers tucked inside thumb in your palm—you know the one), and opened my lips to reveal my clenched, blood-soaked teeth and mean-mugged it for the memory. While I would absolutely feel it later, in that moment, I was far more upset that I was missing "Daylight Dancer" at the end of the set than at leaving the venue with less blood than I entered it.

At some point the next year, I would drive Cristina and the band's bassist Marco back to their hotel after a free outdoor festival in Manchester, New Hampshire, and they would go flipping through my little photo book.

"What the fuck is that?!" Marco exclaimed, coming across the photo of my bloodied face.

"'Tight Rope!' New Jersey!" I shouted back with glee.

"That's fucked up," he said.

The year after I graduated from college, my buddy Bork asked if I wanted to go with him to Germany to the world's largest heavy metal festival: Wacken Open Air. Uh-huh. Yes, I do. Only, one problem: I was working one full-time job at the time, earning twenty-four thousand dollars a year before taxes. In college, I worked whenever I was home for summer or winter and saved my money for shows since I had loans for room and board. But a year after graduation, I couldn't afford to go to Europe, even though the lineup featured the two bands I traveled for the most: In Flames and Lacuna Coil, the latter of whom I saw in their home country of Italy when I studied abroad in 2005. I had caught the train from Perugia to Bologna for a weekend trip, saw the band, which by that point had become my favorite underground band, and soaked up the atmosphere of a European metal festival, complete with some random guy giving me free beer in the pit during Slayer's set just because he approved of my enthusiastic headbanging. Bless your drunken heart, sir.

Even though I lived at home as a twenty-two- and twenty-three-year-old in 2007, I still had college loans, weekend parties, a new band to pay for—not to mention on top of all that, my never-ending concert habit, which by that point had taken me, over five years, into Canada three times for shows in Toronto and as far south as Greensville, South Carolina. All of that just screams privilege and recklessness with money—both of which are completely true—and some form of obsession. I was looking for a means of self-expression at a time when I was scared to death to come out, so I channeled that into emotional wanderlust, hitting up venue after venue looking for my weekly if not nightly fix, whereas most casual music fans might go to a show or two per year. For them, it's a night out. For me, it was *taps forearm with two fingers twice* ←that.

My grandparents on my dad's side of the family were voracious travelers, having visited all fifty states, many of which they did in an RV. When Granddad and Nana died in 2006 and 2007, the inheritance I received from them wasn't much, but it was enough for me to at least afford my first trip to Wacken Open Air in 2008. I reasonably deduced that two people who spent so much of their lives taking in what the world had to offer would have appreciated that I spent that money on making experiences in faraway places.

Live music made me feel good and connected with people in a way that nothing else could match. Festivals magnified that with tens of thousands of people seeing sometimes twelve-plus hours worth of bands in a given day. I had attended every Ozzfest since 1999, including twice in 2002 and three times in 2004, so by the time I made it to the Gods of Metal festival in Italy in 2005 that was headlined by Iron Maiden—and, I swear, of the 35,000 people there, 17,500 of them had to be in Iron Maiden shirts—I was well versed in festival etiquette and knew to look out for someone's Doc Martens boots colliding with the back of my head in the front row.

What I didn't get to do at Gods of Metal, Ozzfest, or any other festival, though, was camp out, which is what Bork insisted we do when we finally made it to Wacken Open Air in 2008—headlined by, of course, Iron Maiden, only in front of 85,000-plus people instead of a measly 35,000.

It's the biggest metal festival in the world, and the energy is like nothing else as 85,000 metalheads take over the tiny cow town for one week, getting obliterated on 5 percent ABV German beer and seeing the world's best metal bands all day and night. There is a vast sea of dirty-ass people as far as you can see in any direction, and every one of them is Ready. To. Party. Including the seven-year-old wearing a Wacken shirt I saw on my first visit there who came into view and immediately threw me the horns. The other incredible thing about Wacken is—perhaps surprisingly—how friendly and open everyone is there. Many people come with maybe a friend or two, so the first day of the fest is generally people bonding with strangers over bands, or, in my case, a bottle of Jägermeister I carried around to share. It's generally easy to make friends at metal festivals where you camp out in tents next to one another because you know the entire rest of your year, you won't see that many people in black T-shirts together. It's vacation, so spirits are high to begin with, and making conversation is as easy as making a Play-Doh snake: "Hey, I like your shirt! [Name of band or album by band] rules! Want a beer? Right on! I'm [name]. What's your name? Nice to

meet you! Where are you from? Oh, yeah? Nice! I'm from Virginia
in the United States, about an hour outside of Washington, D.C. All
right, bottoms up!"

I value experiences over tangible items in general, and the party
in the campgrounds of a festival mixed with the live music itself in
the main concourse is just that: it's living in the moment at its most
genuine. When you're finally experiencing the bands right there in
person—the way the sound hits your eardrums, the visual spectacle
of watching the music being created before your eyes, the show that
goes with it—and the people around you are experiencing the same
thing at the same time, it requires presence in that moment. When
you're seeing your favorite bands perform your favorite songs, they're
interrupting all those memories you've stored from your past of listening to those tunes enough to hum the melodies in the present.

Eventually, through traveling to shows and spending hours in the
one-upping championship that was trading jokes on metal message boards, I'd built a little community of friends who went
to shows and—notably—ran up legendary bar tabs together. On one
such fateful night while on a break from school, three of us left Jaxx,
the local Northern Virginia metal venue, absolutely bombed and
went to sleep it off in my car in the parking lot. We awoke to a cop
knocking on the car window, who told us to get out of the car before
quickly ascertaining just how drunk we were . . . which probably
became obvious when one of my companions tried to casually sit on
the bumper of my car and slid onto the ground instead and threw up
in front of the cop, who not long afterward threatened us with jail
(presumably for being drunk in public) until the owner of Jaxx saved
our asses. That experience taught me the most important thing I

needed to know about being twenty-one: Always carry sixty dollars with you to get a cab ride home so you don't spend ten thousand dollars on a DUI. Subsequently, that night started a series of jokes (on Myspace, no less) that led to us starting a band called Cab Ride Home, which would be the most dominant part of my twenties apart from my journalism career.

MUSIC HAS BECOME AN INTEGRAL part of my personality. For those of us into metal, it's more than a preference or an aesthetic; it's a lifestyle. It is what you put on display for the world. It's how you relate to your friends. The lyrics of some of my favorite metal songs have inspired my life and they have become the way I tell my story.

Truth be told, one of my biggest worries going into campaigning in 2017 was whether I would lose that sense of identity, whether spending an entire year campaigning and then absorbing legislative work into my life would mean I would abandon my friends, bandmates, and the live music I love. I didn't think about how being in the public eye would change me as much as how other people would react to me. I figured I could potentially be left wanting everyone to see the same ol' me, but being treated differently and being the subject of rumors and gossip because "Oh my God, we're, like, soooo close. One time, she picked up my beer thinking it was hers . . . and then put it down, said, 'Oh, sorry,' and picked hers up! So, yeah, we're basically like best friends." At the end of the day, no campaign and no amount of TV time changes the fact that I'm still that kid from Manassas; I just represent the area now in Richmond, that's all. I still like the same music I did before and still talk to my friends the same way. The only differences are that I stopped drinking and I know a little more about parliamentary procedure now. (I can't wait for the day when I get to open up a committee meeting via power metal vocals: "I call this meeting to orDERRRRRRRRRRRRRR-YAAHHHHHHHH!!!")

One of the things my black hoodies and metal connections kept alive for me was my sense of community; that just because I earned election (and then reelections), it didn't mean I was leaving behind the people who got me there in the first place—leaving behind who I really was, even if I was spending a lot less time with my friends. When I visited SiriusXM *Liquid Metal* host Jose "Metal Ambassador" Mangin in early 2019 for a "hostile takeover," where he let me play whatever Virginia-based metal bands I wanted for an hour and tell stories of being a metalhead in politics, I was like a kid in a candy store run by a super-nice, heavily tattooed, heavy metal DJ. When I visited St. Bonaventure University in April 2018, nearly twelve years after I graduated, I spoke to a surprisingly packed Dresser Auditorium in the Murphy Professional Building, where I had sat through a number of classes as an undergraduate. I had a lot of fun telling stories, especially during the Q&A.

I made a promise to the crowd: I would take a photo and chat with every single person who wanted to chat with me afterward, no matter how long it took. That's been a staple of the speaking events I've done across the commonwealth and country since 2017, and it's a work ethic spawned from something I saw about Metallica as a freshman in high school when their VH1 *Behind the Music* special aired November 22, 1998.

Lisa Millman, a publicist from Metallica's label at Elektra Records, said something that stuck with me from the minute I heard it: "They'll leave a venue, like, at four o'clock in the morning and there's kids still waiting out there? Doesn't make a difference how tired they are. They'll talk to every single one, sign every single piece of paper. They're incredibly gracious and generous, and their fans know it and appreciate it."

James Hetfield then added, "We're just four lucky fans that got together and started playing; this could be you."

That last line is something I've paraphrased at the microphone since I've been in office on more than one occasion. I want people to genuinely believe about themselves the thing I've repeated hundreds of times in stump speeches, interviews, and writings throughout the last four years: that you can succeed because of who you are, not in spite of it; that quite often in our society the people we've put on pedestals in fact weren't born into old money—though certainly there are plenty of examples of that, especially in politics and music alike.

I say all of that with the caveat that even without celebrity parents or endless streams of cash, I've still benefited from a lot of basic privileges of being born into a white, middle-class suburban family in the Mid-Atlantic. After my dad killed himself, my mother saved up Social Security benefit checks that came in until my sister and I each turned eighteen and used them to pay for our Catholic school tuition, which led to us earning our high school diplomas. That then put us in a position to earn our college degrees. My ma could have easily found a way to squander that money, but she used it to invest in her kids, even if both of us hated the uniform and rigidness that comes with a Catholic school education.

I saw metal as an outlet of expression in a suffocating Catholic school environment of uniforms and conformity. Little did I know that my interest in it would directly lead to my run for office, as I learned onstage how to project confidence through visual storytelling, appear in front of a packed room to rile up a crowd, and work my ass off in order to land a high-profile, albeit low-paying, gig. There's something about standing on a table-turned-makeshift-stage in a packed room the night of your election victory that just makes you want to stage dive, especially when you see some of your metal buddies out in the crowd. Instead of jumping, though, I started ticking off a list of thank-yous to supporters, including one I just had to do: "To the metalheads, like Chris!" At that point, the bearded, long-haired proprietor of the *DC Heavy Metal* blog rocking a black hoodie over his torso and a bottle of beer in his left hand threw his right-hand horns in the air high above his well-north-of-six-foot frame and bellowed, "Yeaaaaaahhhhhh!" That just felt good. I wanted my underground community to know that I didn't forget where I came from—or where I still reside.

What I didn't realize until I grew up was that my rebellion was born not of a desire to abandon a community but to find one. Like pretty much everyone, I longed to be able to picture myself as part of something bigger—a macro structure of purpose and power and meaning—and I couldn't see my place in the world like most of my classmates could. I'm lucky I found a place in a community that's supportive; many alienated kids in America today are finding one somewhere far more sinister.

If you're interested in being a leader and creating change, the most important thing you can offer people is a big story in which they play an important and meaningful role, just like metal did for me. Fail to do that, and you'll lose them to someone who will.

CHAPTER 4

HACK

We wanted to endorse Danica Roem. Heck, she's a journalist. What more could we ask for?

Well, unfortunately, we have a second requirement for endorsing a candidate: Comport yourself in a manner appropriate to the office you seek. And, in that regard, Roem falls short . . . Roem also lacks experience, something we consider vital. Interviewing legislators doesn't qualify you to be one, any more than being a sports reporter would qualify you to quarterback the Redskins.

—InsideNova, *a community newspaper, in an editorial withholding endorsement in the race for delegate, October 19, 2017*

When I declared journalism as my major at St. Bonaventure in 2002, I didn't expect to pursue a career that included watching people die and writing about their deaths, other than, say, heavy metal musicians. I wanted to be around music and journalism facilitated that goal—though it didn't take long for the intrigue of actual news reporting to capture my attention. At the start of my first semester when I attended a general interest meeting for students to work at the college radio station, The Buzz—88.3 FM WSBU, I did it with the sole intent of landing a heavy metal radio show. That had been a fantasy of mine during my junior and senior years of high school, imagining my introductions on air for bands like Nevermore, In Flames, and, of course, Metallica, as I would drive through the winding back roads of Clifton on my way to high school. Only once during a midday dream did I skid on black ice and drive right through a wooden fence post before two more vehicles behind me did the same thing. I missed a nearby utility poll by just a few feet, which was fortunate because no one envisions their last words alive to be "Ahhh, shit . . ." as mine were at the moment.

Little did I know that just walking in the door to the Murphy Hall auditorium on campus for the general interest meeting with my hair down to my chin would capture the attention of my eventual best friend, Lauren, who was seated in the room, and that the news side of the station would be a natural fit for someone majoring in journalism. Soon, my desire to be a part of the radio station extended beyond being just a disc jockey, though that was still priority number one. I knew I needed to earn one hundred on-campus hours of working in journalism in order to reach the four hundred total hours required to earn my bachelor's degree, so learning how to be a radio news reporter seemed like an easy way to check off those hours while learning the trade and still being around music.

Learning the trade at my small, private school in the mountains of Nowhere, New York, however, included "back in my day"–era equipment issued to the reporters for our field pieces: a rectangular, black plastic box you had to hold with two hands called a Marantz that recorded whatever someone was saying onto an audiocassette tape. The reporters would then take that hunk of junk into the sound studio, hold a microphone over it, record it through a piece of software called Cool Edit Pro, save it, upload it, and play it on air, so you had that good ol' analog white noise of the cassette sound rolling on any given recording. *wipes tear* Such precious, obsolete memories . . .

Being a seventeen- or eighteen-year-old freshman asking older students and professors random questions was awkward enough; holding a sound system the size of a Personal Pan Pizza box up to someone's face as you do it is even weirder, given that we didn't have the microphone extension (or the cheesy bread) to make it more appetizing.

Awkward field stories about snow on campus or whatever not-so-hard-hitting news aside—("Hi, I'm with the radio station and you and I don't know each other, so I'm allowed to interview you. Can I ask you about it being . . . ummm . . . cold as balls every day? I'm from the South, so not being able to see my car under a snowdrift is new to me")—reading the news scripts on air also introduced me to my own overcompensation techniques, like trying to work cuss words into newscasts. In late 2002, when my coanchor and I had a news script that called for "happy talk" during the entertainment section—which is a short, improvised, lighthearted conversation—I remember my producer let me work in a piece about metal bands.

"Oh, they just kick ass!" I said at one point about a band from back home called Darkest Hour, before doubling down on the "ass" part to stress just *how* good it was that an Atlanta-based band Mastodon was dropping their debut album *Remission*. I had seen both bands live in 2001 and very much felt the need to share that with everyone in the five-mile broadcasting radius of The Buzz. Right before we went into the mic break to play whatever PSA or ad, the producer's eyes bulged out as he loudly whispered to me, "You can't say that on air!!" When I reminded him that "ass" was not one of George Carlin's "Seven Words You Can Never Say on Television"— that, I knew for a fact, as Carlin made a point in the 1970s to note "most of the time, 'ass' is all right"—he simply replied, "Yeah . . . not during a newscast!" As it turns out, Riki Rachtman's etiquette for hosting *Headbangers Ball* and Cokie Roberts's evening news anchor etiquette were . . . ummm . . . let's politely go with incompatible.

Yet on the DJ side of things, I thrived in the dead-middle of the night, taking on my first shift from 2:00 to 4:00 A.M. on Wednesdays. For a college radio station overwhelmingly dominated by indie rock, giving the token metalhead quite literally the worst shift—middle of the week, after everyone's gone to bed and before everyone's woken up—seemed appropriate, but I took full advantage, walking over from my dorm with a crate full of CDs, which is heavier than you'd think and quite a fun way to tread the icy sidewalks 1.5 hours south of Buffalo.

During my first show after training, I'm sure I messed up hitting the buttons on the mixer console—but I shoved the CDs into disc players and barked with full energy, "It's the Wednesday Morning Metal Meltdown!" and subbed out the DJs' scripted line of "Rock Radio" with "You're listening to *Metal* Radio, 88.3 FM, WSBU, Saint Bonaventure!" as the intro of a song kicked into high gear. I absolutely loved it, even if maybe one person somewhere in the void was actually tuned in to the show. However, when the 4:00 to 6:00 A.M. DJ stopped showing up after me, I asked production if they minded me taking over that slot, and they told me to go for it. Then I found out the Friday morning 4:00 to 7:00 A.M. host wasn't showing up either, so I snatched that one up, too, and suddenly my dead-of-night, got-to-store-the-metalhead-somewhere show had seven hours a week uncontested on air in which I could spread metal to the masses throughout my freshman year. By the end of my senior year, *Loud Rock* had a thirteen-hour block on Fridays from right after the noon news broadcast all the way until 1:00 A.M., with my show being the prime-time anchor after the 7:00 P.M. newscast, which I oversaw as news director during the fall 2005 semester.

I nearly had that taken away from me at some point my freshman year when I decided to play thirty-two Metallica songs in a row throughout the duration of the four hours of my show and—key mistake—I was stupid enough to actually write every song down on the log. So I got a call from the station manager telling me I had enough violations to get me fired three times—"Six by my count . . . ,"

I thought—but for reasons I'll never know, he let me off with a warning. Bless.

Away from the radio station, even though my freshman grades were absolute shit, I didn't skip class other than taking a four-day weekend once, during which I missed each of my classes one time. Rather, when I was done with classwork, I would pour myself into writing about metal, finding new bands, and going to shows all over the Northeast, Midwest, and Mid-Atlantic, always making sure to be back on air at 2:00 A.M. twice a week for my radio show and whenever I had news stories to read on air during the noon or evening cast.

I took the freedom that came with being able to experience new things as an eighteen-year-old, exploring whatever I could within a seven-hour radius of Olean, New York, and didn't balance it out with that other part of adulthood: work. In this case, homework. My lack of homework cost me dearly, and even when I recovered academically during my second semester with a spot on the dean's list after earning a 3.48 GPA, I still lost half of my scholarship because my cumulative freshman year GPA fell under the 2.5 GPA I needed to keep it. It turns out that a 1.1 GPA your first semester is—and, kids, please highlight this on your reader or dog-ear this page—a bad thing. That wouldn't come back to haunt me until I graduated, but it's something I've tried to pass down as a stepparent: don't make the same mistakes I did.

When I did graduate in 2006, I knew I needed to pay back more student loans than I originally anticipated due to my freshman fuck-ups. Still, I kept on my career trajectory as a journalist who was hungry and eager to speak truth to power as I wanted to emulate my college mentor, Pulitzer Prize–winning investigative reporter John

Hanchette. And I brought that hunger with me to my early newspaper reporting.

U pon entering college in 2002, the basis for my knowledge about politics was whatever *Saturday Night Live* parodied and Jon Stewart's brilliant, engaging, and funny as hell criticism on *The Daily Show*. Being close to my grandfather, who read the news every day, I would read the sports and comics sections of *The Washington Post* and our local newspaper the *Potomac News*, with my favorite comics being *The Far Side, Mutts, Garfield*, and pretty much anything else involving animals. *The Far Side*'s completely out-there brand of WTF humor was by far my favorite thing to read and, coupled with my steady diet of my best friend's George Carlin cassette tapes, led me to search for edgier work. Enter Comedy Central reruns of *Saturday Night Live* and *The Kids in the Hall*, Fox reruns of *The Simpsons*, and late-night comedians like Jay Leno in middle school—including (and I swear this is true) writing down his monologue jokes on a ripped sheet of paper to bring to my basketball games on weekends so that I could recite them to our point guard Chris during warm-up shooting drills. I wasn't just a natural benchwarmer; I *earned* that role. No one teaches you that. You have to *strive* to be the worst.

The funny thing about being a closet-case teenager watching these shows is that the "gay" scenes were etched into my mind: male sheriffs dressed in chiffon dresses in *The Far Side*; Scott Thompson's recurring gay socialite queen Buddy Cole and the *Kids in the Hall* sketch called "Steps" where gay men discussed marriage equality in Canada; the steelworkers who "work hard" and "play hard" on *The Simpsons*; and probably the first time I saw an on-screen gay kiss courtesy

of a *Saturday Night Live* make-out between Will Farrell and Chris
Kattan that left the audience howling with both laughs and cheers.
Rarely, though, were lesbians portrayed, other than an *SNL* bit here
or there; for whatever reason, men making out just had more of a
punch-line effect than women. Such is the world of "feminizing"
hypermasculinity . . . or something Gender Studies 101 like that.

Eventually, my comedy bingeing led to rabid consumption of *The
Daily Show* and *South Park* in the late '90s, so much so that satire
became an easier way to digest the news as a teenager than actually
paying attention to the real news, which was dominated around the
clock at the time by Bill Clinton's affair with Monica Lewinsky and
the 2000 presidential election, where George W. Bush ~~seemed to be~~
was a bumbling dipshit who couldn't string a sentence together and
Al Gore ~~appeared to be~~ *was* a wooden, windup puppet. (Recall uber-
nerd Martin Prince from *The Simpsons* lamenting how he spent his
last ten dollars on a talking Al Gore doll that said only one line
when he pulled the string: "You are hearing me talk." What parody?)

In hindsight, that's probably why I wasn't interested in politics at
the time, beyond what I could laugh at through comedy sketches, so
political journalism wasn't an obvious step for me. Instead, my love
of heavy metal is what pushed me toward wanting to learn how to
write, so I could spend my time reviewing and discussing my favorite
songs and albums with the goal of spreading metal to the masses by,
of course, sitting alone in a dorm staring at a computer. The radio
station didn't interfere with that at all either; it actually gave me
another creative outlet as Lee Coppola, the then-dean of the Russell
J. Jandoli School of Communication, told us that what print, radio,
television, and online journalism all had in common was the need
for reporters to write the news before they reported it. It was the
nearly top-ranked radio station that drew me in hook, line, and

sinker when I toured the campus in the spring of 2001—but what I didn't realize at the time was that working for the radio station would actually help me as a news writer even more than as a broadcaster.

The heavy metal magazines I spent my teenage years reading for hours on a bench at the Barnes and Noble along Sudley Road in Manassas also drove my interest in potentially pursuing a career writing about music, along with making friends through heavy metal forums online. Those forums had led me to writing for a heavy metal news site, which gave me the platform to elevate whatever bands I wanted—and it became an outlet for my all-things-metal nerdom, albeit with the street cred of a Catholic high school haircut that couldn't touch the collar, a yellow button-down shirt, and an after-school, part-time job of filing land surveys into folders and operating a blue-line machine that ran on what I'm pretty sure was pure ammonia.*

Even with my burgeoning love of heavy metal reading and writing, journalism wasn't always my guaranteed major. For a fleeting moment in high school, I actually considered finance. During my senior year economics class, we would play this fun, educational game about the stock market where we had to evaluate price-to-earnings (P/E) ratios and all this other stuff. Every week, our teacher would post our rankings. For the first week, I actually came in first . . . and never again, as noted in a report about one of my stocks failing, which I led off with "AOL: You little bitch." (*I* thought that was funny. *My teacher* disagreed. Apparently, that language is frowned upon in Catholic school.)

---

*My lungs will pay for that when I'm eighty, I'm sure.

Some magazine or book that I remember reading in the back seat of my mom's Subaru station wagon on our way to tour Shippensburg University in Pennsylvania—one of only two colleges I toured— comparing average salaries of different majors also made a hell of a case for finance, with the starting salary coming in at something like three times that of a journalism major. Given that I exited my newspaper career with 10.5 years of experience and making the same twenty-four-thousand-dollar salary as a news editor that I made a decade earlier as a rookie reporter, I would say the book I read in my mom's back seat lowballed it. You don't pursue a career in newspaper journalism for the money because, honey, it ain't there. Pursue a career in television and land one of those jobs reporting about pizza cat chasing pizza rat through the New York City subway or whatever, and maybe you can afford takeout on Fridays while working for one salary.

The thing is, though, my interest in stocks only went so far—the game was really fun, but it wasn't an around-the-clock obsession like heavy metal. I'm much more driven by authentic adventure and live-in-the-moment/reflect-on-it-later-to-friends experiences, like breaking my nose in a mosh pit.

WHEN I ENTERED THE *GAINESVILLE TIMES* newsroom in Warrenton, Virginia, in June 2006 as a full-time newspaper reporter a month after graduating from college, I saw political yard signs all over the walls of the two-desk office that was the entirety of our editorial staff: just my editor, Tara Donaldson, and me. Clearly, covering politics would be important there and given that my interest in politics took off during the 2004 presidential campaign, I had no objections.

Not coming out at work made sense for practical reasons: It would be more than four years before I had my first kiss with a guy and 6.5 more years until I started therapy. My band was just starting—we didn't even have a drummer yet—so that was my focus outside of work and I was desperate to be taken seriously as a reporter. In my twenty-one-year-old mind, that meant keeping personal matters personal . . . even if my boss had her wedding photo of herself and her wife on her desk. So if I was going to talk about anything with her, it would be politics.

That's what I knew best. And Swedish melodic death metal, sure. But suffice it to say, I was lucky in the newsroom to meet just one photographer in nearly ten years who had even seen Metallica live—Greg Nash, who later ended up working in D.C. at *The Hill* news site—and one other who was an exceptionally good jazz bassist, Mark Mulligan, who would later end up shooting for the *Houston Chronicle*. He even stopped by my band's first "live rehearsal," as we called our warm-up to our first live show. There wasn't going to be anyone who had even heard of In Flames, let alone debate with me whether *The Jester Race*, *Whoracle*, *Colony*, or *Clayman* should be considered their greatest album.*

My editor's music taste was . . . not that. And it was just us—we were a two-person editorial staff with one single doorless, windowless room on the side of a ramp that led into the main newsroom of the *Fauquier Times-Democrat*, the flagship paper of our regional chain. That meant finding other things to discuss, which isn't hard in a newsroom. After all, the 2006 congressional midterms hung in the air, and my first assignment on June 12 was to cover the U.S. Senate primary between Jim Webb and Harris Miller, a nomination contest with less than 5 percent statewide turnout. The winner was

---

*It's *Colony*. Fight me.

going up against incumbent Republican senator George Allen, a former governor best known for abolishing parole in a punishment-happy southern state that led the nation in all-time executions. (That was the "macaca" election where Allen made a racist slur on camera in an anti-Republican wave election. Webb won and flipped the Senate majority from red to blue while doing it.)

One of the things about covering local governments as a newspaper reporter in small-town America is that it's half Forrest Gump—"You never know what you're gonna get"—and half pantsless-man-seeks-town-council-seat.

The thing is, when I interviewed Haymarket Town Council candidate Ralph Ring in 2012, I very much did know what I was going to get: someone who, to his credit, attended town council meetings constantly and videotaped them with a camera set on top of a tripod, which was an unusual level of dedication to local government back then before smartphones really took off.

At the same time, it didn't matter what time of year it was, Ralph always arrived in shorts—and not shorts that came down to the knees, but, like, 1970s-style shorts. He had a great sense of humor and just so happened to be the father of a close friend of mine from the Northern Virginia heavy metal scene, so when I interviewed him about his run for office, I told him the headline of my story would be "No Pants, No Problem: Ralph Ring Runs for Council."

He laughed and dared me to do it.

As he quickly learned: never call my bluff.

On the one hand, covering the Haymarket Town Council was sometimes as exciting as flipping a pen in the air repeatedly, as I watched one of the other reporters do constantly at town hall whenever he lost interest.

On the other hand, watching one town councilman point and

yell across the dais, "That's obstruction!" at another town council-man, who then slams his hands down and replies, "OBSTRUC-TION, MY ASS!" back at him is really fun for the whole family, especially considering the obstruction-my-ass guy earned the most votes of all six town council members in the previous election.

At its core, town government is the closest government to the people and, accordingly, you truly get a flavor for the residents of the town by watching their best-and-brightest elected leaders reviewing rezoning applications peacefully during one meeting and cussing one another out at the next. Oftentimes, members conduct them-selves just as professionally mundane as in any other form of govern-ment, but when they do flare up, it's the sort of rocket launch that occasionally gets the cops and/or the courts involved, as I covered multiple times in Haymarket. (My favorite, of course, involved a town council member being found guilty of "using abusive language" following a dispute about what synonym for testicle he told the mayor to suck during a parade.)

After all, nothing exemplifies former U.S. House Speaker Tip O'Neill's famous observation that "All politics is local" like town government, especially with the more modern take that "All politics is personal."[*]

Being a news reporter covering government at the town, city, county, state, and federal levels for more than a decade taught me what I needed to know to serve in office, and even most of what I needed to know about communicating what was important to me and our community during a campaign. I learned the value of in-tently listening to what someone was telling me, asking follow-up questions, listening more, asking more questions, and taking notes

---

[*]And sometimes pantsless.

in the moment—with a notepad as a reporter and with paper on a clipboard. Oftentimes, my listening led me to exposing the truth—and in political reporting, that meant holding people accountable. It's one of the things I loved most about the job—being able to give people a real window into the candidates and elected officials who were supposed to be there to help them and sometimes had the opposite intentions.

One of the dumbest examples of this is when Tareq Salahei—star of the *Real Housewives of D.C.* and infamously known for infiltrating a White House state dinner in 2009—ran for governor of Virginia. I had been working two full-time journalism jobs for more than three years by the time of the 2013 campaign—evenings, late nights, and weekends for the newspaper and mornings and afternoons for *The Hotline* in D.C.—so I had 6.5 years of interviewing experience under my belt by that point. True, Salahei wasn't a typical politician, but his antics became absurdly impossible to ignore when he arrived to my interview at the Watergate in a white stretch limo with his campaign logo on the door. As an independent candidate, he was trying to qualify for the ballot (he didn't), so participating in this interview would help get his name ID up. My interest was in trying to find out if he could pull support from either the Democratic candidate, Terry McAuliffe, or the Republican candidate, Ken Cuccinelli, as that could make a difference in a super-tight election. (Turns out, the Libertarian Party candidate ended up playing spoiler instead, allowing McAuliffe to win via plurality.) It seems Salahei was unaware that some reporters would actually ask hard questions and not treat him like he was special because he had been on a reality show.

I wasn't having that shit. I wanted to grill him on policy and let the results speak for themselves. So I posed to him a question common for any statewide Virginia politician: whether he supported the proposed transportation funding bill for the year in HB 2313 and how the regional funding mechanisms in it differed from the failed 2007 transportation bill HB 3202, which had been ruled unconstitutional by the state supreme court. His campaign manager offered to answer as he froze.

"My question is for the candidate," I replied.

Most people don't need to know about court precedents for transportation funding. Candidates for governor absolutely do—hell, even candidates for the House of Delegates do—and his deer-in-headlights look back at me suggested he needed to get out of the newsroom and back into his limo.

Whether at the local, state, or federal level, I sincerely, genuinely enjoyed interviewing candidates for office and covering public policy and politics. In Prince William County, I earned the reputation of being the toughest interviewer in town as state legislators and county supervisors alike told me to my face. Neutrality was easy to maintain when focusing on public-works projects, budgets, taxes, etc. Yet I also found out that the political and the personal can and do collide in ways that test your resolve to stay a dispassionate, third-party observer. During my first year at the newspaper in 2006 a ballot referendum authored by my then-delegate sought to ban all legal recognition—not just marriage—of same-sex couples in the constitution of Virginia. There was never any doubt the referendum would be approved by the voters; the margin being 57 percent to 43 percent, in the same year that voters elected the Democrat Jim Webb over the Republican George Allen, just reinforced that thousands of left-leaning voters still weren't comfortable with the idea of full equality for their LGBTQ neighbors and family members. While I can't say what the thing was that finally got me to come out to my boss, this at least made it easier to broach the topic. As usual, I used sexuality as a stepping-stone to get to gender identity—I had first come out as bi, then gay, and then finally trans.

"Wait, you're gay?!"

"I thought that's why you hired me," I replied in jest.

"No. I hired you because you're from here," she said.

Oh.

My boss did explain early on, though, that we had to be careful about who we talked to about our private lives so that the *Gainesville Times* wouldn't be branded the *Gaysville Times*—though I want that newspaper to exist *so* badly. ("Gays-ville! Gays-ville!" I would later chant.) Still, a couple of queer people producing the news every week together for nine years and two months was unique in our area, if not the country.

For the first 6.5 years I spent at the newspaper, having a gay editor just meant she was cool with me—when I wasn't chronically busting deadline. Our relationship was much more her telling me, "Where are my stories?! Deadline was an hour ago! The printer's waiting!" and me telling her, "They're coming! They're coming! I swear, hold on, I'm almost done!!!" than it was "Like, oh my God, could you believe she wore an open toe with that dress?" And, to be honest, the part of me raised by a no-bullshit Bronxite mother preferred that. (Do threats count as a love language?)

The best part about working for my boss, though, is that she will always be the single most resourceful person I will ever know. Ever. No matter what stupid situation I put her in or what happened beyond her control, she could always, immediately, seemingly reflexively pull out a plan B . . . or C . . . or D . . . from thin air and figure out what to do in the time it took her to process: "Okay, shit, well, hmm . . . here's what we're going to do." Bam.

That resiliency is something I adapted to my job as a general assignment reporter who not only covered politics and stuff around town but, functionally, was the entirety of the sports department, too.

What she didn't expect to have to process, though, was a call from me one day in December 2012.

"Hey . . . soooo . . . I started therapy last month to deal with lifelong gender dysphoria. Soooo . . . I'm transgender and I'm going to start transitioning soon."

She breathed exactly once.

"Okay," she said, the resiliency portion of her brain immediately kicking into high gear. "Be smart, don't do anything stupid, and I've got your back."

It would be another year before I started hormone replacement therapy in December 2013, and another 0.75 years after that before the way I presented on the job changed. By that point, I was still wearing pants, but stretchy, flowy black pants you could easily wear to work or yoga. Gone were my button-down shirts; in were my scoop-neck, cap-sleeves, and gray, white, and black shawl over my shoulders. My black shit-kicker shoes gave way to gray and white sneakers with neon-pink lining.

Just getting to that point took a professional transition within my personal transition.

Throughout my time at the newspaper, I had worked two full-time jobs for four out of five years. In May 2013, I had lost my second full-time job at the *The Hotline* due to another round of mass layoffs that resulted in three of us being given our severance. My last day of work was a Friday, and I started practicing yoga that Monday, which led me to apply for a job as a content writer at Yoga Alliance, a nonprofit organization based in Rosslyn, Virginia, that credentials yoga teachers. Even though I wore a button-up shirt and tie to the interview, I told the group interviewing me that I was trans and planned to start transitioning physically later that year. They were cool with it and brought me on as a part-time writer that summer, and then hired me full time in May 2014. A content writing job opened up and I started working in an office that was almost entirely women—and one man, the CEO of the organization (*of course*), before a second man, who was gay, took a job in customer service.

Presenting as the woman who I am full time, every day in person at my Yoga Alliance job in an environment of super-supportive women while working on a topic that I just loved—writing about the yoga industry—was such a natural fit, even if it was a step outside of news reporting. The pay was good and an eight-hour workday really was that: work seven hours, take an hour for lunch, and then I could go home to pick up whatever stories for the *Gainesville Times*. Amazing. This was the first job that let me use my chosen name—Danica—instead of my birth-name nickname, which just felt right.

The catch was, I was still writing under my old name at the *Gainesville Times* and leading this double life of full makeup, hair done up, work-professional dresses during my mornings and afternoons at Yoga Alliance, and then either ambiguous or guy(ish) clothes during the evenings and weekends on assignment at the newspaper. I would often change my clothes in my car in the parking lot or even on the road in bad traffic, until it got to a point where my body was clearly changing after 1.5 years of laser facial hair removal and nine months on hormone replacement therapy, meaning that my breasts were becoming noticeable, even if I hid them under a zip-up hoodie or shawl.

By the time the spring sports season of 2015 came around, I wasn't willing to hide my feminine expression at the newspaper anymore. My aesthetic was clearly feminine, though bland: solid colors, usually black and blue. I was only missing the makeup, skirts, and name change at that point. In fact, things got so weird with my name that I started flipping my credential that dangled from my neck so people could see the *Times* logo but not my name or photo. I would introduce myself to potential sources by saying, "Hey, I'm *mumble* Danica with the *Gainesville Times* . . ."

Finally, one day as I covered a high school varsity boys lacrosse team in Nokesville at Brentsville District High School, I was interviewing one of the players and he was super respectful and formal with how he would answer my questions: "Yes, ma'am . . . No, ma'am . . ."

I kept my cool and kept asking my questions and taking notes while, internally, my mind exploded in a chorus of "OHMYGOD, don't correct him because there's nothing to correct! Actually, he's the first one to get it right! OHMYGOD, OHMYGOD, OH-MYGOD!"

Then I was at a varsity girls softball game at Osbourn Park High School in Manassas. I approached a coach after the game to ask if I could interview the pitcher, who had just put on a dominant performance as the team's ace.

"Sure," he said.

He called her over.

"She wants to talk to you. She's with the paper."

Cue up my internal monologue again: "Yes, *she* would! *She* very much would! That is correct!"

Being recognized as a woman without needing a twenty-three-step makeup process, skirts, dresses . . . just my natural self, facial hair long since gone, eyebrows thinned, with an otherwise distinctly feminine outfit that looked and felt right—that's who twenty-one-year-old rookie reporter me wanted to be nine years earlier in 2006.

I can't describe that feeling to a cisgender person of being identified by your actual gender for the first time without it being from someone you're already close with who knew you before you transitioned; or someone showing sympathy or empathy, trying to get it right.

Just—naturally. No questions, no second thoughts, no ulterior motive. Just someone who looked at me, recognized my gender, and got it right. For all the gender dysphoria trans people live with, to be genuinely seen and heard as who you are by complete strangers who aren't just trying to be nice or kind but authentically perceiving you for who you are is, in a phrase, gender euphoria. Dysphoria can be isolating and lonely; that sense of euphoria, even fleeting, is celebratory and affirming, and even if you swear to yourself you don't need to be validated, it really is that, too.

Unfortunately, even if you get used to it after a while, someone else getting it wrong can absolutely wreck your day. By the time I left my job at the *Gainesville Times* to start working as the news editor of the *Montgomery County Sentinel* in August 2015, I was living, presenting, and working full-time as female, no questions, no doubts—wearing whatever I wanted, first name legally changed to Danica, a year of voice therapy completed, gender marker on driver's license changed, and all. But, even then, I remember being on the work landline phone one day, sitting near some of the reporters, when someone called me "sir" on the phone—even after all I had gone through.

As much as hearing shit like that just messed with that part of my day, it's not like that was the first time I was called something I didn't want to be called on the job, so I had to develop a thick skin and a sense of purpose. In journalism, you absolutely cannot let trivial bullshit and petty insults get in the way of pursuing a good story, just like in politics you can't let distractions knock you off message.

I said after my 2017 election that I would "always be a reporter before I'm a politician," and I like to think that I've kept that mentality. In fact, passing my Shield Law (HB 113) in 2020 to prevent reporters from being jailed for protecting the identity of a confidential source finally allowed me to put my heart at ease and my mind at peace for leaving the newsroom to pursue a political career. That bill does more to affirm the value of journalism in the commonwealth than any story I could ever write. It tells reporters, "You're welcome here and you can do your job of holding people in power accountable here."

Nothing prepares you for public service like getting to know every square block of your community as a reporter for more than nine years. Being a reporter, I learned a lot of what to do and not to do from observing public figures. I've seen good and bad alike from municipal leaders all the way to U.S. senators, up close and personal. I could always, 100 percent of the time, count on Tim Kaine—from the time we first met when he was lieutenant governor and I was a twenty-year-old freelancer home from college in the middle of summer—to be prepared to answer anything on any topic without ever being rude or condescending toward me, even when I dug in and challenged him. At the same time, I saw exactly who not to emulate in Corey Stewart, the Prince William Board of County Supervisors chairman who, after eleven years of knowing me personally, just couldn't help himself from making transphobic comments about me during the 2017 campaign. Pick your phobia, of course, but those comments always say more about the person making them than the person targeted by them.

As a journalist, I shadowed candidates from state delegate to governor who were out knocking on doors, picking up little tips from them along the way about how to interact with whoever answers and the importance of attaching a personalized, handwritten note to the flyer that candidates leave at the door when no one answers. I also covered people who were serving in office at all levels of government and got to know well the ways in which they would (or wouldn't) effectively pass legislation, how their constituents respected their work (or didn't), and how they would then try to communicate about their work to the community. I learned so much about what worked, what didn't, and what I would do differently if in their shoes— something I thought a lot about long before I ever considered running for office. It was just always so clear to me what could be done differently and done better.

My skill set honed throughout 10.5 years of interacting with other human beings daily in pursuit of news became directly transferrable when I made the jump to running for office, which is probably why, subconsciously, the idea of interacting with other people on the campaign trail never bothered me. I was much more worried about what opposition researchers and campaign ad makers would manufacture about me than I was about how individual people who met me would react. I spent my entire career talking to strangers; I could handle what I could hear and see, though I was admittedly super nervous and even scared my first day out knocking on doors in Manassas because, well, when you're trans and asking for votes from people who've elected and reelected someone who's explicitly anti-trans, you have no idea who might flip their shit when meeting you. After all, some people must have voted for the anti-trans dude *because* he was anti-trans.

And when I did make the move toward public service, I found that I enjoyed it. A lot. It kick-started the seemingly dormant, strategizer part of my mind, the one that learned chess as a fourth grader in 1993 and took my band to the UK in 2012. By the time I got the phone call from Democratic state delegate Rip Sullivan on August 5, 2016, I was ready for the challenge and the consummate strategizing it takes to run for office and to really start thinking big. After all, not only did I know the Republican incumbent and the community from covering them for years, but I knew politics, campaigns, and government. I knew the press. I knew every reporter in town. I knew, even if it was scary as a trans woman and no one else had done this before, that the fundamentals of a campaign still stood. Who better to execute them than a reporter?

I could take all of the lessons learned and skill sets developed as a reporter holding politicians' feet to the fire and actually be that person in office who I thought should be there—honest, transparent, accountable, and, above all, real.

CHAPTER 5

DRUNK

Danica Roem, in 2008, was videotaped performing a "keg stand" as people chanted "suck it" and then "proceeded to pick up the keg and chuck it through the window. Seriously." (Facebook, August 7, 2008)

> —*Friends of Danica Roem self-opposition research for 2017, conducted by Grindstone Research*

Waking up wearing your socks from the prior night isn't a problem in and of itself, especially when you're in your own bed. People get tired. It happens. Nor is it problematic to see your black Jägermeister wristband still on your right arm, albeit with the fuzz imprint making for a nice bumpy-flesh jigsaw puzzle when you peek underneath it. So what?

When your mind starts to wonder is when you wake up *only* wearing two damp socks and a wristband and there's no heap of discarded clothes anywhere in your immediate vicinity, leading you on a mental frolic through the adventure theme park of piecing your night together. This, of course, comes complete with a carousel of questions: How did you get here, who brought you home, where is all of your other shit, what the hell happened, and just where, exactly, did you put your damn clothes?

So you look under your sheets, under your bed, on the floor, in the hallway outside your door, and . . . nothing.

"Oh, boy. This isn't good."

Finally, you head downstairs, head pulsating with everything but memories, and there they are: pants, shirt, and underwear; last night's attire rolled up on the bathroom floor and with the door wide open, leading to an obvious conclusion. "At some point last night, your journey to bed involved this room. . . . And whatever happened, it didn't go well."

The point of telling this story and the ones that follow isn't so much to glorify the time I spent at the bottom of a bottle throughout my late teens and twenties. Of the actual alcoholics who've gone through AA compared with my drinking years from 2002 to 2015, I realized a key difference: they would *need* alcohol, often when they were by themselves; I was just a party drinker who used alcohol as a social lubricant to invite attention and spectacle. The funny thing is, legislators in general rely on the power of spectacle to get voters' attention. People gravitate toward bold, bright, memorable leaders who take charge of the atmosphere in the room. I learned how to use spectacle to capture people's attention from my party days—performing onstage at the mic with my guitar and a beer helmet featuring two cans of Schlitz on both sides of my head, straw in my mouth, and brew leaking down my chin and shirt. Some days, we'd have a friend bring beer bongs to us onstage midsong; other days (or sometimes the same day), I'd call for the crowd to join us onstage as we held an impromptu cancan dance to our anthemic closer, "Drunk on Arrival." Spectacle came naturally to fronting my metal band and I used it with glee. It didn't even always need to involve alcohol—we once had a real-deal Irish step dancer Riverdance that shit for about twenty seconds during the bridge of our song "Into Oblivion" and it was *so cool*. You had to try not to have a good time at our gigs because, whether or not you liked our music, we knew how to put on a show.

Alcohol, though, is a two-headed beast. It can be the initiator of good times to bring a room of people together and unite over a shared interest in having a party—and, believe me, I had a blast more times than not, and this isn't going to be the book where I'm going to tell you to not have a good time. Rather, my ask is for you to also recognize when either you or someone you know is drinking because they're using it as a wall to hide, and sometimes die, behind. While an alcoholic may develop a dependency on drinking in order to get through the day, "party drinkers," like yours truly, would use it as a means of expression—"If they can't see me for the woman who I am, then they can get to know my other side as the consummate entertainer and we'll all still have fun"—and that can lead to over-compensation for self-perceived inadequacies, which was the story of my twenties in a nutshell.

I could never drink the most: most of my guy friends could throw down way harder than I could. I never got a DUI or anything like that—in fact, the second woman I ever dated, albeit briefly, initiated our first long conversation when she spotted me outside of a bar, sitting alone in the passenger seat of my car while reading a newspaper, waiting to sober up. I spent many, *many* nights alone in my car in parking lots or on sides of streets all across the Mid-Atlantic, Midwest, and New England, sleeping off whatever I drank the night before.

Another thing about my drinking days: I rarely ever had sex—let alone while wasted, though the one time that did happen was hilariously bad. ("Shhh, you're going to wake up my roommate!" "Pretty sure your head hitting the wall just did!") This, in an oddly fortunate way, kept poor decisions from escalating while I was inebriated, though it also fueled my deeply seated feelings of inadequacy.

I had a weird, though occasional, habit the morning after parties of cleaning up the mess created by the whole party—not just me—in whatever house I'd crashed at that night. I always wanted to be a pleasant fun drunk rather than someone who's nasty or surly, though that weirdly surprised my hosts, who weren't aware they invited a single-person maid service from Manassas to crush a keg with them.

In order to live the authentic life I wanted to live, I had to choose to get out from behind that wall I created, using alcohol as a means for tolerating living like a man, and get real on a number of fronts. Perhaps most telling is that from the time I started going to gay clubs when I was eighteen until I stopped drinking at thirty, I would *never* get completely sloshed drunk when I presented as female. Ever. However, when I presented as male in my mid to late twenties, I drank my way through summer trips to metal festivals and shows abroad through Germany, France, the Netherlands, Scotland, England, and Northern Ireland, taking photos of each brew along the way. The more ridiculous the photo, the better. Ever drink from a mechanical beer bong with so much alcohol in it that it required a release valve? Wacken Open Air 2008, my friends.

Back home in Virginia, after turning twenty-one, I'd routinely overspend whatever I budgeted for the night at the bars over the course of a weekend, which, in hindsight, contributed to me living at home until I landed a second full-time job at age twenty-five, when I could split my time between home in Manassas and a pied-à-terre in Alexandria. Still, my life was in Manassas, and in Manassas, well, I could always find friends to drink with there.

At the time, it was actually more socially acceptable for me to get hammer-smashed shitfaced while presenting as male than to be this super-shy, insecure young woman at gay clubs just hoping I could find a guy—or, really, a guy who would find me—who wanted to dance. I was too scared to come out around my guy friends for fear of what they might think of me, of local right-wing bloggers who might find out and start writing about the secret life of the local community newspaper reporter, or, above all, of word getting back to my ma and my disappointing her. But being a loud-as-possible, turn-the-speakers-up-to-eleven, total jackass? Totally fine, as long as I wore my oversize metal shirts, baggy pants, and no makeup.

When I would present as myself—aka female—for the night, it's not like I was averse to alcohol. I was just on constant high alert: first and foremost, hoping some Prince Charming would sweep quiet, insecure lady me off her feet, which absolutely never happened; second, for whether anyone recognized me lest I be outed and ridiculed; and third, hoping no one would hurt me for being obviously trans without "passing privilege." Rather than drink that insecurity away to loosen up, I would go in and out of the restroom fifteen times in a night, fixing my hair, doing something to my makeup, or just recalibrating as I wondered why another night was going by without finding some guy to hold my hips and dance with me. There wasn't an alcohol available that could drown that insecurity and inadequacy away; I just wanted a guy to find me attractive enough to say hello.

All that said, going out with my girl friends certainly involved booze; I just didn't have a lot of it. My (mostly) straight girl friends, however, got so tanked they were one-on-top-of-the-other macking it in the back seat of the taxi, breasts exposed, as we rode home to Virginia over the bridge from D.C. during my transition party in 2013 and I flat-out refused to join in. The amount of liquor that it would have required would have needed to exceed my twenty-fifth birthday and I wasn't in the mood for replicating that disaster.

I celebrated that birthday in 2009 performing the only gig in my band's ten years of playing live that I abjectly did not remember playing the next day. In the run-up to our performance at the now-defunct dive bar in Manassas called The Clubhouse, I set a personal record for most drinks consumed in a night, with more than twenty forms of alcohol entering my roughly five-foot-eleven, one-hundred-forty-pound body as my friends, bandmates, and anyone who found out it was my birthday decided to test the limits of my brain's ability to count and my liver's ability to process.

When my friends from Iris Divine asked me to sing along to some Metallica and Iron Maiden covers with them, my mind started going fuzzy as I fell a beat and a half behind. Then, as my band set up our gear, my ears still worked just fine while my brain turned into broiling cheese in a brick oven, losing any ability to translate spoken words into things that made sense. At some point, the club manager walked up in front of the PA speakers and said something my hearing recognized as English, but my brain reported back to my lips a 404 error message: does not compute.

So I replied into my microphone with the one thing that came naturally to someone who fronts a self-styled "drunken thrash" band: "You said a lot of words, but 'free beer' wasn't one of 'em."

Never mind that "free beer" is, well, two words, the crowd cheered *loudly*, so that's all the validation I needed, English lessons be damned. It was time to start the show.

As my four bandmates (drummer, bassist, and two guitarists) kicked into our opener, "Bullets and Pepperoni"*—written about Arnold Schwarzenegger running a pizza shop, based on a parody performance of the "Ah-nold" voice someone did during a radio show once—I, of course, reached for a pitcher of cheap-ass beer. My guitar buddies in the band Division (using pronouns based on my

---

*Go figure, this would be one of the songs I would get attacked for during the 2017 campaign. This was also our most-requested song by a friend of the band, Jae Curtis, vocalist of the Maryland band Silence the Blind, so I like to think we got some good mileage out of it.

gender presentation at the time) observed the slow-motion train wreck unfolding before their eyes:

"Is he . . . puking into the pitcher?" asked Noodles.

"It's just Miller Lite," replied Mike. "Probably made it better."

Sure enough, I finished vomiting and, without missing a beat, immediately started barking out the first verse while running around the linoleum floor on a partially emptied stomach. My mind at this point goes completely blank. Total, utter blackout. I'm operating entirely on autopilot and, lo and behold, the pilot's flying solo on a separate plane, just absolutely bloody drunk. This being my birthday show, it was one of the few occasions I had invited my ma out to see us play. . . . annnnd I threw up in front of her feet. I then wanted a hug, so I jumped onto another friend while saturated with my own bile, kicked off one shoe that would later end up on top of the PA speakers, and began calling for songs twice in a row:

"This next song is about brawling at a bar! It's called . . . 'Brawl at the Bar'!" I ecstatically proclaimed.

"We just played that!" snapped back one of my guitarists.

"Oh."

Rinse and repeat, two songs later:

"This next song is called. . . . 'The Gorilla'!!!!"

"WE JUST PLAYED THAT! WE *JUST* PLAYED THAT, TOO!"

"Oh."

It wouldn't be long before someone did the one thing we were asked not to do—per our tradition whenever a member had a twenty-fifth birthday—spraying or pelting a member of the band with some sort of food or otherwise foamy substance. Cupcake to the face of one member in October 2007; Silly String to another in January

2009; a gallon of water and four pounds of flour from four one-pound bags for yet another (which was, admittedly, excessive) in March 2009; and then, that night, whipped cream pie to the face, midshow, which resulted in me wiping out to the ground and my friendly assailant—also wasted—falling on top of me.

"Beautiful you . . ." a friend would later text me, attaching a photo of my body on the floor, whipped cream smeared all over my face, still holding the microphone to my mouth, and my missing shoe on top of the speaker.

Meanwhile, the less lucid I got, the rowdier the crowd got, egging us on until management finally had enough. In all due fairness, they did book us because we were from the area and could pack the house with a ton of people who would spend a ton of money at the bar—not for our talent. ("In Cab Ride Home, no talent is no problem," I told our rhythm guitarist when I was recruiting him to join the band before he replaced me on the six-string 2.5 years into me performing double duty, so I could just focus on vocals.) But that night, we were just a little too rowdy. Suddenly, no amount of money brought into the bar was enough to deal with us.

It's not like we were complete amateurs at that point. We did record an album together that we had released earlier in the year. We had played more than sixty shows since 2007. We knew how to put on a good, entertaining gig and stay relatively in the pocket while playing it. This, however, was not one of those shows. This was like putting a moon bounce in a chicken coop.

Eventually, my bandmates had enough of my shit and the ensuing chaos of the others, leading our drummer to throw his sticks in the air and walk out from behind the kit. I went outside and left the concrete a different shade than it started as the tears from my ugly cries and the third round of vomit from the deepest recesses of my bowels darkened the sidewalk. A friend consoled me and drove me home, where I gave him pretty decent directions until I told him to stop the car . . . one house before mine.

The hints were all there: There was a gravel driveway instead of pavement; the lack of a garage door I was accustomed to entering through to get inside the house; and the sidewalk to the front door going to the left instead of the right.

"Goddamn it," I mumbled, blaming the house for not being my own at two-something in the morning, leading me to relieve myself in the driveway as an I'll-show-you-for-not-being-the-right-house. (Sorry, former neighbors . . .)

I got back in my friend's car so we could go one more house over and then required assistance just to get the key into the deadbolt lock so I could enter, since my hand-eye coordination had by that point achieved "can't-insert-key-into-lock" status. At this point, I staggered through the kitchen, turned left, and allowed the mysteries of the universe to unravel, leading me to wake up the next morning only in the aforementioned wet socks and wristband.

I took what seemed like an hour-and-a-half-long shower that couldn't wash away the shame from what I could piece together that morning. I knew something had gone wrong, even if I could only remember bits and pieces, and sure enough, the day wouldn't be through until I apologized in person to three of my bandmates who were furious at me for, as I found out, getting us banned from The Clubhouse. Aside from Jaxx, that was our best place to perform and they paid us well—we got to keep our share of the money at the door from the five-dollar cover charge, which would often be a few hundred dollars—and my antics, along with some other unruly shit that was part of the melee, cut us off from our home venue.

While the guys did accept my repeated apologies, that night

would eventually lead to friction for the band that snowballed weeks later and resulted in our first of many lineup changes to come by the end of the year. Meanwhile, the guys gave me strict orders that I was not allowed to drink before a show ever again. It would be nearly eight years before we played our final show and I kept true the whole time, having at most one beer before a gig and only if my bandmates were cool with it. Needing a babysitter in your late twenties to tell you when you can and can't drink? Decidedly un-metal—but well deserved.

The other, more covert, part of my private life away from work and my band involved frankly too much effort that didn't leave much time for alcohol abuse. Getting ready to go out to gay clubs involved the same things that a lot of other women who get dressed up and femme-out for a night on the town do: either trying on one thousand things at my best friend Lauren's house before heading out to D.C.; spending hours with one of my dearest friends Kristina to do up my hair and eyeliner (like when I went out as Amy Winehouse for Halloween in 2008 in Buffalo); or knowing exactly what I wanted to wear, styling my hair in various updos that would inevitably come undone, or failing miserably to make a good smoky eye look (I didn't get good until I actually transitioned, thereby missing that part of my party-time teens and twenties). The kicker, though, is that I'd have to do one thing that most women didn't do to get ready: I'd sit in front of the mirror for 4.5 to 5.5 hours with a pair of tweezers, pulling out every single hair from my face until I turned beet red, then slip on some heels and cross my fingers as I got into the car, desperate to be acknowledged and embraced as a woman for just a few hours. The tweezers mattered because razors would just result in a five-o'clock shadow at some point after midnight and waxing my face wasn't something I could do myself without literally ripping off my skin. (I conducted that science experiment and drew the same conclusion more than once.) I did get my face professionally waxed twice, but the money, hassle, and inevitable regrowth of hair just didn't make the pain worth it.

Tweezing my entire face when I had coarse hair wasn't fun at all—a massive understatement. At the same time, the feeling afterward when the hairs were all gone and I could slap some foundation and concealer over it at least gave me a genuine, physical feeling of femininity. My face was smooth. I hated, hated, *hated* having facial hair and the tweezers made it go away, even if just for a couple of days. That gave me at least a little confidence going out into the night, with the ironic hope of wanting some guy's razor bristles to cut up my face without feeling my own. (My preference: grown out just long enough so I can slide my fingers through it or none at all. Just not the little face thorns, though that mental image is decidedly metal.)

Once I did go out, my alcohol preferences changed rather dramatically based on whether I was presenting as male or female. In guy mode, I drank what has to be an entire vat worth of Sam Adams beer throughout my late teens and twenties. I liked Sam because one person in my family drank it and it was better than canned beer, yet not as expensive as other brews, so I could be a little bit snobby about my beer preferences in college without the prerequisite bro beard and flannel shirt. The only time I used my credit card in college for something other than gas or food was in spring 2006 for my last huge party weekend on campus, so I needed a case of Summer Ale Sams. If Sam wasn't available, I would find some form of a hefeweizen, American amber, or lager, with Pabst Blue Ribbon being my last-resort, piece-of-shit canned beer of choice. (At Jaxx, it was possible to get a $6.66 tab from PBR purchases, which my metal friends and I exploited for all its \m/ potential.)

Party-mode me in male form also relied on Jägermeister, hence the aforementioned wristband. At some point around 2003, Jäger started pumping a ton of money into advertising at metal shows, the bands they sponsored all seemed to love the hell out of it, and I happily obliged when it came to pouring this otherwise pretty gross licorice-flavored BS down my throat. Cristina Scabbia from Lacuna Coil even told me she took a shot of it before shows just as a little liquid inspiration. I had some very light experience with Jäger in high school at a couple New Year's Eve parties, but once I got to college, Sam Adams and Jägermeister fueled my liver punishments. After college, my band used and abused the worst-tasting shit ever created: Old Grand-Dad whiskey. We drank it *because* it was horrible, if for no other reason than to try to cowboy-face it (blank stare) at the bar. We also used it to reprimand band members who spoke about politics for more than five seconds during band practice, as we all had wildly different political views, with me being the resident lefty.

Lady me, however, didn't drink for the social aspect of it and definitely not to be "one of the guys." Rather, it was to have something in my hands with just a little bit of a kick to move around the dance floor or chat at a table with friends. Oddly enough, I drank vodka-and-Sprite as my go-to because I saw Machine Head frontman Robb Flynn with one in his hands at the 9:30 Club in D.C. during my senior year of high school in 2002, so it's not like it was an inherently feminine drink, but more a way I could almost keep some sense of heavy metal normalcy while wading into the new territory of, even for one night, living as a metal chick. Vodka, like chicken, seemed to go with everything. Unlike chicken, however, it was nasty as hell on its own. Rum-and-coke was my second drink, followed by 007: Bacardi orange, orange juice, and 7 Up. Notice the theme of mixed drinks, which I think I gravitated toward because I didn't feel like they were going to mess me up, they tasted good, and they fell into the stereotypical trope of what counts as a "bitch drink." Granted, that's an inherently sexist term but one I embraced because, well, regardless of "femininity," it completely removed me from the mind-set that goes into men (and male-presenting women in my former case) drinking and raging together. It just felt like a different night out and that's what I really wanted: getting away from having to pretend to be male, shed any lingering clutch on the "normal" security blanket of masculinity, and genuinely embrace being a woman, even if that came with accepting some stereotypical nonsense while doing it.

In short, I didn't have that truly exploratory phase of discovering what it meant to live as a girl or a woman in my childhood and teens beyond just raiding my sister's closet when she or my mom weren't at home. As I grew up and looked for excuses to be the woman I wanted to be, I had to figure out who she was first, and that meant, before anything else, that I wanted to get away from living as a stereotypical guy. Going out to dance, I would warm up in my car by listening exclusively to female-fronted metal bands—especially the Genitorturers, led by their dominatrix frontwoman Gen, who openly embraced all forms of sexuality and alpha femininity in the most overt way possible onstage.

When I was on the dance floor around 2011, I didn't even want to hear metal for those few hours. I was perfectly happy moving to "Judas" by Lady Gaga, "S&M" by Rihanna, "Firework" by Katy Perry, and, my favorite dance floor track for reasons I still don't understand, "Blow" by Ke$ha. I lived with this internal dichotomy of wanting to distance myself from the masculine part of heavy metal with a female gender expression while still holding on to just enough of my metal sense that I could feel like I was being true, that something as little as holding on to that vodka-and-Sprite kept that metal spirit alive in the only way that I knew. It also didn't hurt that Lady Gaga and Ke$ha were both on record explicitly supporting metal— Lady Gaga enthusiastically so with her public love of Saxon, Metallica, and Iron Maiden (even in 2021, she posted a photo of her in a Biohazard shirt designed by Life of Agony's bassist Alan Robert in 1989 when he was a roadie for them), while Ke$ha wore a Judas Priest shirt during her 2010 It Gets Better video meant to encourage LGBTQ youth. I took that video as a subtle nod to queer metalheads given Judas Priest frontman Rob Halford—*the* Metal God— being out as a gay man.

I don't know what it's like to feel like my exterior matches my interior, even on my most glammed-out, feminine days, like on the American Music Awards red carpet in 2017 as a guest of Demi Lovato (more on that later) when I had a proper makeup and hair team, an entire wardrobe to pick out my dress from (that I immediately had to return afterward), and what seemed like an entry into the celebrity D list while standing next to a quintessential A-lister. Some photos afterward looked nice, but other videos and photos still highlighted the parts about my face or build that just tampered with my dysphoria, something that I've learned to live with but know won't be "cured." These are some of the same insecurities I wrestled with as a closet case clutching that vodka-and-Sprite on the dance floor, and I still live with them as the history-making, first out-and-seated transgender state legislator in the country.

A friend once told me that anxiety is a replacement emotion: it's something you cling to when the real feelings you need to feel are too big and unpleasant. I would argue that being a human dumpster fire of conflicting emotions and dichotomy is kind of the same deal. If you lean hard into being a hashtag Hot Mess, you can tell yourself and the world that you're reeling because you didn't like how your dressed hugged your body, that no guy kissed you on the dance floor, or that you vomited in front of your friends and family—not because of the way you go to bed every night feeling alienated from your own body. It takes recognizing the insecurities behind your actions and appearances to understand how to live with or address them. I spent three decades falling short of that.

Running for office, in a therapeutic way, put me out there to let what seemed like the whole world pick apart what I felt drove my fears and feelings of inadequacy. That allowed me to see that, hey, being critiqued and criticized sucks, but it's bearable; I can handle it, especially when it's a transphobic attack that I know comes from a place of malicious intent. At the same time, it didn't remove my dysphoria. Even after twelve rounds of laser facial hair removal over eighteen months from 2013 and 2014, I still carry one set of tweezers with me in the driver's-side door pocket of my car so that I can pick and prune those few hairs that are left when I'm in the parking lot.

When I stopped drinking at thirty, that in a way removed one of the strongest vestiges of my masculine-presentation twenties. That was something within my control that I could handle on my own without needing help—not wanting the alcohol to compete for liver space with my hormone replacement therapy prescriptions and becoming a stepmom who never wanted the kiddo to see me drinking or drunk gave me the motivation to cut out that portion of my life. Running for office and serving openly allowed me to confront my insecurities about what other people would think about me living as an out transgender woman.

But those tweezers in my car are a little reminder that there'll always be insecurities somewhere within that I have to live with and I can't permanently change, no matter how much I may want that change.

Perhaps it's for the best. After all, driving around with a vodka-and-Sprite in the cup holder wouldn't be a good look.

CHAPTER 6

VAGABOND

Does Virginia's 13th House of Delegates district want a delegate who praises violence, getting drunk and other unsuitable behavior when representing the families of Virginia?

Danica's band sings the praises of drunkenness and violence with such provocative song titles as "Slaughter Brew," "Bullets and Pepperoni," and "Assassins of Innocence." . . . What message does this send young people who attend Danica's concerts and listen to her songs online?

—Prince William Times, *"Letter to the Editor: Promoting violence and vulgarity in Virginia," October 15, 2017*

t wasn't at the top of the "Occupied" Bank of Ireland, overrun by squatting anarchists right in the heart of downtown Belfast, where I could see the mountains to the west, the sea to the east, and the burial site of the "Occupigeon" below—aka the bird who gave up a perch on the 1 percent to poop among the commoners.

It wasn't at the Glasgow casino called the Corinthian Club in which a woman convinced me to tell the patrons that I was the American DJ musician Skrillex because "they're all a bunch of poseurs and won't know the difference anyway!" (Until one woman did.)

It wasn't at the docks in Edinburgh, where I unwisely picked up drum cymbals in the one part of town known for gun violence shortly after watching my bassist perform DIY foot surgery with an instrument that clearly needed a bath in grain alcohol.

And it wasn't at the pirate bar in Aberdeen, where a question of "Do you have any tea?" turned to "How about just some hot water?" and an earnest, determined bartender who answered, "I'll see what I can do."

No. The part of my band's UK tour that meant the most to me

was the two-hour ferry ride from Northern Ireland to Scotland under utterly gray and miserable but perfect skies, where I sat alone inside, looking out the window, over the deck, and into the sea, while my bandmates drank enough Strongbow cider to grow an alcoholic orchard in their intestines.

On one hand, the moment was precious because it was a moment of calm, moving meditation, a respite from a raucous tour where I could sit and catch my breath. It was my first and only opportunity to submit to the satisfaction that was finally sinking in that I had gotten us, all of us, to this place. At the end of the ferry ride from Belfast to Cairnryan, all the chaos would start up again: catch the bus to Ayr, catch the train to Glasgow, and then rock out three shows in four days, complete with the high-energy partying and performing that would propel us through Glasgow, Edinburgh, and Aberdeen. But this was the one moment I got to myself, to savor that we were getting to do the thing we'd set out to do—my bandmates' sobriety notwithstanding.

On the other hand, that blissful ride was my favorite because it was the one and only moment where I didn't have to Do. Jack. Shit. For this one, fleeting moment, in the eternal fog of the Irish waters and in the presence of the first alcoholic drink consumed by my nineteen-year-old drummer (such a sweet Baby's First ornament), I could just stare out the window and do absolutely nothing else.

It had been a months-long logistical marathon to book the tour, four shows between Northern Ireland and Scotland, with flights in and out of London, England. I financed most of the tour. I performed each night of it. I made our travel arrangements that included three planes (excluding the one we missed), one ferry, two trains, and taxis and friends' cars in two cities. Planes, trains, boats, and automobiles: we really did it all. I found the opening or headlining bands for every night, and secured the entertainment visas and lodging for five people while helping the other band who traveled with us to figure out their own lodgings. And I did every other thing on the frickin' planet to make it happen, including a mad dash from D.C. to New York City the morning of our flight so that I could scream bloody murder at the British consulate when they didn't turn my drummer Jacob's entertainment visa in on time and forced the issue then and there . . . and then vomited profusely that evening after three liters of beer and one missed flight.

My band Cab Ride Home's Sonically Intoxicating Britain DIY 2012 tour with local metal band Cammo Shorts was the first time since I was sixteen that I demonstrated to myself that if I wanted something badly enough, no matter how insane or impractical it seemed, I could actually make it happen by working hard and putting the hamsters that run the logistics portion of my brain on their loop-the-loop wheel to power up the chess game of decisions that lay before me. I had really, truly applied myself in a similar fashion one time before, in 2001, but only for what amounted to a single day and night's journey to western Pennsylvania and back home. This time around, I could do things that were supposed to be impossible just by focusing on them with an intensity that was insane, relentless, and possibly a little alienating for months at a time. That mentality stuck with me far beyond the tour and ended up propelling me through the early years of transitioning. It also led me to run for office, though unlike my 2017 campaign, it took quite a bit of liquid courage to get through it.

All of that is also the message I want to get across here (sans daydrinking as a coping mechanism): There's nothing inherently wrong with pursuing what someone else might think is impractical when it's what you love and want to do with your life. Finding the time to actually live in a punch-in, punch-out, structured existence when there's no break from the mundane to chase the magic just isn't something I subscribe to with my one shot at life. This mentality first manifested itself in high school, when I skipped my junior prom to drive more than three hundred miles each way as a sixteen-year-old (who had never driven farther than the next county over) to meet my fifteen-year-old first love. Eleven years later in 2012, this was my second big dumb idea, taking two bands on an international do-it-yourself tour with no big-name promoters, booking agents, record labels, or other industry people other than club owners, bands, sound engineers, lighting techs, bartenders, and the internet to fall back on.

My third venture into the unknown was, and continues to be, every single aspect of transitioning: from my first psychology appointment and my first endocrinology appointment, to a dozen facial laser hair removal sessions in a year and a half and starting hormone replacement therapy. Then there was the scariest part of all: coming out to my family at home, to hundreds of my friends online through social media, to my newspaper readers, and to potential employers.

Finally, the fourth mountain I convinced myself to move came nearly sixteen years after that three-hundred-plus mile trip in 2001, 4.5 years after the Sonically Intoxicating Britain 2012 DIY Tour, and 4.2 years after my first therapy appointment. It was deciding to run for office as an unemployed, uninsured, thirty-two-year-old out transgender woman against a seventy-two-year-old thirteen-term incumbent Republican state delegate who had been in office since I was seven years old.

I'm not the person who's going to tell you that you shouldn't chase your dreams and should keep your head out of the clouds. Absolutely not. Rather, I'm going to tell you to visualize your end goal, come up with a list of obstacles you'll need to overcome to get there, and then figure out how you'll clear those hurdles—*not* finding reasons to avoid it but determining what you can do to make it happen.

For the first of those four mountains, I had an excuse to be out of school for a prom I never planned to attend in the first place. I had a way to get where I was going with the Metal Mobile—my charcoal-gray '97 Nissan Sentra with the Metallica and Slayer stickers, Lamb of God decal, and CD album covers on the back. I had printed out driving directions from the Ye Olde Mappy Map Place* on the internet from back in those days, while also bringing a backup atlas just in case (which I very much did use); and I had a twenty-dollar bill my grandfather had given me that would cover the tolls and gas round trip because *cue ol' timey voice* that's what a Jackson got ya back then. I lied to everyone I could think of about what I was doing that night—"Going to an after-prom party at . . . *darts eyes back and forth* . . . Johnnnnnn's." *Mission Impossible* this was not, as I left one of the atlases on the floor outside the bathroom like a total dumbass (which my ma very much did find), drove six hours for a four-hour rendezvous, and drove six hours home with confidence I had never known before, which was only possible from experiencing your first kiss.

When my ma figured out where I had gone, she yelled to a family member, who in response told her—oh, precious irony—"Good! It's time he grew some balls!"[†]

My first love and I shared a ton in common, chief among them George Carlin's comedy and Metallica's albums. One of the most

---

*Before there was GPS and Google Maps, there was . . . Mapquest. *cues Iliza Shlesinger voice* Gather 'round the 56K modem, Gen Zers. I have an Elder Millennial story for you . . .

[†]Some trans women might find that uncouth, but not me: when I heard that story years after it happened, I cackle-laughed. That is hilarious.

powerful parts of heavy metal that drew not just me to the music but, I think, a lot of metalheads in general—as was certainly the case with both of us—was that the musicians don't typically come from a lineage of money, fame, pedigree, or prestige. Our favorite bands took over the world as entirely self-made artists who often started from trauma and tragedy, something that was more powerful for me than I realized as a young teenager. I think I was missing that technical intensity from grunge and that emotional intensity that comes from heavy and hard music, which resonates in my mind as coming from the most real place of an artist's soul. I mean, that and it's loud. Loud was/is good. Shake your blood, as Lemmy wrote.

That's what drew me to the backstory of Black Sabbath as I adopted them as my favorite metal band at first: when he was young, left-handed guitarist Tony Iommi accidentally cut off two of his right-hand fingertips—his fret hand—while working on a factory assembly line and was told by his doctor that he would never play guitar again. Yet that didn't stop him: he cut up a leather jacket, molded fingertips out of it, down-tuned his guitar anywhere between one and three steps to relieve the tension of the strings on his fingers, and found a way to make it work. You could beat someone to death with a steel pipe wrapped in Cannibal Corpse tour shirts and I'll still tell you Tony Iommi down-tuning his guitar so what remained of his appendages could grip the fret board is the pinnacle of metal.

The story I really latched on to, though, came from Metallica frontman James Hetfield. Not only did Metallica write the biggest heavy metal album ever created (the self-titled black album), but they also got to the top of the world after experiencing death, loss, struggle, and turmoil—and that was just James, let alone the rest of the guys. I didn't even know who Cliff Burton was when I was fourteen, listening to songs like "The God That Failed," which was written by James about how his Christian Scientist mother wouldn't be treated for cancer because she believed God would cure her until she died when James was sixteen years old.

What's more, his father walked out on the family three years earlier and never returned, leading James to tell his father years later that he blamed him for his mother's death because she didn't know how to take care of herself alone. That part . . . that death, that loss, that anger . . . made James Hetfield—the multimillionaire, world-touring, festival-headlining, top-of-the-world musician—relatable to me. Bonding with someone I've never met over loss demonstrates not only the power of music (and, frankly, celebrity, if I'm being real to myself) but also storytelling, opening up. Being vulnerable about abandonment. Emotionally bleeding over *real* trauma, not bullshit like "My teenage girlfriend dumped me and I'm so mad!" (Though, a couple years later in high school, that would also be . . . relatable.) That's what spoke to me as a high school freshman—an expression of pain that wasn't based on bitching, whining, and stupid shit, but authentic, raw reality with the heaviness, technicality, and aggression in the music to back it up. It felt like I wanted to hurt with them and they let me in.

The story of James Hetfield goes to show that no matter where life takes you, you carry your scars everywhere you go. The fact that he's been in and out of rehab for alcoholism—I totally get why. Trauma manifests itself in weird ways and at weird times and it can leave you looking for an outlet. Party drinking, like Metallica was notorious for in the mid-1980s (they were called "Alcoholica" in the press), appealed to me in the 2000s, in part because it's a raw celebration of living, completely caught up in the moment of having a good time and embracing the opposite of death. It makes you feel alive when you're around a bunch of other people who are also having a good time. That's how I spent my twenties. Metallica was known for their excessive drinking far more than for drug use—though they certainly weren't strangers to the latter, it just wasn't a part of their image.

Clearly demonstrating my perception of their influence, I decided in my late teens that when I got to college, I would pick my one poison—drinking—and become good at it without any of the other stuff. No drugs. Ever. To this day, that's held up. Being around my mom's ex-boyfriend in the early to mid-nineties kept me from ever wanting to smoke a cigarette, but I also had no interest in any drug other than alcohol. Instead of using drugs, I've let music serve as my escape when I just want to melt into oblivion.

I've also come to learn from my heavy metal icons that there's a thin line between addiction and a personality type that is prone to addiction. Acting on addiction, though, is also a form of self-expression in its rawest sense, and having other, healthier outlets of expression to occupy your mind and body during your most turbulent times *can*—though not always *will*—help keep that at bay.

Hence: Music. Guitars. Traveling. Journalism. That's what I fell into more than anything else in college and I'm glad I made the decision at age seventeen for my only vice to be drinking, with the goal of getting good enough at it to keep up with the people around me at parties. That, of course, went terribly when I drank myself into the emergency room at age eighteen. In the most political sense of nonaccountability through acknowledgment possible: mistakes were made.

What I also did right at age seventeen was to develop a much healthier addiction than alcohol could have ever been: live music.

In 2002 alone, the year I graduated from high school and went off to college, I put more than two thousand miles on my car just traveling to and from In Flames shows, let alone every other band I saw in what was the most instrumental year for my music development. It didn't matter where it was, as long as it was within a day's drive: I wanted live heavy metal in my life and I wanted as much of it as I could get, often alone, though sometimes with friends.

Like cats, you can never have *too many* metal shows in your life—until you begin to smell like one. Coming home from Jaxx before Virginia banned smoking indoors, I always smelled like the ashtray of a mound of cigarettes, zero of which were mine. Despite that, I kept going and going and going to shows, so it became only logical at some point that I would actually pick up my guitar again, after years of not playing it because of my aforementioned deep-seated feelings of inadequacy, and give it another shot. My college band, in a word, sucked. But among the thirteen shows we played from 2005 to 2006, we at least got to travel three hours to Cleveland for a show in our drummer Jim's hometown, even if it was on a stage that was basically a windowsill onto which we crammed three guitar players (JB, Adam, and me), a bassist (John), and Jim. That marked my first time hitting the road to play my own music—and I loved it.

A friend from home, who I met online through a metal forum and went to shows with in the area, suggested we form Cab Ride Home after the aforementioned run-in with a police officer outside of Jaxx Nightclub shortly after my twenty-first birthday resulted in us having to take a sixty-dollar cab ride home. He played bass. I wasn't any good at guitar or vocals but took him up on doing both anyway. He had a friend Enock who played lead guitar and could write music pretty well. Once I showed the third partier from the infamous cab-ride-home night, James, how to hold the AC/DC drumbeat—"One, two, three, four on the high hat. Kick on one, snare on three. Kick on one, snare on three. Crash on four. Okay, here we go . . ."—we had our first lineup by the end of 2006.

By April 2007, we were ready(ish) to play live, having learned a handful of covers and written about four or five originals. Our first show was an open mic night at Jimmy's Old Town Tavern in Herndon—no stage, no pay, just plug in and play for half an hour. I brought my double-neck guitar to that show for the sheer extraness of the audience seeing it live, not for any ability to play it well given that I could barely function on the six-string neck, let alone the twelve-string one.

From there, we booked a couple Localpalooza gigs at—where else?—Jaxx, to finally come full circle. Other musicians bitched about the venue because it was essentially pay-to-play for local bands—you had to sell so many tickets to justify the space you were given. But for us, it just forced us to build a fan base among friends, who we hustled to buy ten-dollar tickets over a *lot* of drinks at Patriot's Café in Fairfax. We also knew that if we were even remotely competent, we could eventually play as openers for some of the national bands that came through the venue.

And "competent" was an ambitious enough goal for us. We wanted to be a thrash band—and although we didn't have the talent to play that fast, what we did have was the spirit and attitude. Our songs were party songs and what we lacked in raw skills we made up for in pure theatrics: a song called "Brawl at the Bar" was exactly what it sounds like. Another crowd favorite was a song called "Retox," because "when you're with Cab Ride Home you don't detox you RETOOXXXXX. . . ." Just to really make it clear that at the ripe age of twenty-two I was leading a beer-drenched party metal band, at one Jaxx show I let my guitar ring out for a moment as I reached behind my Marshall cabinet, lifted up a red plastic beer helmet complete with cans of Schlitz on both sides, and—with only the finest malt beverage dribbling down my chin, onto my chest, down my guitar, and onto the stage—proceeded to drink through the plastic straws while yelling into the mic and playing the guitar . . . simultaneously. Some would call that messy. I called it multitasking, my chin thrusting back and forth from the mic between streams of Schlitz Schlitzing down my face. "Beautiful you," indeed.

Despite all the ridiculous antics, though, the goal from the start was to make a living doing music. We knew the longer we played together and the more we practiced, the closer we'd get to a place where we could put on a tight musical performance that was still high-intensity, goofy, and heavy live; a show people would want to see. I remember the first time I got up on the stage at Jaxx. We arrived to the *Terminator 2* theme and for the final second walking on I thought about how nervous I *should* be. The rest of the guys had been onstage already. Friends and strangers were in the crowd. But the moment I arrived at the microphone and yelled "WHAT THE FUCK IS UP, JAXX!!!"—I was home. After six years of going to shows there, my band—*our* band—was now the show. It was all the energy. I wanted to do that forever.

When you have the kind of charisma that it takes to front a band while wearing a leaky beer helmet, you can use it in different ways. You can use it to manipulate, to charm people into fulfilling your own needs, which is a dangerous game not only because it's wrong to do but because tempers are short and memories are long when it comes to crossing over people in the music industry. You can use it to hide or mask an inadequacy or insecurity, both of which I left neatly packed away in my guitar case and microphone box when I was onstage. And all these things are very much linked together. But another thing you can do, and my personal favorite wielding of this tool, is put on one hell of a party. In those instances, it's pure reciprocal energy between the audience and you—the more you put out there while you're up on the stage, the more it's reflected back at you by the crowd. If they felt good, I felt great. And it was intoxicating.

We did gradually start to get better, more technically proficient, thanks in part to our experience in the studio recording our first album, *The Intoxicated Massacre*, with the gothic band Bella Morte's then-keyboardist Micah Consylman producing, engineering, recording, mixing, and mastering the album. He helped us deliver our best performances, and by the time we escaped from his studio in Charlottesville in October 2008, we had put together our best song, "One Last Round." Enock wrote most of the music and he and I paired up at a bar in Manassas called Mackey's to hash out the lyrics about wanting to have one more drink with someone who died. He had lost a close friend in Iraq in 2006. I had lost my grandfather earlier that April, and the lyrics that we didn't complete at the bar, I did while sitting on his tombstone plaque at Stonewall Memory Gardens. Micah helped us turn a decent concept for a song into a genuinely good piece of songwriting, complete with a multilayered, instrumental intro where I actually carried the guitar melody to Enock's rhythm and then harmonized it on the lower strings—the only time on any song I would do anything like that before giving up my guitar playing to focus on vocals the following year.

It started to feel like the dream could really happen, that we could maybe get signed and go on tour. We developed a solid local fan base and were outselling the other local bands. We became a mainstay at Jaxx, assisted by my mom's boyfriend Scott, who was a friend of Jay's, the owner of Jaxx. He got us hooked into a local festival. When

Jay saw our ticket sales and the fun show we put on, he came up to me and said, "You can play here whenever you want. Keep doing what you're doing." Whenever there was a local TBD listed on the Jaxx calendar as an opener for a nationally touring metal band, we often had first dibs, along with a small handful of other high-drawing local bands like Division and Apothys. Our lineup switched a couple of times, like when we picked up our rhythm guitarist Chris following his stint in Apothys, and we started getting serious about practicing, putting together press kits, and sending out our music to a heavy metal label.

Our record-release show was the same day that a national talent group was coming through town. We wined and dined them (okay, Sam Adams and Yuengling–ed them) and not only had a blast but thoroughly caught their attention as the promoter would help us land shows in New Jersey and Ohio later that year.

By 2012, though, we'd been playing together for six years. Our lead guitarist Enock and I were the only original members of the band left, as we were now on our fourth bassist and second drummer. Jay had sold Jaxx, and the management that replaced him had a completely different vibe and the venue just wasn't quite our home anymore. While we did have another solid venue for playing shows at Ball's Bluff Tavern in Leesburg, we couldn't possibly have the audience size of a good night at Jaxx and we had few national bands come through for the Monthly Metal shows at the Bluff. Most of my bandmates were broke—our new drummer Jacob was still a college student, Enock and Chris weren't making much money, and we had to rely on extended temporary help from friends to fill in on bass. We had all sunk a lot of money into the band, and I—working two full-time reporting jobs, not exactly rolling in it—was the most steady one of all of us financially.

Given that I hadn't dated since 2008, the band was my partner. It was my passion, and my best distraction from the rest of my life. I had even created an LLC under my name. I'd wanted to step up; I was taking voice lessons and devoting more time and energy into figuring out how to get us to the next level. And, all the while, I was on a collision course with gender dysphoria. All that intense energy I was bringing to the stage was also, in a way, about distracting myself. If no one was going to love me as the frontwoman I knew I was and wanted to be but felt I couldn't present as—then I would make them love the facade of the frontman I presented to them show after show.

I t was Wacken Open Air and Hellfest—the European metal festivals I camped and partied at each summer from 2008 to 2011—that inspired the UK tour. With Ozzfest going kaput stateside after Metallica headlined the one-day-only festival in 2008 in Dallas (I had a blast there), European shows had provided the thing I circled on my calendar every year as "I am doing this." I had first traveled to the UK as a little kid in 1992 and then went to my ancestral homeland of Italy to study abroad in 2005, where I took a weekend to catch a train from Perugia to Bologna for the Gods of Metal festival, headlined by Iron Maiden and Slayer, with Italy's own Lacuna Coil also on the bill. That whet my appetite for Euro fests, and after two Wackens and two Hellfests, I wanted much more than just seeing the shows; I wanted to be a part of it, even if it was at tiny clubs in front of twenty people.

Each of those four metal festivals I partied at in Germany and France also meant that I kept meeting new people, making new friends, and getting especially close with my Scottish crew, who'd show up to each festival and travel with Bork and me throughout whatever countries we'd visit in the run-up to the festivals. They'd be key to bringing my band and our touring partners across the pond for our shot at ~~running up my credit card debt~~ touring overseas and ~~leaving me with 51 weeks of payments~~ doing something truly special for an unsigned band from Virginia with no record label, distributor, or agent and three out of five members earning between squat and squat-and-a-half for income.

From the time I was twenty-one years old I had wanted to play a festival, with my dream being performing on the side stage at Ozzfest at our local amphitheater that was not even ten minutes away from where we rehearsed in Bristow, Virginia. To play overseas felt like a new challenge, and a new level beyond all that we'd accomplished as a band so far. I wanted my European friends to see my band. I wanted to have experiences that felt like they were uniquely mine. I wanted to live out my twenties.

On a 2011 visit to Scotland before attending Hellfest in France, I was hanging out at Bannerman's Bar in Edinburgh, a low-key place with couches and stools around the bar itself and a side room with a stage under a centuries-old brick archway, marinating in my Scottish friends' ridiculous, Olympic-level sarcastic banter (and in Scottish alcohol), and I looked around and thought: We could play a show here. It felt like something that was absolutely achievable as the venue itself wasn't much different than the scores of bars and small venues we played at back home. I had the friends, I had the connections, I had the money . . . why not? By this point I was close with a couple of friends in three Scottish cities, all of which had thriving metal scenes and bars where we could put on a great show.

So when I got back home I floated the idea to the band, who knew I had wanted to do this before but was now serious about it.

They were with me in theory, but I knew I'd have to finance the trip for all of us if I wanted to make it happen. Some other friends told me I was out of my mind but knew better than to try to talk me out of it. When I was locked on a dream in my twenties, I would do what I had to do to achieve it or drink my guts out trying. Though our forward motion as a band was flagging, I couldn't let anything get in the way of this quest.

Given that my other dream, transitioning, was quickly approaching a breaking point where I knew I was going to have to do something soon, this was legit the healthiest thing I could do to keep my mind busy and off the thought of wanting my skeleton to jump out of my skin like a cartoon character holding a live electrical wire. And I thought: Maybe this would tip the scales back for us as a band, help us get signed, and open up new worlds of possibility. You never know who you're going to meet on the road, let alone abroad, and "toured Scotland and Northern Ireland" sure as hell would catch someone's eye on the band's CV . . . right?

My friends from Edinburgh, Mike and Aisha, in particular, went to bat for us in the run-up to the tour, too. They both would scout out bands and venues for us while also giving us places to crash, which was huge for cutting costs during the two nights we spent in Edinburgh. Mike even convinced his police officer father to serve as our sponsor for immigration officials to contact, putting his own reputation on the line for his son's friend's band. Fortunately, he had met me once before on what turned out to be an absolutely batshit long commute to and from Wacken in 2009, when we departed and returned to the Netherlands in what my friends from Canada, Scotland, and I quickly turned into a party van. Traffic was so bad on the way back to the Netherlands that cars would park on the two-lane highway and people would literally step outside, pull a hookah out from the back seat, put it on the hood, and puff away, waiting for vehicles to move again. Mike's dad did eventually call home and, in his Scottish accent full of rolled *r*'s, said, "We're in grave danger of missing the ferry!" Indeed, they did—but at least we got to spend some quality time together that, three years later, helped us fly over.

So I had solid good friends I would keep in touch with over Facebook who pitched in while I contacted the immigration attorneys to secure entertainment visas to make the tour work. Six people showing up with guitars, microphones, and even some portable drum equipment would be what you might call suspicious at the immigration gates if you didn't have your papers in order.

As far as I was concerned, I wanted to do everything possible by the book and with the lowest margin for error, which turned out to be more time and effort than I ever could have imagined: emails, online portals, *all six of us* not only answering fifty-plus questions but also providing eleven different forms of scanned documents and pieces of information, then re-collecting all of those documents to send the hard copies to British immigration, PLUS paying thousands of dollars.

As I was the organizer of the trip who was handling all of these logistics, it all made me want to jump through my PC screen in my ma's basement, swim through the underground fiber-optic cable network to London, and throw the largest American-made temper tantrum directed toward the British government since 1776.

K eep in mind: At age twenty-seven, I had no work-life balance. I was writing for *The Hotline* in the morning and afternoon and writing for the *Gainesville Times/Prince William Times* during the evening, at night, and on the weekend, still holding band practice and playing shows and spending every other waking hour setting up this tour. That meant not only dealing with the logistics, but locking down venues that would actually book two unsigned American bands without a preexisting footprint on the promise that we had friends in each town and we drank enough for the bar to at least turn a profit by night's end.

Landing our first venue confirmation of the tour in Edinburgh at Bannerman's Bar from a man named Chris made the entire rest of the tour possible, as other venues wanted to know that we had a tour route but didn't want to be the first to say yes. With the help of Mike and Aisha, who were able to put in a good word, as locals well known in their metal scene along with their crews and friends' bands, Bannerman's came through for us. I remember getting the confirmation email while at work in D.C., complete with a letterhead that we could use for immigration, and I just pumped my fists with absolute joy under the fluorescent lightbulbs of the fourth floor of the Watergate's office suites.

Next came the (coolest-looking) letter from the Moorings Bar in Aberdeen, complete with pirate-skull-insignia letterhead to prove the gig was official. That came about because of a promoter named Brian and my friend Richard, who had introduced me to Brian in the first place. Our friend Hannah, an expat from Maryland, came in clutch in Belfast, helping us book a since-defunct venue called Auntie Annie's with a couple of local bands for the first show of the tour. In Glasgow, Mike and some of my other Wacken friends managed to help me out with a vegan restaurant that had a stageless venue in the basement (and the sweetest Marshall JCM 900 electric guitar amplifier you've ever heard in your life . . . *drools in Scottish Gaelic*) and two super-aggressive local bands willing to serve as the main draw—Citizen Death and Circle of Tyrants—on July 4, our American Independence Day.

We had no such luck with any venue anywhere at all located in England. Whereas Scotland welcomed my bandmates and me with open arms behind the keg of our choosing, England welcomed us with a middle finger and a KICK ME sign stapled to our—and I do believe this is the proper English term—arses. A dear, dear friend of mine, Dan, who I had known for eleven years at that point and who happened to live in northeastern England and played bass in the grindcore band Dawn of Chaos, put in a good word for us at his hometown venue, to no avail. Neither did we gain traction in any city from Reading to Newcastle to Hartlepool to . . . anywhere, usually in the form of no response. Not to make it too political, but I like to think of Scotland as a country that embraces the underdog and will give you a shot to prove yourself without pretension.* Of course, I could be very wrong and just lucked out three times in three different cities with well-established metal scenes . . . or I could just be right.

The thing is, I had so many setbacks booking and arranging the tour that I didn't have time to mope. To quote one of my favorite phrases that I learned covering politics as a reporter, I was a seething cauldron of anxiety for roughly half a year. By the time April came around and I was in the thick of booking everything, we still had two months to get our shit together before the tour at the end of June and the first week of July. That included figuring out where we would crash at night—Hannah's flat each night in Belfast; a cheap-ass hotel in Glasgow for two nights; with Mike in Edinburgh, and

---

*"O' Flower of Scotland, when will we see your like again?"

an upstairs apartment above Bannerman's where bands typically slept after shows; and at the venue-provided flat in Aberdeen, which one member of the band would so gallantly grace with his drunken presence by pissing on a bicycle on the floor in the middle of the night after the last show of the tour as the rest of us tried to sleep in the bunks around him. (Damn it, Enock!)

Then there was the gear. Just how in the High Holy Hanneman's ghost is a metal band with no tour van going to get around with their gear? I told each member that they could bring their instruments, which they would carry with them (guitars, bass, microphones, drumsticks, and double bass pedal), and that the local bands or venues in each city would provide us the backline (amplifiers and drums), because the local bands Cursed Sun and Stand with Heretics—all of whom were super-cool dudes—hooked us up with their gear, especially in Aberdeen, where they provided everything you could think of onstage. In Glasgow, I had to rent out a backline from a company that dropped off the gear (and had to pay them a fine afterward for a damaged drum stand following a full-frenzied Scottish mosh pit that spilled *into the band as we were playing*). In Edinburgh, however, I had to take a bus with Mike to a warehouse at the docks in the one place around town where Mike told me there had been a shooting that he knew of (a little taste of home cooking for our American visitor . . .) to rent drum cymbals for a night and return them in the rain the next morning. That of course required a taxi to and from the Edinburgh Waverley train station, driven by a cabbie who knew every nook and alley of that city from a lifetime of living there, which was super cool since he weaved through driveway-size side roads to get me back in time to catch the train to Aberdeen.

Of course, to even perform the tour at all required us—by which I mean me—to buy plane tickets. I bought four tickets—our tour mates bought their own—which meant we would have to drive from Manassas, Virginia, to Newark, New Jersey, so that we could fly to London; catch a hopper flight to Belfast for the first show; take a ferry across the Irish Sea to a port in southwestern Scotland,* where we could catch a bus to Ayr and take a train to Glasgow for the second show; take another train to Edinburgh for the third gig that I switched out at the last minute for a bus when my boy Dom from Citizen Death told me I could save a shit ton of money doing that, much to the chagrin of my bandmates—which actually led to a stress-induced meltdown from yours truly in the bus terminal as I threw a shit fit for any of them even daring to critique my management skills; and finally a train to Aberdeen for the final night.

Soon enough, the calendar flipped from April to May and May to June, and there was one big, glaring problem: We were finally finished getting all of our hard-copy supporting documents ready after the fiasco with the online portal. I read online that if I wrote "urgent" and "priority" on the package, they could be turned around within days, which would help us . . . until I realized after sending them that was only if we included a $150 expedited-processing fee.

"Oh my fucking God," I said to myself. "We're fucked. We're fucked. We're fucked."

With the resilience I learned from my editor at the newspaper, my brain quickly shifted from panic to determination and I sprang into action. I called a 1-900 number, emailed everyone who could possibly help, sent $150 for each visa to be expedited, re-sent documents, and—the night before we were supposed to leave—finally got confirmation that our passports were arriving overnight . . . except for Jacob's. One. Passport. Short.

---

*So grim. So tr00. So metal.

The next morning, Jacob—my long-haired nineteen-year-old drummer—and I set off on an adventure to New York that included a stop at my job on the fourth floor of the Watergate to wrap up everything before leaving for the trip, a cab to Union Station, and a ride on Amtrak, arriving at the British consulate with my Bronx mother's million-miles-per-hour New York intonation, explaining in rapid-fire speech why I needed to go upstairs to sort out my drummer's passport problem, only to hear that *Jacob's passport hadn't been processed yet.*

At this point, I switched tactics toward a clerk named Andrew, from enraged-spawn-of-a-Bronxite New Yorker to slow-paced, pure southern hostility. "Okay. Here's what's going to happen. It's noon. I'm going to head out. I'm going to come back here at three o'clock on the dot. When I get back here, that passport's going to be ready with the entertainment visa. Understood?"

I needed a drink. More specifically, I needed a drink several times over.

While I have no empirical data to back up this claim, I do have reason to believe that my 2.5-hour binge-a-thon led me to become the first (unsigned) heavy metal vocalist to blackout at the British consulate in New York City. It was a hard-fought and well-deserved victory, given the amount of bullshit I had to get through that could only be relieved via anxiety-induced day-drinking, which, nine years since that moment and six years since I stopped expressing myself via shit-facedness, I still find to be a reasonable response to the situation.

Day-drinking for three hours may not seem like the best pre-game approach to facing the British government on their property when they control whether you and your band get to go on tour, but if nothing else, I had learned to mask fear with an overcompensatingly high level of confidence. From what I've been told, I exuded that by high-fiving the security guards in the lobby, taking the elevator upstairs, seeing my best-good-friend-in-the-whole-wide-world Andrew, receiving Jacob's passport from him with the entertainment visa inside, sticking the tips of my right-hand fingers under the glass slot for a down-low high five as I considered all fences immediately mended, and heading out the door so I could go down the elevator and high-five the security guards again while yelling, "We're going to the UK!!!!"

Pieces of that sound familiar and I can almost draw them up in my mind. What I absolutely have no recollection of whatsoever is what followed.

Jacob had never been to New York City before. I had been a number of times and ridden mass transit enough in my life to figure out what subway trains we needed to take to get to the airport in Newark.

We boarded a subway train and sat. . . .

"Jacob. . . . What time is it?"

"Four o'clock."

"JACOB! We have to get to the consulate! Get off! Turn around! We have to get your passport before they close!"

"But we were just at the consulate!"

"Ohhhhhhhh!"

Apparently, in my effort to take the R train west and south toward City Hall so that we could transfer for the airport in New Jersey, I directed him to the other R train platform—toward the *other* airport . . . eastbound . . . in Queens.

LaGuardia.

"Jacob! What time is it?"

"Four-thirty."

"JACOB! THEY'RE GOING TO CLOSE UNTIL MON-DAY IF WE DON'T GET THERE BY FIVE! WE HAVE TO GET YOUR PASSPORT!"

"We already went to the consulate! We already got my passport! It's right here! I'm holding it in front of you!"

"Ohhhhhhh!"

Apparently, I renewed my earlier high-five celebration from the streets, only now underground, blitzed into oblivion and provoking some not-so-happy campers.

"You need to get control of your friend!" one guy barked at Jacob.

"I don't know him!" Jacob shouted back.

I don't blame Jacob for that response, despite his unbeknown misgendering; I would have bailed on me, too.

Eventually, I did come to at some point and we got to Newark early, where we waited for the rest of the crew, passports in hand, and everyone ready to go to London!

Except . . . not so much.

While my bandmates and Jacob's crew did arrive before the plane took off, it was after the gate had already closed. As we stood at the ticket counter, the staff wouldn't let us board, so I had to shell out another $636 to change our flights to the next day out.

Fortunately for all of us, I suspected months prior that if any-thing was going to go wrong, it would likely be in transit to Belfast, so I scheduled an oh-shit day, which we very much used. It turned out to be for the best, as my head began pulsating on the van ride to the local Econo Lodge motel. I got inside, vomited in a trash can, and passed out next to my guitar player.

Finally, after a fairly obnoxious run through multiple terminals of Heathrow airport due to changed gates, we arrived in Belfast, meeting up outside of the most historically bombed structure in Europe—the Europa Hotel—before settling in at Hannah's flat the night before the first of our four shows. We were ready to take on everything the tour had in store for us, even if that meant trying to sleep on top of a coffin-shaped guitar case stacked on top of other guitar cases in front of a single-cushion seat.

Writing this nine years after that tour, when I tried to think about what went on during that trip, what really motivated me to drop so much money just to play shows "over there" instead of "right here," I actually came to realize that I had answered that question before I even thought of it.

While we certainly had a ton of fun everywhere—we went on that tour with a bunch of rowdy friends showing up to support us—the entire tour was really built around the Edinburgh gig. That's where the greatest number of my Scottish friends lived; that's where I had partied the previous year; and that's where I had looked at that stage once before and told myself that the next time I saw it, I'd be on it.

Sure enough, as we prepared our closing anthem "Drunk on Arrival" at Bannerman's Bar on July 6, 2012, my bandmates and I were just about to complete a blistering thirty-three-minute set, all soaked in our own sweat from what was truly our strongest performance of the tour. That's when I shared a moment of candor with the crowd of headbangers before us:

"By the way, this week was our Independence Day week," I said into my wireless microphone, American flag hanging behind us as our banner. "Nothing more American than living the American Dream—overseas touring with my band and performing for you motherfuckers here in Scotland! Goddamn right! Our stage is your stage; come on up!"

It's hard to hug your friends when you're thousands of miles away—but it's really easy when twenty of y'all are crammed on a small stage together, sharing a moment that you know, deep down, you'll never live again, as close to the pinnacle of "carefree twenties" as you're going to create. I look back at that tour now and as much as I cringe at the all-out assault and abuse I leveled on my credit card, it felt totally worth the digging out I'd have to do on the other side. That's not the most practical thing—and was also entirely a function of my having two solid jobs and the privilege to know that I could pay it back eventually. I know a lot of trans folks who struggle to find work at all, as would be my situation not that long afterward. But at the time I could swing this impractical thing, I could afford to be poor for a while and do the thing that, to me, was what life is supposed to be about.

Figuring out how to move all the figurative chess pieces that made up the tour wasn't just good for me testing out whether the human-anxiety volume control knob does, in fact, go up to 11; it taught me a ton about time management, human management, transportation management, legal manuevering, international relations, virtual networking, and executive decision-making. That last part is key when you're Queen Shit in politics, as a candidate campaigning for office, and a legislator serving in office: you've got a ton of people putting their trust in you to keep them safe and they're willing to offer you guidance on seeing your vision through to completion. At the same time, you realize that there's no safety net at that point—you're at the top and if you mess up, you're hurting not just yourself but all the people counting on you to make good decisions. Achieving a once-in-a-lifetime dream is the antithesis to wasting time because you'll remember not just how it felt when you did but the work that went into it, too. Hopefully you can develop a skill set or two that's transferrable to whatever it is you want to pursue afterward—even if, God forbid, you decide to become a low-life, stinking politician.

In the end, applying yourself to chase something wild is about more than money.* It brings fulfillment, proving that when you set your mind to something, the pursuit in and of itself is worth it, even if other people may think what you're doing is impractical. Your dreams just don't always translate that well for others—yet achieving that major milestone of your life can have a lasting effect beyond the moment. It manufactures hope for the future, too. It tells you that the task in front of you may be hard, but if you've moved mountains before, then it's at least worth a shot. With hope comes ambition, and with ambition, confidence—the self-assuredness that win, lose, or draw, it's going to be okay.

When you find your once-in-a-lifetime adventure, just make sure you take your credit card with the 0 percent APR with you.

You're going to ~~want~~ need that.

---

*Debt!

WHORE

Marshall Ad Accuses Roem of "Lewd Behavior" in Old Video of Her Band

John Findlay, the executive director of the Virginia Republican Party, criticized Roem on Wednesday "for being featured in a video where it is clearly implied she performed group oral sex in a public restroom."

—The Washington Post, *October 25, 2017*

My back hurt so bad, I cringed. I gritted my teeth and squeezed my eyes shut hard enough to raise the apples of my cheeks.

At twenty-six, not only was I experiencing the back pain of an eighty-year-old former coal miner, but my band's show just an hour or so earlier had sucked so much, I hated everyone. In a farmhouse affectionately referred to among friends as "Chokesville," I sprawled out on the floor, trying to go to frickin' sleep while everyone else partied inside and outside the house, deep in the rural farmland of the western edge of Northern Virginia.

My back was in the kind of pain that even my dear hoppy friend Sam Adams, and a number of his higher-proof relatives, couldn't negotiate away. So when a friend of mine—a super badass, funny, and all-around beautiful woman who was so fun to hang out with through all hours of the night—crouched down next to me and asked if I wanted to face-plant on her bed instead of the floor, I didn't refuse. Nor did I refuse when she offered to help ease the pain in the way only your best stripper friend could.

There was just one problem: I didn't want to look lustfully *at* her, I wanted to admiringly look *like* her, flowing, curly dark brunette hair and all. The few times I had seriously tried to date women, none had lasted more than two weeks before I was inevitably dumped for reasons that—and this is completely true—include "I want you to tell me you think I'm *hot*, not that you like how I wear my eyeshadow."* I could always connect with the women in my life on a mental level. Physically, though, the same primal urge my guy friends had to, like, bone (huh-huh-huh) just wasn't there.

That night with my beautiful friend, looking up at her, just felt so off. Oddly enough, it wasn't just because her Army Ranger, Iraq war veteran husband walked in and said, "Oh, sorry . . ." as he reached for a roll of condoms in his sock drawer and tiptoed back out. (Swingers work in mysterious ways.)

For a while, I had tried to convince myself that penis-in-vagina sex was okay, as long as I was on the bottom. (For some reason, that way it was a little easier to convince myself I was acting as my partner's girlfriend rather than the other way around, which internally made it a . . . lesbian hookup? Hey, that's affirming. I'll take it?) When I wasn't looking up, I had tried to clench my eyelids as tightly shut as possible and pretend I was role reversing. I had *really* tried to enjoy sex with cisgender women who wanted to enjoy being with me. But I just couldn't keep bullshitting myself.

By that point in April 2011, five years after graduating from college but still 1.5 years before I started therapy, I couldn't even pretend to pretend anymore, even with a friend I trusted, admired, and adored.† So I rolled my head to the left on the pillow and turned my

---

*In my defense, her smoky eye was—and always is—on-point. We're still friends.
†Still do. She's so cool.

body with it as this woman with her absolutely gorgeous blue-green eyes lay down next to me and asked what was wrong.

Finally, I said the words every woman who just dismounted from her partner longs to hear: "I'm so sorry. I have a major case of the gay."

Okay, so maybe I *wasn't quite* done pretending. "Gay" is not exactly what I am, or even what I was. I'm a woman who's trans and is physically/sexually attracted to guys—cis, trans, and nonbinary alike. I've A/B tested this enough to know how my body just swoons after the way a guy kisses so, so much more than with women. Mentally, though, romantic attraction for me is much less gender based and much, much more personal. I'm pretty straight sexually for a woman in that I physically prefer a masculine presentation but pansexual romantically in that someone's gender doesn't determine my ability to fall in love with that person. But in that moment more than ten years ago, I was using humor to navigate a situation that could otherwise have been awkward and unpleasant for us both. It was a lot easier to explain "gay" than it was to explain "I'm a closet-case trans woman hiding behind stubble hair, caterpiller eyebrows, and a security blanket of beer because I'm too scared of what other people would think of me if I transitioned today."

It didn't take me long to learn that humor can and will save a story (and possibly a life) when you're figuring out who you are as a sexual being. It's an analgesic—a way to be tender and true with others without drowning in something too deep or humiliating. I can never decide whether it's saving my life or limiting it. Maybe both.

It's also something I used to convince myself that pursuits I knew wouldn't go anywhere were still worth my time in the moment because I wanted the story that only a good laugh can provide. Cracking jokes to try to make my sexual partner laugh through first, second, and third base became more important than "scoring." Connecting with my partner and being able to be vulnerable and silly with them matter infinitely more to me than anything else in a relationship. That, of course, is exactly what sex-ed classes don't teach you how to do.

Figuring out that I really liked guys went from a decade-long thought experiment to "Yes, please" after I finally graduated from college. As a brand-spankin'-new college graduate at age twenty-one, exactly four people had ever kissed me, and each time we had stopped right there at first base—not even rounding the basepath, taking a lead toward second, or any other gripping baseball metaphor of your choosing. It was more like getting walked on four pitches, trotting to first base, and then heading back to the dugout when the coach subs in a pinch runner.

My first kiss was, of course, passionate: I was sixteen years old and we were both wearing Metallica shirts. Teenage me couldn't have scripted that better. The goodbye kiss, though, leaning through my driver's-side window as I was about to back down the driveway in my car with "Baba O'Riley"—better known as "Teenage Wasteland"— from The Who cued up just at the right moment on the radio*— absolutely took my breath away.

The second person to kiss me entered the picture months later via a friend of a former colleague from my first job. I had come out to her as bi. She took it well, which felt like some kind of connection to teenage me, and she was a blast to hang out with. We'd make out in her car or her house on random occasions and . . . *poof,* by that

---

*The second—and I mean *the* second—I got to the bottom of the driveway, I cried and cried and fucking cried. It was simultaneously the most beautiful moment of my life with the exact perfect soundtrack from my early childhood's favorite band and my heart being stabbed with my own vertebrae because I had to leave.

December, it was over. That's what happens when you quasi-date instead of actually commit. "Don't worry," I told myself. "You have one more semester left of high school and then it's time to hit the reset button."

But in college things didn't really reset in a big way. There were two instances of "Hey, you're drinking, I'm drinking, we're at a party together and we're low on options to keep up this facade of hetero-normative behavior. Cool with you? Okay, same for me."

five minutes later

"Well . . . that was . . . a thing that happened. Neat. Let's drink more and not do that again. Cool with you? Okay, same for me."

And so I stayed celibate during my last 3.5 years of college. Any time I thought to break this pattern, my brain took a quick exploration of every possibility of how anything involving me presenting as female and hooking up with guys could eventually make its way back to my family. So I kept up the facade in front of my guy friends while coming out in private to most of my girl friends, one at a time. While I heard about one kind of micro gay bar near campus existing, that was way too close; what if someone who knew me saw me go in? They would know!*

At shows, I projected this image of a crass-humored, hard-partying, heavy metal frontman in black slacks, a plain black T-shirt, and a wallet chain hanging out from my right pocket, who would down flaming beer bongs and become the life of the party offstage. At my journalism jobs, the persona I projected was one who would interview politicians with a sense of command that only comes from when you're on a mission to hold someone accountable—never preparing questions

---

*It got better, eighteen-year-old me. It really did. After all, at age thirty-seven, you're now driving a '98 Honda . . . what an upgrade from your '97 Nissan!

ahead of time because I wanted to really listen to what they were saying so I could ask follow-up questions, poke holes, and reveal that the person either knew their shit or didn't know shit at all. Yet until I turned twenty-two, my sex life was so empty, I was once rejected on a Buffalo dance floor by a guy dressed in all black who said he just wanted to dance by himself . . . *and he actually did.* (Little did I know, that's apparently normal at goth clubs.) Finally, though, I started to take baby steps. Two weeks after graduation in May 2006, I headed out to Nation, a large, now-shuttered music venue in Southeast D.C. for gay night.

I dressed up in my size 1, stretchy, skintight blue jeans (I don't think my ankle would fit in them now) and favorite scoop-neck, cap-sleeve black T-shirt with a guitar on it, threw my hair into a loose updo, patted on some charcoal-colored eye shadow, and went out by myself. Sure enough, this woman came up to me on the dance floor and asked to dance . . . and then to kiss.

I obliged.

And then a second time.

At this point, while I appreciated her directness, I wasn't going to gay clubs looking for women even though . . . I was at a gay club . . . while dressed as a woman. . . .

No shit, Madam of the Mixed Signal me. Can't imagine why that one went awry . . .

Still, I was curious what her rationale was, so in the midst of whatever existential crisis I didn't know I was having but was clearly underway, I asked the bespectacled young woman before my twenty-one-year-old self whether she was gay, bi, or . . .

"I don't like Doritos."

Hmm . . . ? It must have been the loud music.

"I don't like Doritos."

I was truly stumped. What did that have to do with . . . anything? At all? My brain hurt.

"Neither do I, but . . . what?!"

"I SAID, I DON'T LIKE LABELS."

"OOOOOHHHHHHHHHHHHHHHHH!"

I f nothing else, that night at least reactivated whatever sense of sexuality I had in me, insofar as I was actually trying to make a physical connection with people who I hoped against hope would find me attractive as the woman in front of them, not a guy in girl's clothes. By night's end, I would dance with four different guys. However, one guy immediately backed off when his leg went way too high up my own and he clearly figured out I was trans. Another guy I had to forcibly move when he tried to slide his hand down the front of my jeans. He came up to do it again, too, so I slapped his hand, walked directly up to security, and asked if someone could walk me to my car since this guy was creeping on me. The guard declined and, sullen, I went by myself.

However, one dance in particular went especially right that night. The man I found wasn't exceptionally attractive; his main draw to me was the fact that he had on a black T-shirt of the old-school rock 'n' metal band AC/DC. I thought my shirt would catch his eye, so I approached him and asked for a dance before stepping in front of him, pressing my back against his chest, the back of my hips pressed against the front of his. As I swayed my hips and looked over and down from my left shoulder, he placed his hands under the bottom of my shirt to connect his palms with my bare skin along my waistline. He held me from my sides as he gyrated side to side, his hands feeling warm and strong but not overbearing or threatening. Just . . . sexy. Really, really sexy.

For the first time in my life, a guy was touching me like he meant it.

Any questions that lingered about "Well, you've only dated one person, who was a girl . . . and you made out with two women in college . . . are you reaaally sure you like guys?" flew right out the window and into the late-spring air.

"Fuck, yeah, I do," I thought. "His hands are *amazing*."

After the song, I kissed him on his cheek as a thank-you and we went our separate ways, though if he had asked me for anything more, I would have consented in a heartbeat. Alas, it was a live-in-the-moment episode of my early twenties, something that I'd take some more time to experience again.

Years after I graduated from college, started playing live music, and dated two women on and off from fall 2006 until some point in 2008, I kept two distinctly different profiles, from 2009 to 2011.

When I was off the journalist clock and on the heavy metal front-man clock, I would make myself out to be the exhibitionist and thrill seeker who would gladly exchange third-base pleasantries in the parking lot behind a Bowl America (stay classy, NOVA) or on the side of a dirt road in southeastern Ohio the morning after one of my band's road-trip shows opening for our buddies in Black Dragon, where I made quick friends with a bi woman who was super laid-back with a distinctive laugh.

"Ahh, hell, you're bulletproof!" one of the guys told me about her. Why?

"She's pregnant."

Well, then . . .

Even in metal-guy mode, the one perk I could offer as a closet-case trans woman who had spent time researching gender affirmation surgery was that, in the most dispassionate, medical sense possible, I had done my anatomical analysis homework. And, credit where it's due, read plenty of "spice up your sex life" style women's articles in *Cosmopolitan* because, well, it was easy to buy at the store or get from one of my girl friends. The other thing about being a trans woman dating cis women: I would quite literally ask, "What would you like me to do?" It's amazing how good you can make someone feel by simply asking what works for them rather than poking and prodding around, hoping to luck out like you're waving a metal detector along the beach. In the end, I just viewed a lot of fooling around as a fun activity between friends. As long as whoever I was with was having a good time, I was happy for them.

My other profile—the one that inched me more toward the person I knew I was—was the one I kept secret. This was the ever-present part of me approaching my midtwenties that had never been kissed by a guy before, a streak I badly wanted to end. So I set up an internet dating profile. Ever wary that either someone I knew from the metal scene, someone I went to high school with, or someone I considered a source or a colleague at one of my news reporting jobs would find me, I decided not to mark "female" and instead clicked the boxes for "gay" and "male," especially given that "transgender woman" wasn't exactly available as an option on popular dating sites at the time. I then wrote that I was a trans woman but clicked "male" just so people would know I wasn't cis—which, in hindsight, was absolutely stupid but somehow seemed to make sense.

I correctly deduced that this would limit the pool of people browsing and ferret out any straight people I knew—which was just about everyone I knew—from finding my profile. Next, I got dolled up for an amateur photo shoot, just looking pretty and, frankly, insecure as hell, before posting two of the dozens of photos my dear friend and stylist Nora snapped of me. "Please let him be bi . . ." I would think anytime a message came in. I just hoped that whichever guys would be interested in me, even if they liked other guys, would be able to see me as a woman before they saw me as a gay twink and that they would like what they saw.

Sure enough, I started receiving messages, and they all, without fail for a long while, seemed to lead to exactly the same place: treating me as a fetish. That said, being twenty-four to twenty-five and completely in search of validation from men, I would at least look at the ones I thought were cute and then chat with them, knowing full well that it would lead down a hole of them wanting cybersex right on the spot because they saw me as a sexual curiosity more than an emotionally frail trans woman exploring her sexuality and trying to figure out who she was and who she wanted to become.

The anonymity of an internet dating service also allowed me to explore my word choice and projections of femininity. So I let my mind run free and I started envisioning myself in romantic situations as a fully transitioned woman. Routinely, I found the guys who were not particularly creative with language, so I would take control of the fantasy narrative, putting all of my skills as a feature writer to use: describing the sheen of my lip gloss and its subtle cherry taste, the scent of my Pure Romance perfume, and the silky texture of my lightweight, periwinkle-blue dress.

Keep in mind, this was all over the chat function on a website with a better-than-even chance that the photo of the guy I'm talking to isn't even of the right guy. As long as he was my age or older and wasn't completely repulsive, I would give it a shot and more or less try to figure out which feminine qualities men liked so that I could project toward them those that were authentically mine. In my mind, if a guy was looking at my photo and reading what I was writing with a DO NOT DISTURB sign hanging on his doorknob and duct tape plied over his webcam, then, well: a *guy*—a cisgender, straight, or bi guy!—found me attractive as a woman, even if over the internet without a webcam. I wanted my femininity validated by men so badly, it hurt in the most cringeworthy, insecure way possible.

A few times, I did actually message with guys who would talk to me about, well, normal stuff like work or how their day went or whatever was on their mind before they inevitably turned toward wanting to cyber. With one guy, I decided I wanted to be hyper feminine, more than I ever had the opportunity to be in person, and just highlight that part of my personality, without bordering on caricature, to basically see if that fit, if it came out naturally. He was a time zone away from where I was—or, at least, so he said—and we actually shared a moment of affection, made possible through me wondering what it would really mean to just talk to a guy like I was his girlfriend.

And then, of course, he wanted to wank. Welcome to the internet.

On a small handful of occasions, messaging online actually did result in real-life dates with guys who weren't disgusting—few and far between as they may have been, they did in fact happen. What they all had in common, though, was that I presented as male in some of my photos and on each of our dates. The first guy I had absolutely no connection with whatsoever, physically or mentally. The second guy really seemed like my type: well educated, well traveled, metal fan, tall, long blond hair, late twenties . . .

The morning of our date, we talked on the phone. As we were hanging up, he said, "Okay, we'll see you then."

Wait . . .

We'll? As in, *we* will???

Sure enough, he brought his open-relationship girlfriend with him for brunch. Let's just say he wasn't looking for a forever companion. Scratch that one.

The third guy, my sense of humor absolutely did not mesh with his. He seemed nice, if not overdressed, but when he asked me what my goals were, I told him I could only dream of one day becoming as successful as Lady Gaga, so I, too, could get paid to pose nude on a magazine cover, sans exactly one vinyl glove draped across my breast for all the world to see.

"I see . . ." he said, definitely not laughing.

Shit.

Finally, the fourth time was the charm in terms of actually meeting someone who (1) looked like his photos; (2) was a stand-up comic, so he could take a joke; and (3) lived close enough for us to meet in D.C. but far enough for him to not know my crew or sources from work. On top of all of that, I explained to him that while I wanted to transition, I wasn't there yet, so I would be presenting in male mode, just with, y'know, long hair and cleaned-up eyebrows.

We went to a bookstore on our first date and to the underground music club and restaurant DC9 for our second date, where they played Brazilian thrashers Sepultura over the speakers, so I took that as a good omen. I ended the night trying to slyly lean up against his car parked on the street and promptly wiped out after misjudging the distance between the curb and the car as being considerably closer than it was actually was. Suffice it to say, Date No. 2 didn't end with a kiss.

The third date, however, changed the entire equation.

It was October 2010 and we met at the queerest place in D.C.:

Dupont Circle, the District's largest gayborhood.* If nothing else, going on a third date with a guy while I was presenting as male meant that in theory we had a chance to make this work, and I didn't want to get punched in the face for being queer in public. So we hit up this restaurant, sat at the bar, and the bartender asked me what I was ordering. I told her lasagna and then she asked a question that made my heart flutter: Two forks? As in, you and the guy you're so clearly here with are going to share that together from the same plate?

Yes. Good lord, yes.

Now, at this point, with a male gender expression, I thought it was only proper for my date to know one key fact about dating me: "At some point, if some woman comes up and compliments my hair, it's cool. Just go with it. It happens all the time."

Sure enough, about ninety seconds later I heard, "Excuse me, I just wanted to tell you, you have such beautiful hair!"

The first woman of the night stopped by to say hello. I chatted as Italian-descent extroverts do and she went on her way.

"Hi, I'm sorry!"

Welcome, No. 2.

"Your hair is just beautiful! Can I touch it?!"

My date is now looking flummoxed. Pretty soon, so was a larger guy in a red-and-white Washington Capitals hockey jersey who put his arm around her shoulders and shot out this glare of death.

"Oh, hell . . . I'm with him!" I declared, pointing to my date.

The hockey fan in question immediately flipped his mood and started yakking it up. For once, coming out to a straight guy was actually a lifesaver instead of a life ruiner.

---

*Shout-out to Word for not putting a red spell-check squiggly line under gayborhood. Our home has made it, queer folk! We're spell-check official!

Despite common sense after an Italian dinner, my date and I went to a gay dance club down the street called Apex. Once we hit the floor and started dancing, the music was so loud I couldn't really hear what he was saying. . . . except for one part:

"*Blah blah blah blah* make out now?"

I thought you'd never ask.

At age twenty-six, I was finally kissed by a guy. His stubble was a little bit prickly and the gel in his spiky, bleach-blond punk-rock-style hair was a bit hard, but it didn't matter. I had waited so long to finally be with a man and here he was, lips locked with mine.

Neat.

So we then headed out of the club, reclined the passenger seat in my Subaru battlewagon parked alongside the road near a sidewalk, and—fully clothed—started making out again until the windows fogged up . . . then three quick knocks on the back passenger-side window shook up everything.

"Ahhh, fuck. That sounds familiar," I thought.

Much to my surprise, however, there wasn't a badge and a flashlight when I sat up and looked out. Instead, there were two guys walking their dogs, scampering away down the sidewalk.

Whatever. Back to business.

It wasn't long after that, though, when a sedan pulled up to the driver's side and parked, and we could both just feel multiple sets of eyeballs starring through the glass, as foggy as it was, right at us.

The momentum of the night more or less sputtered on from there, leading us back to his place for a movie and a night of sleep. We saw each other once more for a disastrous final date courtesy of yours truly when I freaked myself out about whether I was going to get an STD from him not wearing protection and abruptly stopped the proceedings. I can't even say it was his fault, though; I never thought to ask him. I just wanted to experience *the idea* of what we were doing so badly that, as a twenty-six-year-old who was having her first true sexual encounter with a guy, the part of my brain that stores basic ideas like, I don't know, condom use, had a VACANCY sign in the window.

Before this, all my sexual experiences had been on a spectrum from entertaining and funny to awkwardly hitting a wall, stopping as soon as the word "wrong" came popping into my head as my body had already completely dismissed the concept of pleasure even being possibly derived from that moment. Which is to say, they'd all been with women. It was the final clarity I'd needed. As it turns out, a pretty surefire way to know you like men is when one of them is grinding shirtless on top of you.

I was working eighty-hour weeks routinely due to the impending Republican wave that was about to sweep over Congress during the Obama-era midterms, consuming my day job at *The Hotline* while I was still working at my newspaper full-time on nights and weekends. We were seeing each other once a week because I couldn't possibly make the time otherwise.

Still, I knew I didn't belong with him, and when he asked if we were boyfriends, I wouldn't give him a . . . *sigh* . . . straight answer.* Truth be told, we hadn't connected much during our four dates and I was more interested in the concept of him than in who he actually was as a person, and that's just not right to do to anyone. Whatever fantasy I had left of this gay man seeing the trans woman under the male exterior evaporated when he asked that question, despite me telling him before that I wanted to transition in the future.

---

*I'll show myself out.

Within the week, he called me to break up, to which I replied, "Oh, thank God!"

"Huh?" he asked.

"Oh, we're terrible for each other with no chemistry. I'm a horrible boyfriend and I need to get my shit together," I told him.

I came to realize that I could serve in the role of "boyfriend" when I dated women because I wasn't seeking their sexual validation and in the sad recesses of my mind knew deep inside that those relationships were doomed to fail anyway. Whatever term they used for me, it just didn't matter to me, although I very much wanted other women to see me as one of their own. But for a guy to see me as being a guy with him, it meant that the dream of being the girlfriend of my boyfriend wouldn't be actualized. It dawned on me pretty quickly when that relationship ended that if I was going to date men, I couldn't be presenting as male myself. It wasn't working.

I wanted a boyfriend to see me as *me*—and that couldn't happen as long as I kept living a lie. At the same time, I couldn't blame him—if that's how I was presenting myself each time he saw me, who else would he possibly know me as? I was still just too scared, too nervous about what would happen to my career, band, and family if I took the plunge.

So . . . I stopped dating. Entirely. Instead, I kept messing around with women and men alike but nothing even approached the vicinity of being serious after those four dates in October 2010, all the way until I opened myself back up in October 2014. In my midtwenties it constituted a fun story from a night out when I asked a woman if I could put my tongue in her mouth when she told me I looked like Nathan Explosion (the animated, fictional frontman of the melodic death metal band Dethklok from the Adult Swim show *Metalocalypse*, a huge hit among underground metalheads) . . . before asking her name. It was the easiest way of propping up the image of the cis, straight, heavy metal frontman. I made people laugh, I made myself laugh, she sure as hell enjoyed it, I got a story out of it, and whoever I was with had a good time. As far as I was concerned, as long as we both said yes without ambiguity and both enjoyed the night, then I had no objections. . . . I didn't have to look that deep inside, though, to know that this was shallow as hell—some junior-varsity, PG, not-even-close-to Tucker Max knock-off shit. I just wanted to entertain whoever I was with and make my friends laugh with the story afterward. That's it. That's what substituted for gratification.

Not only was I painfully overcompensating for being a closet case by projecting a cis-het narrative of masculinity that I thought fit in line with how other people thought about me, but it frankly wasn't much different than twelve years earlier on the baseball field, going along with whatever chauvinistic crap the guys said about the one girl on our team or a player's sister, all the while wishing I could look like she did.

That part didn't change at all. There wasn't a single time I kissed a woman where I didn't think, "Wow . . . I wish I could be like her . . ." while projecting something different.

But I felt stuck. It seemed like if I transitioned and actually lived authentically, then straight guys wouldn't want me as a trans woman and gay guys wouldn't want me as a trans woman. I was hoping to find a bi or pansexual guy, someone who would like me no matter how I presented, but that just wasn't in the cards without me transitioning first because I couldn't even see myself for who I wanted to be, let alone expect someone else to do the same.

Still, I tried. I would find the time to get dressed up in lady mode to go out with my girl friends to gay clubs in D.C., Buffalo, and Richmond while hoping to find a guy. Every so often, I could snag a kiss on the floor of a gay club but nothing permanent, especially as I would return to my normal male-expressing life when I was back from the clubs.

Finally, I decided to do something about it. Something actually permanent. I had to commit to being who I was and stop living in these other narratives that had held me back my entire life.

It was time to transition.

CHAPTER 8

DANICA

**Danica Roem, born male, has made a campaign issue
out of TRANSITIONING TO FEMALE.**

*—Mail advertisement, paid for by the Republican Party of
Virginia, authorized by Bob Marshall, candidate for
Delegate, 2017*

was turning twenty-eight and looking down the barrel of thirty. I knew that for most trans people who physically transition, the younger they start, the more likely they are to achieve what you might call desirable results. I didn't want to wait any longer. I didn't want to go into another decade of my life wondering, "What if, what if, what if . . ."

And if I ever wanted to actually land a boyfriend and, maybe, husband, who would actually see me as his girlfriend and, maybe, wife, then I needed to be her. I needed to live as her. I wanted to care as her, to laugh as her, to talk as her, to dress as her, and, being as candid as possible, to have sex as her, too. I wanted a guy to treat my body like he would any other woman he liked and to validate my heart with his mind, affirming to me that I could be loved as the woman I wanted the world to know. I had watched endless YouTube videos from people who transitioned, read so much about what to expect, and really decided for good that while the path I could take might be scary, as it would be unknown, the path I was on was flat-out unsustainable. I was ready to do something about it.

When my band made it home from our 2012 UK tour that July,

I figured I would have four months ahead of focusing entirely on work, with the presidential election coming up and me holding down two full-time jobs. Once Election Day came and went, though, then it would be time for me to actually get real about transitioning and call a psychologist, someone who specialized in treating transgender clients. That person, though, needed to fit three categories: (1) have a doctorate, because in my mind that meant top-shelf; (2) be relatively young, so as to be relatable to my life circumstances; and (3) be a woman, as she would understand what womanhood and the desire to achieve it meant.

Perusing a *Psychology Today* directory, I found someone in Fairfax who fit all three descriptors. She had worked with a lot of trans girls and women, and when, during my first session, she told me that we had something in common—she also liked the thrash band Slayer— I knew I'd found the right person.

Before my third session with her, she told me that she wanted to see me as the woman I wanted to present to the world—only, of course, if I was okay and comfortable being "her" there. I agreed, and that December, came in wearing full makeup, a purple shirt and skirt, black tights, and heels.

"Oh my God, you're beautiful! Why would you ever hide this?!" she said.

I could have fainted. I needed that so much more than even I knew.

From that point on, I only presented as my true self to her. When I first started therapy, I expressed how unsure I was about where I wanted to go with my transition because of practical reasons. If I followed my heart, I would express myself as the lady I always knew myself to be, twenty-four/seven, in front of anyone and everyone. But, though I knew I wanted to transition, because of my job as a reporter and status as a now internationally touring heavy metal front . . . person . . . who very much intended to go back to Europe and soon, could I really transition on the job or expect to keep leading my band? And, above all, could I come out to my family?

It seemed like too much. Maybe if I could find a way to just be her whenever I wasn't on the clock, so to speak. Whenever I was at the apartment I had closest to my D.C. job or in my dating life or . . . just something more permanent than once a quarter at gay clubs.

That day in December 2012, I walked into her office as myself and walked out as myself, too; I knew what I wanted to do, even if it was going to be a while—transitioning is a long process and I would have plenty of time to deal with other people's comfort levels, slowly but surely. That's when I called my newspaper editor to let her know I intended to transition and made an appointment to see an endocrinologist so that I could start discussing hormone replacement therapy.

One thing I knew beyond any uncertainty was that my facial hair absolutely had to go and it needed to go first. I was beyond sick of it. I hated shaving, hated spending 4.5 hours plucking my hair or bleeding during waxing, only for it to grow back out, something I had done since I was in college a decade earlier. That shit grows real old, real quick.

I knew without a doubt that no matter where my transition took me, I could live the rest of my life without facial hair and be just fine. So I looked online for a laser facial hair removal center in Northern Virginia that treated trans women, found one in Alexandria, and set up my first appointment close to the time I started seeing my endocrinologist in February 2013.

My first time at the endocrinologist, however, was . . . awkward, to say the least. I was grateful my best friend, Lauren, showed up with me for moral support, but mortified when I had to drop trou and one of the little pads that accentuated my posterior dropped out from my underwear and on to the floor. We discussed the future of my reproductive organs and how I would have to go to a cryopreservation center to make deposits of specimen before I started hormone replacement therapy, knowing full well that being on spironolactone for an extended period of time would make me functionally infertile.

While I contemplated the future, I spent the rest of that year and all the way until August 2014 paying to have lightning bolts shot into my face for twenty to thirty minutes at a time by a very sweet woman who was as kind as could be while, well, discharging lasers into my flesh. My first time in was a consultation, where I agreed to undergo six rounds over about nine months. One of the biggest problems of laser facial hair removal is that you can't pluck or wax your hair during the six to eight weeks between sessions; you can only shave with a razor, and you're not even supposed to do that much. So that leaves a lot of in-between days, with stubborn hairs hanging around.

By the time my travel buddy Bork and I made our third trip to Wacken Open Air in northern Germany in 2013, I had about four sessions done, so my facial hair wasn't as thick as when I started but definitely still sprouting out. When we arrived in Hamburg on day one, I was still wearing metal guy clothes as we entered the "Metalheads Local 666 Union" part of town, complete with bars that played metal, punk, and hard rock over the speakers.

I pulled up a seat at the bar and struck up a conversation with a blond-haired Finnish woman, probably about ten years older than me. I leaned in close to her to say that I've had a huge crush on some

Finnish metal musicians since I was a teenager, especially Eicca Toppinen from the cello metal band Apocalyptica.

"So you're gay?" she asked me.

"Well, not exactly," I replied. I told her the honest truth—I was just starting my transition—coming out to a complete stranger with the full details because I judged her to be safe. I was in a foreign country, talking to someone from another country, and my friend was out in town. It was worth the risk. Much to my surprise, she took quite a bit of interest in what I had to say—not because she was some woke goddess there to offer me emotional support on my journey but rather because the guy sitting on her other side had been bothering her and she wanted him to leave.

"So I will tell him you are transsexual and I'm a lesbian," she said.

Uh, that's amazing. What the hell else was I going to do? Say no? If you haven't learned by now, I'm *always* up for a good story.

"Game on."

Sure enough, she turned to her right and proceeded to tell the man exactly what she said she would tell him.

"So she is transsexual and I'm a lesbian and I'm going to be with her now," she told him plainly.

I raised my glass of beer by the handle, slightly tipping it toward him in acknowledgment. With that, she made good on her point to him, leaned toward me, and kissed me with quite a bit of grace. She paused and I looked at the guy, who laughed once to himself, shoved the bar to push his barstool out, and walked out the door. Girl power, activate!

By this point, I'd started coming out to different women in my friend groups. It was tougher for me to broach the conversation with a lot of my metal friends—not that they were inherently bigoted or anything even close to that, but rather coming out to men in general was difficult and a lot of the men in my life happen to be metal. Out LGBTQ people in the D/M/V (D.C./Maryland/Virginia) metal scene in those days were few, and not every space I was in felt comfortable for me to be out yet. In general, metal can be a pretty gender-conforming, male-dominated space, black nail polish aside. The music is made and performed so frequently by men that there just tend to be more men in these circles. And, of course, boys are taught that loud and aggressive is who they are—metal is not "supposed" to appeal to us and until there's more visibility of women in the metal world, that cycle keeps reproducing itself. There were, however, a handful of amazing metal women I'd met who were eccentric, cool, outgoing, and who I knew were embracing of everyone after they provided me with chances here and there to feel fully myself with them; it was wonderful. I imagine this is what folks must feel who build their LGBTQ friend-families, though I never quite managed that in the beginning.

In a way, gravitating toward women in the metal scene for being able to open up about my gender and transition made sense. The three women I had ever at least attempted to date seriously were either completely metal themselves or tangentially connected to metal.

In 2001, when I lied about going to my junior prom afterparty, it was so I could drive hundreds of miles to meet in person someone I had met online in 1999 and bonded with over our mutual love of Metallica, Zakk Wylde, Black Sabbath, Iron Maiden, Pantera . . . you name it. She even introduced me to bands like Apocalyptica, In Flames, and Mudvayne and could go toe to toe with me quoting the comedian George Carlin.

The day I pulled into her best friend's driveway to meet her, she greeted me in a black Metallica shirt, black pants, and a pentagram necklace that contrasted with her shoulder-length blond hair, which just made her all the more badass. Her love of diesel engines and mudding in her quad didn't exactly scream delicate feminine flower, which I found wildly appealing, next only to the fact that she was super smart, excelled academically, and could crack me up. Things fell apart a few weeks later because I couldn't handle the distance while being still more than a year away from graduation. I realized from that time in my life that, if nothing else, I valued brains and wit above all else in a partner . . . and, of course, a heavy metal heart.

Five years later, a woman six months older than me, who we'll call Cam, instantly clicked with me in a parking lot outside of a dive bar in Fairfax. We chatted for more than two hours as her metalhead friend sitting next to her in the car drifted in and out of consciousness. When we finally went on a date, I parted the plate and the glass in front of me and told her from the start that I would put all of my dirt out on the table: I came out to her first, talked about my dad's suicide second, and just ticked off all of my eccentricities. It turned out, she had dated a woman before and told me she was bi, so I figured maybe we had a chance to make it work.

And the funny thing is? She was super fuckin' fun. We would go on digressions built on digressions when we talked while cruising around Northern Virginia for seven hours at a time, loudly completing each other's sentences in pure extroverted rage, when we weren't looking for parking lots or the occasional restroom for a third-base quickie before anyone could catch a blatant display of exhibitionism with a high-five at the end. And therein lies the flaw: I celebrated with her like she was my best dude-guy-bro, not my sensual, romantic love interest. That said, I had no regrets about depositing my V-card to her permanent possession in May 2007, which we did over a bottle of red wine and the first disc of the 1999 Metallica *S&M* album

at a Red Roof Inn. (Stay classy, Manassas.) Frankly, I'm glad someone I genuinely think the world of could give it a good forever home
like it's a shelter puppy. It's just that I found out that night that
I didn't like having sex with women. My closed-eye fantasy role
reversal only lasted so long. We tried again but . . . nada. It wasn't
anyone's fault. It just wasn't meant to work.

That October in 2007, I had sworn to myself that I was done dating women when my band played what would be quite the show at
Jaxx and my long hair caught the attention of a friend of a friend, a
woman named Kim who was about fourteen months younger than
me. When some of my friends joined me to meet her and her friends
at a bar in Warrenton on a later date, she out of nowhere stabbed one
of them in the stomach with a pen the second he walked up to the
table.

It was absolutely uncalled for and I was smitten.

Along with the fact that she had been at that Jaxx show to see the
industrial band on the bill, it turned out she really had a thing for
feminine guys, and I told her I was a closet case and asked if I could
raid her wardrobe. She was as wildly unpredictable a human being as
anyone I have ever met, ever. We could be driving down to Richmond for a party, just talking shit and laughing, when she would
burst out "THAT CAR'S FROM ONTARIO!" and then continue
the conversation like nothing had happened.

Of course there's a twist to all of this—what would this book be
without one?—and it came that November. We never had sex—
nothing beyond second base—but that didn't mean we weren't intimate. So one night when we were, she lay on her bed shirtless and
looked up at me with her devastatingly gorgeous, soft blue-green
eyes over a light smile. The hourglass of her body, toned by years of
kung fu practice and working outdoors and standing up as an equine

massage therapist, was objectively like seeing a Michelangelo sculpture before me.

"You look like art," I told her with sincere honesty.

To this day, she'll tell you it's the nicest thing anyone's ever said to her.

Still, as much as she knew something was amiss, she just couldn't put her finger on what it was this time. She had come out of a number of relationships with men that hadn't ended well, and in her mind, she was with a man—albeit a queer, cross-dressing one—with whom things were otherwise going well. Her ever-perceptive dad, rest his soul, figured it out, though, with pinpoint perception: "Have you ever considered the idea that you might be dating a woman?"

It suddenly occurred to her that me liking guys and wanting to wear her clothes meant a little bit more than she originally thought.

"Oh, shit," she told him. "I hadn't, but you might be right."

In my heart, I knew it wasn't going to work out either, though that might have just been from an innate sense of fatalism more than perception. One night, we lay across a couch in her basement together, watching Metalocalypse and laughing hysterically at whatever Toki Wartooth was complaining about. She lay across the front side of me in my arms, both of us still in our day clothes, just smiling and having a good time.

"Enjoy this while it lasts," I thought.

I did. Very, very much so. And to this day, fifteen years later, my straight, cisgender ex-girlfriend exclusively refers to me, as a term of endearment, as her ex-girlfriend, too, including at—appropriately— her dad's celebration of life service.

By that point, we had been broken up for more than a decade but remained close and my transition was well underway. So at the service I was in full makeup and a nice dress, chatting with a former neighbor of the family, when the older woman asked me how I knew Kim.

Upon my triumphant explanation that we used to date, the woman's eyes bulged ever so slightly, just enough to express, "What else don't I know about that nice young lady from down the street . . ."

My dating experience with metal women at the very least gave me an idea that I could be vulnerable around them in a way that was difficult with other people. In 2009, after playing a show at my friend Davis's house, I met his family. His two moms and his sisters Rachel and Anna were all very open, creative people, and their place became a kind of safe house for me. Rachel, a hairstylist, always had bright magenta hair while her mom, Nora, had a dash of purple. Her friend Jeanette—green and black locks complementing her full-sleeve rainforest tattoos—was around, too, another incredible metal chick, all of them tatted up and friendly as could be. By 2011, I had come out to all of them, and Rachel, tired as hell from a long day at work, still took the time to do my makeup and hair for a photo shoot. I felt like I had friends who not only were cool and fun to hang around with but genuinely embraced the idea of bringing out my inner self: not the security blanket of a person I showed to the world on a day-to-day basis, but me. Her. And they, for all the ups and downs that come with transitioning, would be my support, every single step of the way.

In 2013, I was getting really serious about my yoga practice, thanks to Rachel having introduced me to a hot-yoga facility in Fairfax. I needed that so badly in my life, in many ways. On a spiritual level, there was a definite void my Catholic upbringing left in my trans queer lady heart. A yoga studio could give me that place to reflect, to get out of my all-logic, all-the-time mind and enter into some form of spirituality, or maybe even mysticism, that still made sense and allowed me to see beyond my work, my band, and the hindrances blocking my transition. Most important for me from twenty-eight to twenty-nine, I felt that a yoga studio would be the next place (after gay clubs) where I could express my femininity without fear of judgment or reprisal, and actually be welcomed for it.

Despite eating my hair during my first class—that's what I got for not braiding it—I came to love sweltering hot-yoga classes. The women were all kind. I could wear little shorts, a decidedly women's cut tank top, painted toenails . . . whatever, it was fine, even if I ended up using the men's restroom and shower afterward. That first class also marked the first time in public, outside of an explicitly LGBTQ setting, where I publicly acknowledged my chosen name. I was late to class, so the instructor politely asked me as I unrolled my mat who I was as a means of introduction. I looked all around the room and, spotting no one I knew and hoping I was right, said, "I'm Danica." One thing that's common for a lot of trans women is that we'll often feminize our birth name (aka dead name) when we transition if we choose to pick a new name. Well, I used to get picked on as a kid with taunts of "Dan-ielle!" so that name never felt right and it was just too close to my dead name. So I tried on some other names like Dani and Dana, and they just didn't fit right. Then one day at band practice I just blurted out "Danica" when I was being teased about a photo of me winning my college's drag show in 2005. I don't know why I came up with that on the spot other than that combining the "-ica" from Metallica, Apocalyptica, Epica, etc., with the nickname I had gone by since childhood seemed both edgy and pretty at the same time. The extra benefit was that it was definitely a name—the race car driver Danica Patrick being, of course, the most famous one—but not a common one. It stood out. I liked it and immediately stored it away in my mental back pocket.

Declaring myself as Danica at the yoga studio, for all intents and purposes, was a test of how safe a place it would be to express my inner goddess. I also usually had the longest hair there, so I would take a long time to shower after class, which meant I needed to be the last one to enter. Still, I hadn't transitioned physically yet, so I used the men's locker room to change and shower. One time, a guy in the back of the class, who was clearly new, decided to chat with me after class, which was just fine . . . even if he said hello with his towel wide open. I didn't let my eyes wander and stayed focused. It wasn't my first time seeing a naked man in a locker room and I could certainly keep my cool about it.

What I didn't anticipate was that after I finished one of my typically long showers, he would still be there, seated toward the back of the room. I didn't let him see me without wearing a towel—which I wrapped horizontally from my chest to halfway down my thighs. I knew I didn't belong in the men's locker room at all, not by a mile, except that I was so nervous about my mere presence bothering anyone that I stayed where I knew I wouldn't be kicked out as no one would perceive the femme "guy" with a purple pedicure and small turquoise workout shorts as a threat.

"That class sure has me beat," the guy told me.

I made small talk with him, got changed behind a curtain, and walked out to the parking garage to hop into my rusted-out '92 Dodge Shadow—you know, the total babe magnet of 2013. Well, sure enough, the guy comes out in his gray sweatpants and gray hoodie— the hood pulled over his head despite it being late summer—and called my name.

"Danica! Danica!" he called.

By this point, I'm seated in my car, looking for my credit cards, which I can't find in my wallet, and figuring this dude must have found them somewhere and was bringing them back to me. I stood back up to talk to him.

"Hi."

"Danica . . . I wanted to ask you . . ."

"Yes?"

I looked at my console, where my cards were sitting in front of the radio. I looked back at him. Oh.

"Can I kiss you?"

"Ah. Okay."

I first told him I wanted to get to know him for a minute, so I asked him how old he was (thirty-five, when I was a little shy of twenty-nine), what he did for a living (telemarketing sales).

And I wanted to know . . . was he only attracted to women?

"Yes," he said, much to my surprise. He had been with a trans woman once and cisgender women otherwise, and he thought I was beautiful.

Okay, screw it, I could use the validation and I knew it. So, with my driver's door open, I leaned over the top of it and received his kiss for a couple of seconds. I then sat down for a second to put down whatever I was holding. When I turned my head back toward the door and looked to my left, he was standing by the edge of the door, his sweatpants now three-dimensional like a gray pyramid.

There was no doubt that him just standing there pitching a tent in the parking garage wasn't going to be a good look, so I invited him to sit in the front passenger seat. I wanted that affirmation badly, though I wasn't going to be as forward as "Excuse me, kind sir, would you please validate my womanhood for me with your— c'mon, Catholic school, what's the Latin—novitiatus erectio?" I was still a few months away from starting HRT, which I told him, and this man who only dates women still just saw me as this woman who he was sexually attracted to, trans or cis. His age and job and, frankly, personality, mattered exactly 0 percent as I brought myself in to kiss him again. Realistically, I was so in the moment I was probably just seconds away from taking things to the next level—what else is a '92 Dodge made for?—when this SUV pulled into a spot across the deck. All I needed to see was the door open for me to jump back into my seat, turn on the engine, and hightail it out of that garage to the one across the street where he was parked.

Except I forgot that I had been blasting the shit out of the fastest track from Dark Tranquillity's newest melodic death metal master-piece, *Construct*—a song called "Apathetic"—when I pulled into the parking lot to begin with, so my passenger was immediately greeted with pounding guitars and aggressive, harsh vocals the second I flipped the ignition switch.

Ooops.

"Whoa!" he exclaimed. "I like a woman who likes loud music!"

Cool.

O nce we arrived at the other parking lot, something just came out of me. Maybe it was the music kicking in, but whatever pleasure I partook in earlier had done what it needed to do. Our small talk slowed to a stop.

I dodged a number of questions from him, asking for my phone number and when I usually went to yoga. Instead, I just let him go and headed on my way. I can't even begin to imagine how confused he must have felt—I didn't even understand why I did a one-eighty so hard at the time, though in hindsight I think I was just scared of

committing to someone when I wasn't sure where my future was going to take me. HRT was just around the corner, and with it the
chance for me to truly begin what I hoped would be my new life. I
wanted a fresh start, and taking someone along with me from the
final vestiges of my previous life, even someone who, for that one
moment, did all the right things, just didn't seem right.

During that gap, a couple of my other girl friends took me out to
another club, just two weeks before I was going to start HRT for
real. We got dressed up, with me wearing a high-low strapless dress
and a padded bra underneath, and though I was admittedly nervous,
I still took the opportunity to flirt with a men's college basketball
referee, all in an effort to make out with him for the sake of (yet
another) good story. That encounter ended with the referee's friend
getting visibly agitated, eventually so much so that my friends got up
from their chairs and told me, "It's time for us to go," before hurry-
ing my ass out across the parking lot, heels click-clacking across the
pavement, into one of their cars and heading the hell out of Dodge.

I didn't realize it quite so much at the time, but that was my first
encounter with someone meeting my transition with anger that trans-
lated into a "You don't belong here" moment. That unpleasant ending aside, I had now found men twice in a period of just a few months
who were seeing me sexually as a woman worth their attention,
which were like little checkboxes on my card of things I wanted to
accomplish before I went full time.

On December 3, 2013, a small group of some of my closest
friends—including Nora, Rachel, Jeanette, Anna, and Nora's
wife, Connie—invited me over to Alexandria, where we had
a smudging (burning the edge of these rolls of sage that look like

cigars) outdoors to reset my aura before we lit some candles inside. I used the flame from the blue one to light a pink one, took my first 2 milligram pill of Estradiol at 8:24 P.M., and blew out the blue candle. I was ready to firmly, fully begin my transition.

I started the antiandrogen testosterone blocker spironolactone two weeks later and on Day 55 of my transition, while recording vocals for a demo at my new lead guitarist's house, I felt a super-sharp pain in my chest, right under my nipples, that made me giggle like Anderson Cooper saying "Dyngus Day." I could barely breathe as I flew to the floor. My transition was without question underway.

The following summer, I returned to Europe with Bork, where this time we met up with a bunch of our Wacken Open Air friends in Copenhagen to hang out for a few days before the festival. I came out to Bork on the flight over—it's kind of hard to turn around once you're in the air, I justified to myself preflight—and told him I planned for my wardrobe to match. While wearing metal guy clothes at Tivoli Gardens amusement park, I somehow led the conversation to my transition, allowing me to say out loud to my friends that I was transgender and I was going to live my truth. To a T, each one of them either hugged me or offered me a fist bump and a "That's awesome!" which made me feel incredible.

True to my word, I did my makeup that evening, put on my blue and green skirt and blue shirt, and headed into the city to meet up with our crew that was easily pushing a dozen people. While walking on the sidewalk with a couple of friends, two of us stopped to chat with two random strangers on the street. I was a little bit away from them when I heard this guy say, "Danica? Oh, she's hot."

Like a magnet thrown at a refrigerator, I glided over to inspect.

Blond hair. Blue eyes. Nordic.

You have my attention.

We got to chatting for a while.

"Sooo, what are you looking to do tonight?" he asked.

"Blond hair, blue eyes," I said without missing a beat.

He smiled.

"Sooo, what are you drinking tonight?" I asked him.

"Beer."

"What kind of beer?"

"Corona."

"Corona? What are you doing drinking beer from my hemisphere?"

He grinned, and I knew I had to try it.

"Do you still taste like Corona?" I asked with whatever seductively blunt tone I could muster.

"Don't know. Tell me," he said. A surefire line if ever there was one.

Seconds later, my buddy Cullen jumped in to tell me we had to go and he hustled me out of there. Cullen's a super-open-minded guy, so I was a bit surprised but went along with it, knowing there must have been a good reason.

Sure enough:

"Danica! That woman who he was with . . ."

"Yeah?"

"That's the woman He. Is. With."

"Oh, shit!!!"

Okay, sure, I just home-wrecked a straight Danish couple on a sidewalk in Copenhagen without even knowing it—but I was elated.

Men were, for the first time in my life, consistently showing interest in me sexually and I was absolutely there for it. I could just be her, be acknowledged as her, and be affirmed as her—even if it meant a guy sprouting wood through his sweatpants in a parking garage, a college basketball referee hitting on me in a club, or some rando Euro dude cheating on his partner while ten feet away from her on a sidewalk in Scandinavia. By this point, the idea of kissing women, let alone dating women, seemed like a relic of a bygone era of closetivity.*

When we finally made it to Wacken, the 2014 festival marked the first time I actually went as myself to an outdoor metal fest. I felt it necessary beyond words. I was past the point of no return and it seemed like such a necessary part of my journey to come out at a place that was my personal wonderland and such an integral part of my metal life. There was no point in me pretending to be a guy there anymore when I was coming out to new people seemingly daily. Wearing a black skirt, altered Meshuggah shirt, and black eyeshadow and eyeliner seemed like a good fit in a camp that included at least two other bisexual women anyway.

While there, another Danish guy named Jonathan would tell me that seeing me go up onstage to sing karaoke with a live-performance metal cover band in front of a crowd of hundreds of people on one of the side stages helped encourage him to try to tackle his depression and insecurity by being visible onstage while singing Iron Maiden. His vulnerability and sincerity were like elixirs for me. He was a sportswriter who had never seriously dated or even been kissed. I wanted to be that woman for him so badly but didn't work up the courage to tell him, thinking that there was no way I was going to be his first. (Sadly, he died in 2017.)

I was the frontwoman that I'd assumed I'd never be able to be, that I'd always have to hide. My friends were cool with me, and I

---

*Pronounce it "Closet-tivity." I'm proud of myself for that one.

was getting to live my life in a body that was feeling more and more like mine.

From that time onward, things were starting on a collision course I knew I couldn't turn away from. The same month I returned home from Wacken in August 2014 was the last time I presented as male when performing with my band. We had a show in Baltimore at a tiny dive called the Sidebar Tavern, where I drove straight from my Yoga Alliance job, complete with a full face of makeup. I did a video for the Ice Bucket Challenge that evening with my makeup, an altered Genitorturers shirt, and a black skirt as I posed in full lotus on my yoga mat outside the venue.

I changed into dry clothes afterward, which happened to be my stage clothes—guy clothes—and removed my makeup. When I walked back to the entrance of the club, this one bouncer who was obviously queer stared at me with a disappointed look in his eyes and asked, "Why did you change?"

Never had such an easy question devastated me so much, right to my core. I didn't have a real answer. I thought about that question all the way home to Manassas that night and decided that would never happen again.

At my next show a couple of months later, after I had come out to more of my metal guy friends and my ma and sister back home, I committed to presenting as myself onstage for the first time . . . at least from the waist up. I arrived at our gig at a pool hall in Sterling, Virginia, with a load of nerves. I showed up in full makeup, a black cap-sleeve, scoop-neck T-shirt and . . . black slacks. I used humor onstage both to deflect the concept while addressing the elephant in the room, saying, "I'm sure you can tell something is different onstage tonight—we are down a bass player!" Everything was really the same as it always had been. I just looked (and smelled) better.

I also had another incentive for wanting to look the part that night: I had met someone. My friend Metal Mike reached out to me to ask if I could connect with a friend of his named Tal, a burgeoning trans man who had just started to transition (and who would later come out as nonbinary with they/them pronouns).

I was happy to oblige. Scrolling through Facebook photos, I saw this light-haired, blue-green-eyed Finnish metalhead in a Children of Bodom hoodie. "Okay," I thought. "I like what I see." I also noticed they had a young kid, whom I realized I'd seen at a metal show before (because when you see a five-year-old girl wearing protective headphones and genuinely enjoying herself at a metal concert, you remember). I sent them a long message, putting myself out there and trying to be helpful in whatever way I could—and, also, in hopes they might be interested, too. I didn't hear back right away and was starting to worry it had been too much, but then I saw a long wall of text back. "I'm in," I thought.

They asked if I was going to a Within Temptation concert in Baltimore that October 7. I wasn't planning on it at the time, but responded in the affirmative, ready for a first date. It just so happened that Tal asked me about the show just before I came out to my ma and sister on my thirtieth birthday.

Coming out that night was not easy at all. It had been something I dreaded—absolutely dreaded—since childhood and I was finally confronting the very real notion of disappointing my conservative, Roman Catholic, Republican ma in an irrevocable way. What had started brewing when I was caught with my sister's clothes under my bed on the day after Halloween at age thirteen or fourteen had to be put to rest: I had to come out to my ma. Every now and then she'd find women's clothing in my room, and I'd blame it on my best friend, Lauren, or I'd say my sister had left it in there. I know there was some level of denial and dismissal from both of us; she wanted to know why the clothes were in there, but I knew she didn't *really* want to know. And I sure as hell didn't want to tell her.

It was my birthday, I was well into my transition, and I was headed home to have cake with my family. I knew by then that my ma had seen some photos of me presenting as female on my Facebook page, so I called her from Nora's house in Alexandria and told her, "Ma, I'm coming home soon, but I'm coming over as my Facebook self today." She knew what that meant in that I had changed my name and gender marker and kept putting up photos of me out and about with my girl friends, in full makeup and all. I remember calling my aunt, her sister, on the way over, who I'd already come out to—but I was so blasted with nerves that I genuinely don't remember what she told me during that drive. I think she told me to channel my grandfather's calm, cool energy. I am sure I did not.

I knew my sister would take my coming out well; she never even had so much as a homophobic or transphobic inkling. Her favorite musician was and is George Michael, after all. But I decided to save my coming out to her for the same time as my ma just so she wouldn't be burdened with carrying my secrets.

I walked into the house, a ball of anxiety, and entered the living room, where she and my sister were watching TV. They looked at me. I looked at them. I turned and walked back to the kitchen, getting out glasses for drinks to have with my birthday cake. My cat, Sandy, clearly unperturbed, jumped into my lap when I sat down. Once my ma came into the kitchen, I asked, "So, what do you think of my outfit?" She replied, "You can like it and that's fine—but that doesn't mean *I* have to like it."

Heart, meet stomach.

We didn't mention it again until after we started eating the cake and my sister said something about a doctor's appointment. I used that moment to pivot to my gender therapy sessions, figuring that my ma would be more likely to respect what I was doing if she understood the medical component of it first: both the mental health side and the actual science of physically transitioning. I told her I'd been seeing a psychologist who specialized in treating trans people for the last two years and had received a diagnosis of "302.85 Gender Dysphoria, according to the DSM-5," which meant I'm a transgender woman and the way I deal with that is by transitioning. I told her I'd been seeing an endocrinologist who prescribed hormone replacement therapy pills for me, which I had been taking for the last ten months. I even mentioned that I had been going through voice therapy with a doctor at George Washington University all throughout the year. The more medical and dispassionate my approach, I hoped, the harder it would be for her to refute it and the easier it would be to understand.

I'd love to tell you that it all clicked for her and she gave me a big hug and told me she loved me for who I was. But it was hard for her, as it is for a lot of parents. It's difficult to look at your child who you've known as one way for three decades—a being who you had carried, birthed, raised, and loved as your own—only to find out something this startlingly different, in defiance of how you raised your own child. There's a mourning that comes with that.

I had known for years that it was going to suck that day; I'd even planned it on my actual birthday in hopes that she wouldn't be able to yell at me about it, which to her credit she refrained from doing. It was awkward and painful. The last thing in the world I wanted to do was hurt my ma. But in some way, that moment started us on a path to a bigger understanding. She made some overtures I could recognize as a kind of "getting to yes" moment—I knew she was trying to wrap her head around it.

I said before that I'll never say a bad word about my ma. Obviously, I wish parts of moments like these could have gone better for us, but I know that deep down she was trying to protect her child from a hard life. After a lifetime of struggling through all the things she'd had to struggle through, the loss and work and bad luck, she didn't want the same for me—she wanted my life to be as normal and smooth as possible, and normalcy in my own life often felt like the gift I could give to her.

The biggest concern my ma had that she told me about during our 2.5-hour conversation was how I would ever find someone. The last time I had brought someone home was in 2008, so she knew dating was hard for me to begin with. Fortunately, I could answer her with an honest smile: I told her I had a date the following week in Baltimore with a trans guy from the local metal scene.

I don't remember how the conversation ended other than that she moved from reluctance to guarded acceptance throughout the course of the night. When I told my therapist that I finally came out to my ma and sister, she advised me not to offer mixed signals by putting on guy clothes again—that I needed to show her that *this* is who I was and am, and this is who she's going to see me as from here on out. I knew it would be super awkward for a while but within the next week, when she brought home a black dress from Lord & Taylor and asked me to try it on—and it looked good, really good—I knew she had come around. That's when I knew things would be okay. She's bought me a ton of clothes since then.

I think in the modern day, a lot of parents are really expected upfront to automatically be okay and accepting about their kids coming out to them, either with their sexual orientation or gender identity. Of course, I would hope that becomes more and more normal as more people summon the courage to express their truth as they see other people doing so, too. But the reality is that for a lot of parents, it's hard. You're presenting them with a version of yourself that's foreign to them and if it's something they've never had to confront before, there can sometimes be an adjustment period that's difficult. That doesn't mean you should just throw away your family and leave forever; it just means it's going to be hard and awkward, but they at least need a chance to come around.

That said, if someone comes out to their parents and they're met with outright hostility, rejection, and even abuse from which there is no turning back, then people need to do what they must to survive and leave a toxic situation. Some parents absolutely can and do reject their queer and trans children and it truly shatters my heart to think of that as an ever-present reality, even today. Parents of queer and trans kids need to recognize the courage of their children and the trust they're placing in them by being authentic and real to them. Whether that person is a child, teen, or adult, when it's your kid coming out to you, they're doing so as an expression of hope—they hope you'll understand and embrace them. The last thing someone in a vulnerable situation needs is rejection. I wasn't rejected.

That year of 2014 marked a time when I was coming to a new place in my life—that fresh horizon was finally arriving. I'd collected plenty of stories for the road, but I was also excited about the prospect of something steady and real—to stop the partying and drinking, to settle down, to have a family. I had to make peace with giving up what was quickly becoming my past and open the door for something new.

For our first date—which I knew was a date, but which Tal did not—I was still playing the part of transition guide, in a way, and I was a great combination of nervous and excited. Meanwhile, I was also easing into a date where, for the first time ever, I didn't have to do a 101 course in being a trans person. Tal was still ginning up the courage to use the men's restroom, and I encouraged them as we waited for Within Temptation to come up onstage.

I grabbed Tal's hand afterward and guided both of us into the middle of the floor, sliding off my NOVA Pride wristband made from little rainbow-colored rubber bands to give to Tal as a gift. Well, it turned out to be perfectly timed given that Within Temptation's singer Sharon den Adel, who'd been photographed repeatedly over the years holding Pride flags onstage, gave a gay rights speech before launching into my favorite song by them, "Stand My Ground." This kind of overt openness was so atypical for metal bands; I couldn't believe it was happening at all, much less on a date that I was already excited for. Then the crowd started roaring in affirmation. I thought: "Where have you all been for the last fifteen years?!" My whole life and all my worlds felt like they were coming together in one loud, raucous moment, and I moved past a brief twinge of mourning what could have been had I found all this earlier, and I thought, "Everything is going to be all right."

For my one-year "rebirthday" to celebrate the anniversary of my start of HRT, I flew to Scotland to party with friends and see At The Gates headline a metal show in Glasgow. Before I flew over, Tal and I had talked about where we were in our relationship—we hadn't made it official just yet and Tal made it clear that what I did overseas was my business. So the night before the show, I met a guy out drinking with friends, and though I couldn't stop thinking about Tal back home (I am loyal to a fault when it comes to my love life), I just kept reminding myself of what we agreed to before I left.

I did end up going home with the guy . . . and making out with him. It was amazing. This time around, I knew who I was and didn't need a man to make that case for me. I hadn't really realized just how my confidence had sprouted: it surprised me, and it was wonderful.

In the period of about 1.5 years, my sexual awakening had taken full hold in a way that physically and mentally felt totally different compared to kissing random people in bars for one-liners, laughs, and stories. I wasn't just doing it for fun and to impress my friends later. I was hooking up with men now because I could; because they wanted to, without reservation.

That last part though—without reservation . . . I came to realize that, even in the midst of very much wanting to have that experience with him, my heart wasn't truly in it. My heart was an ocean away, with this ever-busied, super-introverted Finn; this folk-metal-loving, third-degree karate black belt who was working at a library, writing novels, volunteering both in the Coast Guard Auxiliary and as a crew member of a historic tall ship docked in southern Maryland, and raising a kid, all while just starting to work as a freelance translator, too.

I knew that's not just where my heart was, but where I needed to be, too. Thousands of miles to the east, as dawn broke over Edinburgh, I gently ended that late-night/early-morning tryst as he picked up his bicycle, walked down the stairs, and rode home, no sex to be had by either of us.

I left the apartment in the early morning, ran into an older woman who offered me a ride to my friend Aisha's home—"Now I get to tell my friend at brunch that I saved an American girl from a walk of shame," she told me, which I thought was royally hysterical—and that night we ventured out to Glasgow to see At The Gates in the front row at a venue called The Garage. After the show, we hung out with a bunch of mutual friends, allowing me to drink up, have a blast, and try not to think about the prior night. While I had been nervous about how my Scottish friends would react to seeing me presenting as female for the first time, my buddy Andy summed it up best:

"I don't care what you look like, mate. I just want to know: Do you still drink?"

At the time: I sure did. Bottoms up.

With that, we partied hard for the night, and the next day I boarded a plane back home . . . back to Tal, ready to fully commit myself and certain that, even though I didn't know what was to come, I did know that being with Tal is where my mind and heart told me I belonged.

CHAPTER 9

SELLOUT

Danica Roem has "a celebrity profile that opens pocket-books and draws attention nationwide."

—The Washington Post, *as quoted in a mail advertisement paid for by the Republican Party of Virginia, authorized by Kelly McGinn, candidate for Delegate, 2019*

T hey say: When life gives you lemons, turn it into lemonade. I say: When life gives you the Westboro Baptist Church standing outside your state capitol protesting your existence as a trans woman elected to the state legislature, turn it into a counter-party of two hundred metalheads drowning out their message of hate with vuvuzelas, paint-bucket drums, and kazoos. (So many kazoos.)

I have a lot of wonderful memories from campaigning and legislating, more of which I continue to make by the day. But I don't think I will ever again experience something as absurdly unique to the experience of being a transgender metalhead serving in elected office as what happened on March 11, 2019. That's when Lamb of God vocalist Randy Blythe and a crowd of more than two hundred people outside the General Assembly building in Richmond drowned out the Westboro Baptist Church's protest by blowing into kazoos for half an hour as a line of paint-bucket drummers pounded away in front of them and the occasional vuvuzela blared out from Randy as he stood near someone dressed as gay Elvis.

Whether it was gay Elvis—who won the costume contest and

donated the few hundred dollars he received from Randy to PFLAG, which provides resources for families of LGBTQ kids—or my former boss Tara and her family doing their part to overcome the hateful message across the street, *my* people stood up for me: metalheads from the underground, queer people from greater Richmond, you name it. That's what happens when you embrace every aspect of your identity instead of running away from it and use it to empower other people who know what it's like to be singled out and stigmatized for being who they are. You create a moment that absolutely destroys the intended bigotry with something truly special.

Beyond that incredible scene, I also used that moment to raise a ton of money for my campaign from all fifty states, D.C., and Puerto Rico—enough money to completely fund my first week of TV ads during the final six weeks of the campaign. Naturally, the Westboro Baptist Church accused me of "greed" for fundraising off of their bullshit. But look: ever since the first week of my first campaign in January 2017, I've flipped the script on hateful rhetoric by asking people to donate to my campaign whenever bigoted people say or do bigoted things toward me for daring to be a trans woman in politics. Some of these people do genuinely think that if my voters only knew that I was trans and supported trans equality policies they would surely, *surely* vote against me.

A conversion therapy advocate from Maryland tested this out in a January 10, 2017, email to the incumbent I was running against, Bob Marshall; the then–Speaker of the House, Bill Howell; and Kari Pugh, the then–executive editor of the *Gainesville Times*—where I worked for more than nine years. This activist attacked my family and me directly, saying that after my dad's suicide in 1987, I "did not receive the surrogate-fathering [I] needed" from my grandfather.

Along with a number of errors in the email, the fact that someone would dredge up an obituary that I personally wrote and try to make my dead grandfather—who I adored and lived with for seventeen years—out as an inadequate male role model showed me at the end of my first week as a candidate that this campaign would get personal, nasty, and downright awful, so I better figure out how to make episodes like that work for me instead of bring me down.

In response, I mentioned it on social media and made a direct ask so I could fundraise off it. When the first twenty-five dollars showed up in my inbox afterward, I knew that truly was the only thing I could do. What were my other options? Write back to the author of the email? Complain to the editor of my former newspaper? Complain to the Republicans? No. Being a trans woman running for office means you need to have thick skin and that you can't ever, ever let the bastards grind ya down.

I know seeing a politician asking for money online is nauseating when there are so, so many other ways to use that money to help those on the margins. In that regard, running for office can be a gut check, especially when you refuse the main source of campaign funds most legislators have accepted since financing campaigns in the United States existed: corporate lobbyists. You then inherently turn to the grassroots, netroots, nonprofit organizations, and individuals who can write four- or five-digit checks because you share values.

At the same time, my vote in 2018 to expand Medicaid also provided health insurance to more than half a million people from the time it went into effect on January 1, 2019, through the start of 2021, with thousands more people still enrolling. My first campaign cost just under one million dollars in order to unseat an incumbent who had voted against and harshly criticized expanding Medicaid, a service that so many people who don't make a lot of money rely on for their health care—trans people included. Meanwhile, in Virginia, we've affirmed that Medicaid covers transition-related health care, which is life-changing for transgender Virginians who've had it even worse than I did. That money we raised and spent during my 2017 campaign to earn election to the House of Delegates and the money we raised and spent during the 2019 and 2021 campaigns to keep me there means I'm in a position to decide where tens of billions of dollars in funding goes through my votes on the House floor.

All that said, running for office is pretty surreal when you don't come from money. There I was, driving a $324 car and just barely raising $10,000 during my first month of campaigning—about 40 percent of my yearly newspaper salary in just one month—which I thought was terrific, yet wasn't even close to the hauls being brought in by two other Democratic candidates running in the same primary election as me. I'd be wondering to myself, "Is it okay to use the campaign account for gas?" (Answer: Yes, stupid, you have to go places) while constantly worrying about making payroll. At the same time, while my message and intent behind the campaign were hyperlocal, I was extremely well aware that being a trans woman running for office against the bathroom-bill guy meant that losing would set back our community, while winning would inspire people across the country. It was a lot to take on.

Entering the race as Potentially Credible Transgender Candidate* meant that there would absolutely be media attention, something I knew as a reporter now running for office. So, I gave the scoop to Jill Palermo at my former newspaper, the *Gainesville Times*, while I was getting my hair done before my first photo shoot on December 30,

---

*Transgender Candidate for short, Transgender Journalist if ya nasty. . . . Such was my life in headlines.

2016, and announced my campaign the afternoon of January 3, when I knew the newspaper was off to the printer. Having satisfied my need to make sure the newspaper I dedicated nearly a decade of my life to as a reporter broke the news about my campaign, I turned to LGBTQ media outlets, calling John Riley at *Metro Weekly*, a magazine in the D.C. area.

Even though I gave my interview to my newspaper alma mater first, John immediately put his story online, so it became the first piece to circulate, with the headline: "Transgender Journalist Announces Run for Virginia House of Delegates." My name appeared in the subheadline: "Danica Roem Is Running in the 13th District against Anti-LGBT Delegate Bob Marshall." As it turned out, that would be a common theme. The *Gainesville Times* headline the next day: "Transgender Journalist Challenges Bob Marshall for 13th House Seat." A couple days later, in the *Washington Blade*: "Transgender Journalist Challenges Bob Marshall in Va. House."

I realized a few things here: (1) My gender was going to be the first thing anyone learned about me through the news. (2) My occupation would hopefully be second, as it was my chief qualifier for office. (3) While I was a "transgender journalist," the incumbent I was running against would be called by his name.

My challenge would be to get people to read past the headlines and actually give a damn about my candidacy, so I had to hit my points and hit them early. Also true: my accompanying photo really, really needed to look good, because with 100 percent certainty, I knew people would give quite a big shit about whether I was "passing" as a cisgender woman—a term I just disdain. Not too far back in my mind was a 2015 sketch on the Comedy Central show *Inside Amy Schumer*. In it, Amy finds herself walking along a trail when she stumbles across actresses Julia Louis-Dreyfus, Tina Fey, and Patricia

Arquette having a picnic with a full spread, wine included, at a table on the grass, under the shade of a tree. Patricia informs Amy, "We're celebrating Julia's last fuckable day." Julia, long removed from her *Seinfeld* days and now in her fifties, soon adds, "In every actress's life, the media decides when you finally reach the point where you're not believably fuckable anymore."

Trans women who put themselves in the public sphere are immediately judged on this criteria, regardless of age: Are. You. Fuckable? It's wrong, it shouldn't be like that, and yet I cannot even begin to underscore the reality of this. The comments that followed the hundreds of news stories about me that year almost universally centered on my looks. While being judged on appearance alone is, of course, an experience shared by cisgender women, the overt intensity applied to trans women is truly breathtaking. When you see cisgender women running for Congress and president, you see this over-analyzing of their entire visible anatomy. For cisgender women running for local office, though, simply declaring their candidacy typically doesn't get one-hundred-plus comments on social media page after social media page, awash in the proclaimed culture war that is the, well, existence of a thirty-two-year-old stepmom's face.

I figured it would get ugly, and so the moment the first "mental illness" comment came up on the *Prince William Times* (*Gainesville Times*) Facebook page under that story, I asked my friends to just flood the comments section with nice things. Even though everyone tells you, "Don't read the comments!" my instincts told me that a lot of people do anyway, so I figured I could influence the social media narrative early. I hoped that an overwhelming amount of positive comments would possibly leave a would-be negative commenter questioning whether they really wanted to stand out as being an asshole.

Meanwhile, undecided Democratic primary voters who read the story and liked my policies but were unsure if anyone would actually vote for someone like me would see all of these nice things other people were writing and possibly think, "Maybe she really does have a shot. People really seem to like her." This was important for managing my rollout in local news outlets, just because it would be highly likely that 13th District voters would, in fact, be reading the comments. Manufacturing a little enthusiasm may seem potentially unethical, but these were people who knew me and who knew I knew my stuff. Considering that the alternative was "mentally ill" being the first impression someone had of me, I'll opt for, as one 13th District resident (and friend) wrote, "She understands the issues in PWC . . ."

Once the news stories started getting out there, I began receiving donations from across the country—more than one hundred totaling fifty-five hundred dollars by the end of the first week. Not bad . . . though it came with a catch: that wasn't nearly enough to finance a campaign, and your opening week is supposed to be your big splash. I took to social media, spreading the word on groups like Pantsuit Nation and other sites where a bunch of Democratic women, pissed off from the 2016 election results, were looking for an outlet to express their contempt, and defeating Republican incumbents in Virginia in 2017—given that the Old Dominion went for Barack Obama (2008 and 2012) and Hillary Clinton (2016)—meant that unemployed, uninsured me taking on an avowed Donald Trump supporter would pique their interest.

Obviously, it wasn't only about the fundraising, though, and it even transcended what kind of legislation I'd be able to pass if I did win. As the first out-and-seated transgender state legislator in American history, I'd be showing other people that we can thrive in positions of power, too. That pressure could be inspiring, but it could also be really heavy. When I say people doubted my ability to win, I mean other transgender people didn't think I could win, let alone the other seven out trans candidates who would emerge victorious that November 7 across the country. Two months into my campaign, I sent an email to a fairly well-known transgender writer and journalist, asking whether she would be willing to cover my campaign.

The reply was truly stunning:

> I have struggled for days to try to figure out how to say this, so I must do it plainly. The real problem in US politics right now is gerrymandering. Marshall won his election in 2015 by 13 points. I do not see a path for you, especially when Virginia's gerrymandered districts are still in court.
>
> Transgender people in America are simply not electable at this time, and certainly not in gerrymandered districts. I cannot help but conclude a better, more efficient and effective outlet for your time, energy, and money would be to find ways to support efforts, both in court and in the legislature, to end gerrymandering which favors rural political parties.

Oh, dear reader, trust me: it gets worse.
She called on me to drop out of the race.

> I wish I could say this more diplomatically, but given the limited resources we have as a community this expends what little we have to no purpose. The visibility gained is nearly worthless: they know we're here, and

are already actively working to wipe us out. Indeed, the transgender candidates in the 2016 election did not win, nor has it influenced the wave of laws targeting us.

This was particularly infuriating. She wasn't looking at the right turnout model and her saying that I would be hurting our cause by running just makes me think: If we're not willing to stand up for ourselves, who the hell ever will? Literally the only way I was going to prove I was viable to some people was to win the primary. Though when the election came around, some celebrities would weigh in with their support, I didn't see a lot of support from other prominent trans activists around the country at that stage. My team and I couldn't expect every famous trans person in the country to tip the scales toward me. We would have to work for the win, just like any other candidate and campaign team.

The first person I hired on the campaign, Ethan Damon, played major roles in Hillary's campaign in my home of Prince William County and later in southern Arizona. In the run-up to my campaign launch, a Democratic staffer in late 2016 told me the two worst pieces of advice I received during that campaign: not to make fixing Route 28 my central issue because transportation didn't poll well in Northern Virginia, and that while field (talking directly with voters by knocking on their doors or calling them) was important, I needed someone who had experience raising money, which Ethan didn't, so I shouldn't hire him.

Following that meeting, I offered Ethan the job of campaign manager and plastered "Fix Route 28 Now!" on my yard signs. (Excuse me while my sixteen-year-old self cranks Rage Against the

Machine: "Fuck you, I won't do what you tell me!") To me, the most important way to win a low-turnout primary in a fairly densely populated, suburban area where you could get from one end of the district to the other in half an hour was through quality conversations at the doors. Ethan had lost his mother, due in part to inadequate health care, and had just come off a stinging loss to elect the first woman president. He wanted a victory and he saw the same plausible route to victory that I did, even while being told by other Democratic operatives in Virginia that there was no way he and I could win the race.

Given that Ethan knew the district from knocking on doors and organizing in it in 2016, he also knew most of our local Democratic activists, and they really seemed to like him, so much so that he kicked ass at recruiting volunteers. In fact, during our first mass canvass event on January 28, we had twenty-five volunteers show up to collect petition signatures for us, which caused me to get super energized and sprint back and forth in the little library room where we congregated like I was running a relay race. We were still hoarding every dollar we raised, so we handed out little photocopies of a flyer my artist buddy Tom Faraci made up for me because we didn't have the money yet to afford full-on, professionally made, union-printed flyers that my direct mail consultant Alan Moore would eventually create for us. In February, when he did deliver them, we looked all sorts of professional, and I was so stoked to share them on the day they arrived, as that also happened to be the first of three days I'd spend training with a group of Democratic women candidates through Emerge Virginia's boot camp.

Emerge Virginia's entire mission is training Democratic women in Virginia to run for office and win, as the state has a chronic underrepresentation of women, even now, so the organization's efforts are absolutely critical to changing that equation. Yet so many of us stepped up to run in 2017 that our collective candidacies became a story in and of itself. I was invited to the training by Emerge Virginia's then–executive director, Julie Copeland, who had heard about me from James Parrish of Equality Virginia. They were excited to support a trans woman candidate and signed me up.

I had trained with the LGBTQ Victory Institute in Dallas, Texas, back in November during their candidate and campaigning training program, which included three or four dozen prospective LGBTQ candidates from across the country, myself included. As it turned out, two of us would be elected the following year, the other being Andrea Jenkins, the first out[*] trans Black woman elected to any office in the United States as a member of the Minneapolis City Council. (That same year, another Victory Institute alum, Phillipe Cunningham, would also win his race to the same city council, making him the first out trans Black man elected in the United States.) Going through that training ended up being the tipping point[†] for the Victory Institute's sister organization, the Victory Fund, to endorse my campaign that spring.

While the Victory training was super intense and really fun, I didn't stay in touch with many of the people I trained with afterward, other than Victory staffers. The Emerge training was more like the development of a sisterhood: Virginia women coming together to learn how to run and win together. The best friends I made that year were my Emerge sisters, especially Karrie Delaney, Jennifer

---

[*]Althea Garrison was elected to the Massachusetts State House for one term in the mid-1990s but was outed against her will while in office by a Republican operative who would later work for Mitt Romney. In some circles, that counts as a résumé booster.

[†]Also, a junior staffer named Vince—whose actual drag name is Sandra Slay O'Connor—went to the mat making the case for me.

Carroll Foy, and Dawn Adams, who I would talk to frequently. Along with the three of us, eventual House of Delegates winners that year who trained in that class included Elizabeth Guzman, Debra Rodman, Kathy Tran, and Wendy Gooditis, with another winner, Hala Ayala, having trained previously with Emerge. Two Virginia Beach Democratic women also flipped seats that fall, even without that training: Cheryl Turpin and Kelly Convirs-Fowler.

Together, we learned how to message, how to fundraise, how to tell your story to a crowd, how to make life on the campaign trail work if you have kids at home, and so much else. The Victory training had a special emphasis on what LGBTQ candidates experience that's unique to us, my favorite being the role-playing when one of the guests, a Black woman pretending to be an old voter judging a candidate, said, "You got a little sugar in your tank?"* (I just . . . died. Amazing.)

At Emerge, we would each give a stump speech and then those around the table would highlight what they liked and offer positive reinforcement for playing to one another's strengths. It was a genuine building-up. I couldn't have been happier then: I could just be a heavy metal frontwoman, full of energy, working in how each of the women around us represented the true culmination of the American Dream and that this year, this time, in 2017, was our time to shine.

Each training I attended also had a moment where I figured out exactly how I wanted to message my campaign. At Victory, lead trainer Joe Fuld played the role of a reporter, asking me whether fixing Route 28 was *really* what I cared about because . . . c'mon . . . a

---

*"Are you gay?"

trans woman running for office? Isn't there . . . something else . . . that your campaign is really about?

"Transgender people get stuck in traffic, too!" I snapped off the cuff, earning hoots and hollers from the audience. Joe's training had been so on point, I ended up using that exact line in interviews and my stump speeches.

A t Emerge, we really focused on the parts of our stories that were unique to us and would speak to voters, allowing us to harness our natural sense of empathy to genuinely hear someone and respond to them. We learned to prepare different types of speeches: an in-and-out two-minute one; a three-minute elevator pitch; and a ten-minute full story, with an emphasis on "body awareness" as we spoke—making intentional motions. This workshop also gave me the space and time to refine what I wanted that message to be. The energy of all these women running for office, challenging other incumbents, writing new stories for themselves while trying to make real change in the world, was a great environment for shaping the kind of candidate—and, ultimately, legislator—I wanted to be.

I thought about two years earlier in 2015, when I had driven out to Dover, Delaware, to pay my respects to the Biden family when Beau Biden died. Beau had successfully fought as Delaware's attorney general for the state legislature to pass a trans rights bill to prevent discrimination in a number of different areas of public life, and he did that before most other Democratic-led state legislatures had done the same, which I thought came from a personal place of genuine support from him. In fact, it did; he had a close friend who was trans, someone who would end up campaigning for me that same spring, Sarah McBride, who in 2020 became the first out transgender state senator in United States history.

When I approached Beau's casket, I genuflected, waited a moment, and extended my right hand out to Joe Biden, then the sitting vice president of the United States, who shook hands with or hugged *everybody* up to that point, holding a conversation with anyone who wanted to talk, even hours into the memorial service.

I started to choke up ever so slightly as I told Joe: "Hi, my name's Danica. I'm so sorry for your loss. In 2013, when Beau fought for the law to protect transgender people, he fought for me. That means a lot to me and I just wanted to thank you for raising someone who would do something like that."

Joe wrapped me up in a big hug. As I turned to go, he held my hand and asked me to look at him. He leaned in and looked into my eyes. Joe looked paler than normal, tired—obviously grieving. Without breaking his gaze, he said: "We mean that. *We*. Mean. That."

He lifted my right hand and kissed it. My jaw fell agape and my eyes widened, bulging forward. I couldn't believe this. In that moment, I had just told the vice president at his son's wake that I'm transgender and that his son fought to protect people like me. He kissed my hand for it. He reassured me that his whole family felt the same way as Beau when it came to standing up for transgender people. This was the vice president of the United States telling me I'm worth protecting.

Whoa. Whoawhoawhoa. Whoa.

We hugged one more time. I hugged Beau's widow and his sister, telling each of the women, "I'm so sorry for your loss."

I didn't know what else to say because I knew they had just heard everything I told Joe. I walked out of the viewing room, turned to the left, and was redirected by a guard to my right; my organs all felt like goo. It was an incredible moment, one so overwhelming that I couldn't even cry. I just gasped and wheezed as I jogged through the rain back to my car, trying to process out loud what just happened.

Once I was workshopping my campaign speeches and thinking about who I'd hope to be as an elected official, that moment came back to me in a big way. At this point, we didn't have someone in the White House who felt that our rights are worth protecting. Meeting then–vice president Biden at his most vulnerable moment had stayed in my mind as a possibility for how those in office—at whatever level—could make serious impacts both as legislators and in terms of visible, audible support.

My speeches in the workshop came to include that moment with the vice president. I made the pitch that when politicians in Washington turn their backs on us, then we have to lead at home in the states—that's where I could make an impact, by unseating someone I sparred with as a reporter, in the state house, and at home.

I had fought Delegate Marshall in the legislature as an activist, and I had won. I had fought him in the press and in front of the Prince William County School Board, when he called transgender people "gender confused." I said later that electing a transgender woman to replace the most anti-LGBTQ legislator in the South would be an act of certainty and a defining moment that would resonate across the country.

By mid-April, I'd hired a finance director, Rohan Ramesh, a reliable and steady field staffer from the Hillary campaign in Prince William County, but we were getting absolutely creamed by two different campaigns that had raised more than $70,000 each by that point, while we had brought in about $27,000. I refused to take corporate money, with the one exception of a $70 check from GWARbar, a dive bar in Richmond run by one of the metal band GWAR's guitar players that brought in more than $700 in revenue on an otherwise slow Sunday afternoon when I held a fundraiser there that February. They donated 10 percent as a thank-you and, hey, I'm pretty proud of that one. After all, what? Am I in the pocket of Big GWAR? Sure. Guilty. Now hand over another Jizmak and cheese, please.

The biggest problem was that I started the campaign saying that I wouldn't take donations of more than $500. I wanted to run as pure a campaign as possible in a commonwealth like Virginia, where there are no campaign finance limits. It's a disclosure-only state, so you can take any amount of money from anyone who's at least eighteen and an American citizen or any American corporation, group, etc., you want. Just report it to the state Department of Elections. That's it. So when the first-quarter campaign finance reports came in and I had collected by far the most donations of any of the four candidates running—in fact, I was number six in the state for total number of donors—I significantly trailed in overall money raised because my money was all coming from $1 to $500 donations, while they were taking in thousands of dollars at a time.

I realized that I had no viable pathway to the nomination with a gulf like that and I had made a huge mistake, applying a different set of rules for my campaign. So I sucked it up and when the first $1,000 check came in from a gay donor in Massachusetts, I signed the back of it and then immediately drove to the Bull Run Mobile Home Community to knock on doors. I wanted to tell myself above all that even if I was getting rid of my self-imposed limit in order to compete, I would at least stay true to my values about making this campaign about the people who don't have a lot of money and not about the donors who do.

While my fundraising gulf made a lot of people nervous, we were winning every single other aspect of the campaign. Our field program had been damned near flawless. Ethan's knowledge ensured that he was sending me only to the doors of people who would likely vote in the Democratic primary that June 13 and would be open to voting for me. He never gave me a bad list that entire campaign. Meanwhile, being the "transgender candidate" had a benefit to it, in that the earned media (news coverage) we were receiving absolutely dwarfed the rest of the field.

I also decided that when Jacqueline Smith ran as our Democratic nominee for a special election for clerk of the circuit court, my campaign would go all in for her to win—which was an investment in our community, a great learning experience for me as a first-time candidate, and an opportunity for me to prove myself to local Democrats that I was the real deal and that I could hustle harder than anyone.

I knocked on doors in Tyler, a swing precinct within the district that also happened to be the community I had covered the most as a reporter—and where I declared to my campaign manager that we would focus and win. I spent time at one house in particular where I spoke with four registered voters, all with shared Democratic values. I knew if they all voted, we could win this precinct, and I told them that they could make all the difference. Sure enough, three days later, the results from Tyler came in: Jacqueline Smith, 85 votes; Jackson Miller, 82 votes.

We had demonstrated the power of our field program with Jacqueline winning Tyler in an area historically difficult for Democrats.

Ethan had trained our volunteers to have quality conversations with voters and really earn their support. My public policy knowledge and ability to connect with people in one-on-one settings also made it clear to voter after voter that when I made the hard ask—"Can I earn your vote this June?"—it would be more likely I could get a "Yes" than a "No" in that moment. For most people, I figured they would be willing to keep their word, and there wasn't a chance I would let anyone outhustle me that spring.

That is, until my second car of the campaign died. My '92 Dodge Shadow finally bit it for the last time while I was driving on the beltway in February 2017. I couldn't afford much, so bought a $1,500 '98 Toyota Camry from someone my ma knew up in Loudoun County. Well, that car sure could haul with a lot more giddyup than the Dirty Dodge . . . and then within two months, it broke down and would need more than $3,000 worth of repairs.

My home was in the woods. We don't have sidewalks anywhere even close to there. Every lot is at least an acre in size, so going house to house took time. Still, my campaign was really, really low on money and I couldn't afford a rental car. So I did the only thing I could think of: I hopped on my bike for two days and went by foot for six, spending more than a week knocking on every single likely Democratic voter's door in all of Yates Ford precinct.

If nothing else, I knew that the dirt roads, hills, and spread-apart houses in the woods of Manassas would tell the two candidates from Gainesville that it wasn't worth their time when they could find much more densely populated neighborhoods closer to home. Sure, they came out to Yates Ford, but not to that extent. In fact, one of their campaigns would just leave literature on people's doors, ring the doorbell, and go off to the next house. I knew that because I heard that story repeatedly at the doors when I would stop to talk to the voters and connect with them. On one street, I kept knocking on doors with another candidate's flyer already on them. The voter would then open the door, the flyer would fall to the ground, and I would extend my hand. "Hi, I'm Danica Roem, running for the House of Delegates. How are you doing? Looks like someone else was here earlier, but I guess they didn't knock. So I'm just going door to door today . . ."

Quality conversations. Quality conversations. Quality conversations. It's a mantra I repeated over and over in the campaign, so much so that when someone wouldn't answer the door, I would leave a handwritten note with their name on it that said "I'm sorry I missed you! I'm running for the 13th District of the Virginia House of Delegates and I would be honored to earn your vote in the Democratic primary. Please vote June 13 at [name of precinct]. Warmly, Danica," followed by my personal cell phone number. I learned to do that as a reporter covering the special election for the 50th House of Delegates district in 2006 when the Republican candidate would leave a handwritten "I'm sorry I missed you!" sticky note on his literature if someone wasn't home. I thought a more elaborate handwritten note to go with my literature would substitute for a conversation if there wasn't one to be had.

(As it turned out, people liked the notes. I got a few phone calls, including a voicemail from a mom in Sudley precinct that was truly special. "That was a nice touch. You can count on three votes from this household: you've got my vote, my daughter's vote, and my ex-husband's vote." There's . . . a lot to unpack there. But you know what? Weird is my normal. I was grateful for their support.)

Anyway, when I got done with Yates Ford, I turned my attention to our adjacent precinct Signal Hill—another largely semirural area that had two main subdivisions where there were typical single-family homes on quarter-acre lots: Roseberry and Arrowood. Again, I hit every Democratic door in those precincts and absolutely crushed it because these were my neighbors; I could talk to them on such a micro level about how traffic from the potential development of a nearby farm could affect our local roads and commutes and about how I opposed the development for that reason.

After the first quarter, our campaign finances were picking up a little bit, but not enough to match the other candidates. While our social media, earned media, and field programs were going well, we needed to catch a few breaks. Winning a local straw poll was a huge one that helped with giving people a reason to believe, which manifested itself with our first game-changer endorsement of the campaign from the national organization of Sen. Elizabeth Warren's supporters called the Progressive Change Campaign Committee (PCCC). Not only did their endorsement come with the validation of me as a "bold progressive," but also for days afterward, PCCC donors pitched in a torrent of small-dollar contributions as they responded to a national fundraising email.

The following week, we received our second major endorsement, this time from the Victory Fund. They were convinced that with every other metric of the campaign going our way they could help us close the fundraising gap enough to make us competitive, even if we weren't going to outraise either of the top two candidates in our field of four. Sure enough, a month later, I got on a conference call with Victory board members, telling them we had already hit our projected win number in seven precincts and all we needed was to raise $8,000 more to afford our fifth and sixth mail pieces.

After the call, I went to lunch at the Chipotle off Sudley Road in Manassas. In the restroom, of all places, my phone kept buzzing.

"Goddamn it, what?!" I thought as I collected myself, washed my hands, and looked in my purse to see my phone glowing as I walked out the door.

It was Ethan. The chairman of the Victory Fund's board of directors, Chris Abele—himself an elected official as Milwaukee County executive in Wisconsin—had asked the board after the call how much money we needed for those last two mailers. Getting his answer, he took out his phone, pulled up our ActBlue page, and bam: $10,000.

The entire primary, we had only received seven donations above $500, all ranging between $700 to $1,000. I didn't even know what Chris looked like and couldn't have distinguished him on the conference call because we did it on Ethan's phone. I exclaimed, "Holy shit!!!!" when I found out.

Being able to afford six mailers meant we could execute our strategy completely, even while being outspent. We knew we had the ground game and a front-page profile from one of our local newspapers, *Inside NoVa*, in April about Route 28, which would include a graphic of me pointing an animated hand at Bob Marshall for not fixing it, meaning I had just won complete control of the narrative of the race. My issue—fixing Route 28—was now *the* defining issue of the campaign. As I knocked on doors in Tyler, I saw the newspaper in the driveway of house after house—yes, people still subscribe to the dead-tree edition—the day the story dropped. I was beside myself with glee.

Meanwhile, several other things were going well, including the attention I was getting for taking on Dominion Energy and using two of Bob Marshall's particularly egregious votes against him—one opposing a bill that would require insurers to cover twelve months of birth control and a vote to defeat the governor's budget amendment to expand Medicaid to four hundred thousand Virginians.

On primary day, with polls open from 6:00 A.M. to 7:00 P.M., I voted first thing in the morning and then drove to Gainesville to spend the next twelve hours at Heritage Hunt, a community largely, though not exclusively, made up of white people aged fifty-five and older, with a historically disproportionately high turnout. My goal: greet everyone possible with the hopes that they would look at me and say, "You remind me of my granddaughter."*

As I yakked it up with voters, my team went to work. The night before the primary, Chris Abele had donated another $15,000 to us out of nowhere. It was the best problem: How could we possibly use that in the primary in one day? I figured the best thing we could do would be to staff the precincts for the day—we were the only campaign that day to staff all eighteen precincts and, sans a small gap here or there, did so the entire thirteen hours.

When all the votes, including the absentees, were counted, we won the primary by 498 votes—the exact same margin of victory Bob Marshall claimed during the 2013 general election. The difference was, his was out of more than 17,000 total votes cast. Mine was out of 4,339 votes—a nearly 11.5 percent victory.

Phone calls started coming in from media outlets across the country and I kept driving my local message about fixing Route 28. Steve Jansen had been such a favorite to win the primary that, after a candidate forum featuring the four of us, *The Washington Post* ran three photos of him and one thumbnail of the rest of us. I had been dubbed in the news as the "LGBT activist" and "transgender journalist" more

---

*No one said that. I was sad.

than as the lifelong local resident who was trying to fix a road and fight a powerful utility company.

Moving into the general election, I wanted to turn the conversation to my roots in the community, to what I would do to change the things we had all struggled with for decades, and draw the harsh comparison between me and Bob Marshall. Of course, that comparison had to include the fact that I was trans and he was the bathroom-bill guy, but my being trans couldn't be *the* story.

At the same time, I still had in my mind every single day what this victory could mean for our community—losing wasn't an option.

Trans and other people who have to deal with bigotry because they've made themselves vulnerable enough to be visible can take a bad situation and make something positive out of it, under the right circumstances and with the right message. As I learned from the great Taoist philosopher Winnie the Pooh, information isn't inherently positive or negative: it's what you do with it that determines positivity or negativity.

There are limits on this, of course. I'm not going to look at the chosen families of the dozens of Black and Brown transgender women murdered last year in this country, and the dozens more who will likely die this year, too—a rate far outpacing that of white transgender people, though the violence against us is also very real and fatal—and tell them that all that's needed for the country's horrendous national issues with racial equity, toxic masculinity, and gun violence is a little bit of positive attitude.

What I'm saying, rather, is this: If you've lived your life on the margins, and you're worried that changing the story about who you are and what you're worth is a kind of immodesty or betrayal—a sellout to your sisters, brothers, and nonbinary siblings who are still suffering—please stop doing that. You deserve to be able to take care of yourself and to use your platform to elevate people who can relate to what you've been through and who need help, too. It's not your fault that society didn't value your life and the lives of people like you properly before you put yourself in a position to take care of yourself and your community.

The voters saw my profile. They knew I was transgender. Hell, they even knew I had a metal band. And they knew I knew my shit; I knew public policy and would bring the fight to Bob Marshall in the fall. One voter told me at her door that she loved what I stood for and liked me personally, but was just so worried about whether someone like me could win, so she planned to vote for Steve since she saw him as the safe choice—a white, middle-aged, former prosecutor working as a university professor with a wife and two kids from a gated community. I asked her to vote her hopes instead of her fears. She ended up doing the latter in the end . . . but when I won the primary, she became one of my most fervent volunteers. The candidate she wanted to win did and it was time for her to confront her fears and make sure I would, in fact, become electable, by doing the one thing every cisgender, straight Democrat before me had failed to do for two and a half decades: win more votes than Bob Marshall—rainbow headscarf and all.

CHAPTER 10

HEADLINER

Danica Roem is making a show of Richmond and Virginia politics.

Danica Roem, when she arrived in Richmond for the start of session, "arrived wearing her trademark rainbow headscarf and leading a trail of news cameras, with the attention focused on her rather than the issues."

—Friends of Danica Roem self-opposition research for 2019, conducted by Reger Research

The sun was rising. The birds were chirping. The teapots were percolating.

And, somewhere in Manassas, my state delegate had, well, *something* on his mind:

"Let me say that your opponent is Danica Roem, a, uhh, sss, uhh, juh, they, she's described—he! It's a guy who dresses like a woman—I don't think there's been any surgery. He's been described as far as I know?" conservative talk-radio host Sandy Rios said to then-delegate Bob Marshall during her September 25, 2017, radio show.

"Correct," replied the thirteen-term, seventy-three-year-old incumbent who had been in office since I was seven years old and had never/will never see my junk. "Right."

sips tea

Just another Monday morning for Transgender Candidate on the campaign trail.

While my mere existence as a transgender woman was just too much for poor Sandy Rios—who in three seconds managed to call me they (no), she (yes), he (no), and it (really?)—headline editors couldn't keep their shit together much better. *The Washington Post* kicked off the general election on June 14 with the headline, "She Is Transgender. He Proposed a 'Bathroom Bill.' They're Running against Each Other in Northern Virginia."

Click. Click click click click

All the noise and stupidity aside, what won the 2017 campaign for us above everything else was our ability to tell stories—to communicate, engage, and connect with people. Every person who knocked on doors for the campaign had a story to share about who I was while asking the voters what was important to them. Every donor to the campaign made it possible for me to make payroll for the people telling those stories and to send out advertising that told those stories, too. All of the earned media I received from newspapers, magazines, online publications, television, and radio, and the social media I used to promote those news stories, contributed to our dialogue with the voters.

None of that would have been possible without a bunch of people who dedicated months of their year to telling those stories. If you can please cue up the Academy Awards music: My campaign manager Ethan Damon, finance director Rohan Ramesh, and our interns Gordon Baer and Kyle Powers made it possible to win the primary. For the general election, we added in field director Chris Vega, field organizers Maria Salgado, Brad Chester, Jamie Landa, and Quinn Dunlea, and deputy organizer Hannah McDonald. Meanwhile, we added some reinforcements for my direct-mail consultant, Alan Moore, as we expanded to television and digital communications under the eye of Scott Kozar, polling by Joshua Ulibarri and Meryl O'Bryan of Lake Research, and a handful of House Democratic caucus staffers: executive director Trent Armitage, deputy executive director Trevor Southerland, communications director Katie Baker, and field director Jessica David.

While Democrats often outspent my predecessor in his campaigns, he always had a robust group of socially conservative volunteers to knock on doors for him. In short, I wanted us to do something that had never been done before in thirteen previous campaigns: outorganize and outmobilize Bob Marshall.

To start, the field program designed during the primary had exploded in a really, really good way with five full-time field staffers and two part-timers, along with our finance director, who was really good at knocking on doors when we needed him to.

We switched offices to work out of the coordinated campaign's Manassas field office, this dump* of a former dentist's office on Surveyor Court across the street from the hospital where I was born in 1984. Our team interacted daily with the coordinated campaign group working to elect the three statewide candidates as well as those of us down-ballot. On days when the coordinated campaign's turf for knocking on doors overlapped with ours, we could visit a ton of people all at once. Also, I'm an easily distracted, chronically late, people-pleasing, extroverted procrastinator who loves telling stories (surprise!), which meant that Ethan often needed to find something for me to do off-site just so I would shut the fuck up and let him run the show without me sidetracking our team.†

Ethan, Chris, and our organizers brought in hundreds of volunteers to have persuasion conversations at the doors, too—so many at one point that it became normal for us to send out fifty or more people to knock on doors on a single Saturday during the last two months. Just to put that in perspective, the 2015 Democratic nominee Don Shaw—the guy who originally asked me to run all the way back on

---

*But it was *our* dump and we loved our dump. Wait . . . that sounds terrible. Scratch that.

†"Ahh, let me tell you younguns about a time called the '90s! There was this one time, at band camp . . ."

August 4, 2016—had a maximum of fifteen volunteers come out for him one time. By contrast, we were running a congressional-sized field campaign for a House of Delegates seat.

At the same time, a group of young adults from Let America Vote—a mobilization organization founded by former Missouri secretary of state Jason Kander—was out canvassing for us, too. And our volunteers were also the people leading phone banks during the week, providing us with food in the office, writing postcards to voters, allowing us to have all-day-long photo and TV shoots at their homes . . . just whatever it took to win.

Our two big endorsements during the primary, the PCCC and the Victory Fund, more than doubled down for the general election. The PCCC would send out fundraising emails for us and they weren't alone: the Democratic blog *Daily Kos* jumped on board with their own endorsement and national fundraising email, resulting in thousands upon thousands of small-dollar donations trickling in by the minute, for three days or more in a row. We added the name of every person who donated to our own email list, where they would then often respond with even larger donations.

On July 26, when then-president Trump tweeted out his ban on transgender people serving in the military, the Victory Fund's chairman Chris Abele was so pissed off that he, as Milwaukee County executive (who happened to be at the White House for a jobs announcement during that ill-fated moment), donated fifty thousand dollars to my campaign on the spot.

Chris got under Bob's skin. Big time. Not only did Bob label Chris—who, by the way, is a straight man with a wife and three kids—a "radical, sexual ideologue,"* but he started making him the

---

*"I don't know what that is but it sounds fun," said Chris.

focus of mailers and other attacks. ("I love it when Bob attacks me. It's my favorite thing," Chris would tell me in a text.) I was totally fine with that: the more Bob was attacking Chris Abele, the less time he was focused on either his message or mine.

Right about then, we tested our message for the first time using polling and found out that we entered the summer campaign down by two percentage points among all voters, but down double digits among most motivated voters. When our October polling came back, however, we had closed to gap to pull in dead even, tied 42 to 42 among all voters, and with a double-digit lead among our own most motivated voters. Democrats were fired up and they liked our message. A lot had to happen for us to actually get there, though, and it took an all-around team effort from a ton of different people.

When Ethan and I started having weekly conference calls with our consultants and the Democratic House Caucus staffers after the primary in June, I made it clear to everyone that on no call was I to be the only woman present. This was important to me because women's perspectives are so often talked over, drowned out, or missing altogether when there are multiple men calling the shots, so I wanted to prevent that from the start. The caucus's executive director Trent Armitage honored that request and made sure we had women from the caucus.

While my team organized on the ground and we kicked ass with fundraising in June, the Republicans flat-out refused to take me seriously during the summer, even when there were warning signs that we were real.

On July 18, *The Washington Post* ran a headline, "Va. Transgender Candidate Raised Nearly 20 Times More than GOP Opponent in

June." Transgender Candidate™ of course being my drag superhero alias; the public believed in what we were doing—just not the Republicans. Three days after that story ran, the Republican Party of Virginia chairman John Whitbeck told political commentator Tom Sherwood on *The Kojo Nnamdi Show* that I, "the Democrat," was smart to talk about local issues like fixing Route 28 "because going head-to-head with Bob Marshall on anything else is [*laughs*] going to be very difficult. He consistently wins in a district that's overwhelmingly Democratic. He's going to win again, he always does, and I don't see that race as competitive. But I do commend, I'll give credit where credit is due: talking about the issues that matter to voters of that district like Route 28 is the right way to go."

There's a saying in politics that you're not supposed to believe your own headlines, so I couldn't just simply take John at his word. I also knew the Republicans in Richmond weren't particularly fond of Bob because he would fight with them as much as he would fight with Democrats. At the same time, could it be true that they genuinely, earnestly didn't think he was endangered, even after he barely won in 2013?

I figured if they didn't see the race as competitive, then we would catch them by surprise and completely flat-footed. If the Republicans had sunk one million dollars into Bob's campaign and hit me with twenty negative pieces of mail and six weeks of negative TV/digital ads, would I have won? Possibly, though undoubtedly the margin would have been slimmer if I had. But that's just the thing: they didn't. On the one hand, Bob told *The Washington Post* in the July article that he had not "yet fully mounted his reelection campaign" but he wouldn't be "in cruise-control mode very much longer." On the other, the Republicans were on record saying that he would win and I would lose. That begs the question: Why bother getting involved in the race if you think it's a done deal? It's not like they had anything to bank that on: an out trans person had never run for office in Virginia before, so there wasn't an in-state A/B test for facing Transgender Candidate.

Yet in the same way women as a whole have been underestimated by men since the dawn of time—think of Ruth Bader Ginsberg graduating at the top of her class in law school and being unable to land a job afterward—so have been LGBTQ people broadly, and trans people specifically. Transgender people are immediately judged by our outward presence and gender expression to see if we fit into the societal standard for what counts as "passing" as the cisgender version of our gender identity. That judgment is cast upon us before anyone even learns about who we are as people. In my case, they knew I could raise money and knew some people would not take me seriously during the early summer—either out of force of habit or from sincerely believing that since no Democrat had defeated Bob before, then surely a trans woman wouldn't be the one to do it.

They underestimated me because I'm different and because they just assumed Bob would find a way to win, running the same campaign he always did.

The scoffing laugh John Whitbeck gave when talking about me to Tom Sherwood is such a great lesson to draw from, even beyond politics. Preconceived ideas of what makes up success may be based on trial and error, but the only way to break that cycle is to challenge it. We can't just assume that because "this is the way it's always been," it has to continue to be like that; we can choose to make ourselves vulnerable enough to be visible, to challenge the status quo, and to try something—or someone—different. Being different doesn't have to be a disadvantage; it can actually be *why* we succeed. Also, it really helps if the people who make up the majority—whether in politics, the boardroom, or anywhere else—are open-minded enough to hear us out and give us a shot. As Chris Abele told *The Washington Post* that August, "Every rights movement that has ever succeeded . . . succeeds precisely and only because it's not just the aggrieved who are active. . . . My world is a better place when people who are not like me have every right that I have."

In the midst of my general election, that very sentiment played itself out at the Prince William County School Board.

You may recall that around the time I was asked to run for office, I was much more focused on my activism work. For sixteen months, I had urged the Prince William County School Board to update their nondiscrimination policy to include sexual orientation and gender identity to protect LGBTQ students, faculty, staff, and really everyone at our local schools.

During the first hearing on the subject, the room was about evenly split between supporters and opponents of the policy change. In the meetings that followed, though, hundreds of opponents showed up, many with horrifying comments, keeping in mind that they were directing their ire toward LGBTQ kids, most of whom didn't speak. The opponents scared some members of our five-to-three Democratic majority on the school board from voting for the policy change, so they punted until the end of the school year. I had to talk and talk and talk to the members, all while campaigning during my primary, until we finally had the votes locked in.

The deciding vote came down to Democrat Justin Wilk. I had been so, so upset with him for being one of the people to change his stance—he had initially said he was in support, and then was one of the Dems who got scared off by the opposition.

Fast forward many months, and just five days before the school board finally voted, Justin wrote to me, "I should have supported this in the fall, but I needed time to do some research and learn more about the community."

Little did I know that Justin not only had a change of courage and mind, but he called all forty-one school districts larger than Prince William County to ask them if they had adopted nondiscrimination policies for sexual orientation and gender identity, to ask if there were any cases of transgender kids attacking someone or being attacked in a restroom since the adoption of their policies, or any cases of boys dressing up as girls to go into the girls' bathroom.

The night of the vote, with a lavender-colored tie over his white shirt and a purple rose on his light gray suit jacket lapel, Justin spoke for thirteen minutes at the microphone, revealing that 3,611,000 students attended schools in districts larger than Prince William County with sexual orientation and gender identity in their nondiscrimination policies.

"Zero trans attacks. Zero boys dressing up as girls," he said, to applause from all of us in purple shirts behind him.

Finally, 1.3 years after I started my advocacy on this issue (before running for elected office even felt like a real possibility), the five Democratic members held the line and voted yes. The three Republican-identified members voted no. The motion carried, five to three.

"The vote is five yes, three no," said the school board clerk. "Motion passed."

The room blew up in a round of "Woooo!" with applause and cheers and then all of us in purple shirts hugged, high-fived, and celebrated in the moment. I lost count of how many people I hugged, but Justin might have received just as many from people who approached the dais just to thank him for his speech. I hugged Ryan Sawyers so hard that we swayed back and forth, incredibly grateful for how bulletproof and resilient he had been through months of threats toward him and his family, all to stand up for LGBTQ kids.

When it was my turn to talk to Justin, I pointed to a group of out high school freshmen and told him, "See those kids right there? You just voted to make the next three years of their lives a little easier." I grabbed him by the shoulders to look him in the eye, just like Joe Biden had done to me two years earlier, and I gave him a lavender-colored, rubbery wrist band for equality.

Before I left, escorted out by my biker drummer and his biker family (as my safety wasn't guaranteed that night), I talked to a gay man from Manassas named Brian Pace. I first met him in 2006 when I covered a debate between him, as leader of Equality Prince William, and a social conservative activist, about marriage equality. Eleven years later, he had gotten married when marriage equality became the law of the land, a trans woman had won the Democratic nomination to represent him in the House of Delegates, and the school board had just approved a change to its nondiscrimination policy to welcome kids like us, who were too scared to reveal our true selves when we were their age.

In two sentences, reflecting on that moment we just witnessed and experienced together, we shared the stories of our lives.

"I wish we had a policy like this when we were their age," I said.

"Tonight we just became the advocates we never had," he replied.

That victory at the school board came eight days after I won the Democratic primary. It wasn't in a vacuum either: Bob Marshall was in attendance. He saw his side lose. He saw my side win. And yet after the vote, he was so confident that he would be returning to the House of Delegates that one of my supporters over-heard him say that he would fix it the next year in Richmond.

Ummm. . . . 'bout that.

That should have been the moment that freaked him out, caused him to kick his campaign into high gear, and made him understand that there had been a fundamental shift in Prince William County, in both politics and ideology. For the first time since the school board changed from appointed to elected, Democrats were in charge. And 1.5 years into their term with a five-to-three Dem majority, they made it clear that the governing policies of Prince William County weren't just for the Bob Marshalls of the town; they were for the Danica Roems and everyone else who was different from us, too. That change really started in 2005, when Lt. Gov. Tim Kaine as the Democratic gubernatorial nominee narrowly won Prince William County on his way to winning Virginia. Jim Webb carried it in 2006 when he won the U.S. Senate race, one of our state senate seats flipped red to blue in 2007, and then-senator Barack Obama and former governor Mark Warner won their races here in 2008 before Republicans took it back with all the statewide races in 2009.

There wasn't another statewide election in Virginia until 2012, but Democrats carried Prince William County then, too, as they did all three of our statewides in 2013. Our school board flipped Republican to Democrat in 2015 and the Democratic presidential ticket won in 2016. All of these should have been clues to someone, some-where, in Republican Land that all was not well for them and a cor-rective shift was about to take place that fall of 2017.

But not only did Bob Marshall not seriously campaign during the summer, other Republicans in the county seemed to be on the same path for their own reelection runs. One incumbent represent-ing Prince William transferred $170,000 toward the clerk of the court special election race he lost in April, lost anyway, and then kept doling out money: $36,000 to other Republican legislative candidates, including one $1,000 donation as late as October 25—two weeks before the election. He was so sure he was going to win, he closed the campaign with $31,000 still in his bank account—which wasn't even the highest among Republican incumbents who lost in Prince William County.

Democrats weren't just catching the Republicans flat-footed; we out-hustled, out-raised, out-worked, and out-campaigned them in every single metric. If there's a life lesson to draw from that, it's that it takes a village to elect a candidate.

A few famous types even helped us out in the general election, like the actor Mark Ruffalo, who urged people to get out the vote, the Funny or Die team who put together an amusing video featuring three House of Delegates Democratic candidates (Chris Hurst, Kathy Tran, and me) struggling through our campaigns as a way to ask for volunteers, and Will Butler of the band Arcade Fire, who shot a Facebook Live video with me at the Verizon Center in D.C. before one of their shows. Sure, we had some big names come to Manassas to launch canvasses or rally the troops, like former Texas state senator Wendy Davis and Tim Kaine. We had lots of help from a bunch of LGBTQ equality groups.

But above all, it was our organizers in Manassas, making thousands of phone calls to potential volunteers and voters. It was thousands upon thousands of small-dollar donors in Virginia and across the country pitching in $1 to $100 at a time. It was our Democratic-allied organizations that contributed thousands, or even tens of thousands, of dollars and rallied their volunteers. And it was just regular ol' trans people and other allies from across the commonwealth and even the East Coast, from middle schoolers to sixtysomethings, who stopped by Haymarket, Gainesville, Manassas, and Manassas Park to knock on doors for us just so they could help.

My own grit was always inspired by the incredible hustle of our organizers—one who saved the life of a suffocating baby he saw on the ground (Brad), one who got chased away from a house by a guy on his lawnmower (Quinn), one who got heckled with sexist comments by tween boys and absolutely was not having it (Jamie), and one who got so soaked in a flash flood that she had to run the heat in her car to dry out her socks and my campaign literature (Maria). They withstood every trauma nature and people alike could throw at them to complete their work, recruit volunteers to knock on more doors, and go back out the next day to keep it going. All the while, they told the story of who I was—a lifelong local resident and long-time local reporter running to fix Route 28, expand Medicaid, raise teacher pay, fight Dominion Energy, and make Virginia more inclusive. In turn, they jotted down the notes from their conversations at the doors and would send me emails telling me to call so-and-so because they had a question about fill-in-the-blank that only I could answer. Running a persuasion campaign in politics, or in any other field in life, is about that personal connection: really getting to understand what's important to someone else as they learn about what's important to you.

My supporters would relay back to us stories they were hearing from Bob and his team. It was particularly amusing to hear some of my gay supporters at different homes in Gainesville tell me Bob's campaign was asking for their votes . . . after he had written the constitutional amendment banning their right to marry the consenting adult of their choice. These were also strong Democrats, so we learned pretty quickly that the Republicans were either really bad at deciding which voters to talk to or genuinely believed strong

Democrats—people who donated to my campaign and volunteered for us—were going to see the light and come around to Bob in his twenty-sixth year in office. Their data was bad, if not their entire strategy, which was even more amplified when the American Principles Project started sending anti-trans robocalls into the district to help him and hurt me.

Then, during the closing weeks of the campaign, our October surprise hit: Bob's campaign had found a video I very, very much knew was on YouTube of my band's 2012 music video for the song "Thrash Mob" and a 2009 video interview my bandmates and I did before one of our shows at Jaxx, when I was an absolutely hammer-smashed-shitfaced twenty-four-year-old trying to make it big in the metal world.

I could have prevented the "Thrash Mob" video from getting out, but there was nothing I could do about the interview. Before I launched the campaign, I called my buddy Greg who had interviewed us and asked if he could pull it from his YouTube channel. He told me that it had been eight years; try and try as he might, he couldn't get the login and password info to work. I told him I would just have to take that one to the face and prepared for impact, knowing that sooner or later, me lifting up my shirt, twirling my index finger around my nipple, and sticking my tongue out at my guitarist would probably end up in a TV ad.

Spoiler: It did.

You know what else did? Something I dismissed at the time as "ehhh" in late 2016 but which became a *Washington Post* headline on October 25, 2017: "Marshall Ad Accuses Roem of 'Lewd Behavior' in Old Video of Her Band."

So okay: I got some 'splaining to do. That summer day in 2012, I had started my morning in Hot Springs in rural Bath County along the West Virginia border four hours from home to cover a U.S. Senate debate between Tim Kaine and George Allen. I was the first reporter to file my story afterward (woo!) and then I hit the road to drive up to the northernmost county of Virginia (Loudoun) to film my parts for my band's first-ever music video. Given that the song "Thrash Mob" is literally a pun I made up from "flash mob," which was kind of a thing at the time, I figured we needed a stupid video to go with a stupid track from our yet-unreleased second album. (Which would come out . . . five years later. Ooof.) So my friend Joe Ciomek and his cameraman Justin came in from Ohio and we shot this thing at Ball's Bluff Tavern, the dive bar in downtown Leesburg that I mentioned earlier.

We loved the Bluff, and the Bluff's management let us do pretty much whatever we wanted. So, for the video, I figured each of the five members of the band could be caught doing something funny in various scenes in between clips of us rocking out to the music on our instruments. We got a bunch of friends to come in as extras, but not everything went as planned, so the team had to improvise. First, our lead guitarist, Enock, started a two-man mosh pit that got him thrown out of the bar; then our rhythm guitarist Chris got abducted from his work as a chef and got hauled out over the top of a bunch of dudes' heads; our bassist Davis stuffed one of our friends into the back of an old-ass SUV, and our drummer Jacob acted as the getaway driver, complete with his I R DRUMR Virginia license plate.

Alas, we needed something to close out for yours truly. Our original plan was for someone to open a closet door and I would come pouring out,* passing out on top of a bunch of empty bottles. Well, we lacked the closet or the bottles, so we had to think of something

---

*A little on the nose.

else. We talked it out and settled on four of our friends and me hiding in a bathroom stall with bandmates outside the door, wondering what was causing all the commotion on the other side.

The door opens and out comes the first guy . . . then the first woman . . . then the second woman . . . as the band gets more confused . . . then the second guy . . . annnnd then there's me, band aghast with their hands up in the air as I slowly wiped the corner of my mouth, flicked my wrist, and walked out with a bottle of PBR in hand. Hilarious! Or something like that.

Well, so I thought at the time. And, hey, that was all in good fun, just a stupid piece of Cab Ride Home history that was entirely and exclusively designed to make our friends laugh. That's all we wanted out of that video. We never expected it to take off, to land us a record deal or anything. We just wanted to bring the funny—and we did. So when I had to decide whether to contact Joe before the start of the campaign to pull the damn thing from YouTube, I thought, "Nahhh . . . keep it. It's funny and who cares?"

Well, turns out, the Republican Party of Virginia, Friends of Bob Marshall, and *The Washington Post* cared, as noted in the fourth and fifth paragraphs: "The snippet shows an unidentified man leaving a bathroom stall, which in the full music video is part of a scene that is suggestive of people having oral sex. Although that context is not clear in Marshall's campaign ad, John Findlay, the executive director of the Virginia Republican Party, criticized Roem on Wednesday 'for being featured in a video where it is clearly implied she performed group oral sex in a public restroom.'

"'That behavior is shocking and her appearance in the video in that role is the definition of bad judgement on Danica's part,' Findlay said in an email."

Whoa, whoa, whoaaaa there! Time-out!

First: "Implied"?! I was pretty direct there, John. And second: Ohh, please. As I told the *Post*, that scene was the equivalent of a spit take on *The Daily Show* or *Saturday Night Live*. I was an entertainer. I entertained. I did ~~who~~ what I set out to do.

As much fun as I had responding to that attack, the reality was it did turn into a distraction. We started bickering it out in the press. In September, Bob said to a reporter at my former newspaper, "Why do you call Danica a woman? Did Danica's DNA change?" In response, my campaign released a thirty-second digital ad called "Inspire," which was meant to be about LGBTQ kids seeing themselves represented through my campaign and election. It was a sweet ad and it showed me taking my hormone prescriptions and applying makeup before cutting to three smiling teenagers outside. You know . . . rising above his bullshit. The problem was, I was told that I had taken my eye off the ball and was making the race about my gender and *blah blah blah*, never mind that Bob could say whatever he wanted that was insulting toward trans people but if I defended our existence, then it was my problem, not his.

In a way, the warning I was getting was that playing on his field would allow him to control the narrative of the race. When Bob's "Bad Judgement" ad (yes, they spelled "judgment" as "judgement" when it first ran online, which a Libertarian friend of mine happily noted in the comments) aired, I started unloading on him over some of his greatest hits, like supporting government-mandated transvaginal ultrasounds. Engaging in that food fight made it clear to everyone but me that I was distracted from my main messages.

My TV ads and direct mail, however, were exactly on message, hitting what we wanted, especially Bob's vote against Medicaid expansion, where we featured a sixty-two-year-old woman from Prince William County who his vote had left uninsured. My positive ad was a piece that I narrated with a specific mention of my reporting that unveiled Amazon as the owner of a controversial data center in Haymarket at a time when Dominion Energy refused to disclose it.

But it wasn't until I saw a comment from a former Haymarket town council member, who I used to cover for the newspaper, that I realized that I wasn't, in fact, staying on message. She said she didn't want to vote for either of us at that point. I called her and she told me that, look, she'd vote for me, but I had to remember why I got into this race in the first place. It wasn't about fighting with Bob over stupid shit, like what videos I did with my band.

She asked me to re-center and figure out my message during the final week and a half of the campaign. I knew right then and there that she was right. In the *Washington Post* story, I hadn't even mentioned Route 28. I was so consumed with calling out Bob's hypocrisy and BS on social media that I wasn't emphasizing my own plans to make people's commutes better. I decided from that point onward, every day for the remainder of the campaign, I would write about Route 28. Bob had declined an invitation to debate me, so it's not like we were going to have a single moment that could alter the race. I just needed to focus on *my* message and *my* story, not on responding to Bob's message and Bob's story.

The thing about telling your own story is that, even when you think you've repeated it ad infinitum and it seems like a pleasant distraction to talk about someone else, campaigns come down to how you can make people's lives better, which means authentically being yourself, not responding to what other people want you to be or think you should be. When you stop letting other people control your narrative and you focus on who you are, what matters to you, and why it's important to share that with other people, then you're going to have a lot more moments when you can unlock your own potential and inspire other people.

That became clearer and clearer as we refocused our message. And there was one overriding theme about understanding who I was up against: it was that Bob was Bob. No matter how much time he spent away from the camera—which was highly unusual for him and a sign he was scared of the coverage he was receiving—one thing would remain certain: "He just can't help himself."

I said that refrain over and over until everyone understood why. It didn't matter how disciplined he would try to be. When all was said and done, he was going to say something bigoted, whether it was transphobic or homophobic. It was just going to happen.

Questioning my DNA was definitely a mistake on his part, given that it helped with my fundraising and earned him some bad press. Where he really, truly threw away the race, though, was when, with about a week to go, I received a mailer from him—because his targeting was *that* good—with quotes I had given to a conservative talk-radio show host about what age it would be appropriate to talk to kids about other kids who are transgender. The radio host was trying to pin me down on this, trying to get me to say that I would "teach transgenderism to kindergartners," when the reality is that, to me, if there's a trans kid in your class, of course there's an age-appropriate way for students to learn to be nice and respectful toward one another. Nothing wrong with that.

Bob's campaign, however, saw a lot wrong with that, and he sent out a negative mailer with the transcript from that interview.

There was just one wee little catch.

He titled it "Danica Roem in His Own Words."

His.

That, my friends, is a transphobic red alert: Raise *all* the money, stat! Get reporters on the line! Brew the tea! Pick up the doughnuts! Let's go, go, goooo, people!

With five days to go until Election Day, he just couldn't help himself.

Sure enough, NBC–Washington reporter Julie Carey came to town to do a story on the mailer. She needed some B-roll to go along with it, so a videographer followed me going door to door in a wooded area in my home precinct after Julie sat down for an interview with me in our campaign headquarters. My team and I made sure to place my purple-print-on-white yard sign behind my left shoulder for effect. My journalism training—call it home field advantage—also informed me that at most, I was going to get fifteen seconds of actual speaking time on camera for this story, so I better make the most of it.

"My legislative focus is what's on this sign, right here," I said, extending my left hand backward to my "Fix Route 28 Now!" slogan. "Because Delegate Marshall won't do it, he hasn't done it, and he can't."

Over and over during that interview, I pointed to that sign, knowing that it made for good television—y'know, motion and all—along with a few sharp barbs that didn't detract from my main message. They were all based on job performance and the issues, which was exactly the contrast we wanted in a story that highlighted not one but two transphobic mailers sent out by the opposition. The other mailer Julie covered had a black background and was headlined in all caps with scaaaary red font, TRANSITIONING TO FEMALE, to make sure everyone knew I was trans.

Egads! Transgender Candidate is transgender!

"When Delegate Marshall realized that he cannot win on public policy issues—on traffic, jobs, schools, and health care—he resorted to trash," I said, instantly realizing that that sentence would make it on air the second it came out of my mouth.

The closing of our news story from Julie was far more devastating for Bob than our negative TV ad could have ever been. As she walked up a street in Old Town Manassas with Republican campaign yard signs, Julie said the two sentences that marked the unofficial end of Bob's twenty-six years in office: "We can't tell you what Bob Marshall had to say about the controversy. Until this campaign, he's always been very willing to do on-camera interviews with me, but he declined our request to talk about that campaign mailer and he declined a chance to debate his opponent."

I have to break down what just happened here, because it was so important: Julie Carey, one of, if not *the* most respected veteran TV news journalists in the D/M/V, on the highest-rated local newscast in the region, said at 6:10 P.M. on a Thursday—aka dinnertime, when people would be looking up at the television—that not only was Bob ducking her questions, but he was ducking debates, too.

Both were completely accurate. In fact, Bob had ducked a number of press requests toward the end of the campaign, leading Michael Pope from the Virginia affiliate of NPR to quite literally play the sound of crickets chirping in lieu of a response from Bob on a story about Route 28 and then call him out again for declining an interview about the mailers.

Meanwhile, Julie's ninety-second story ended up airing three times between that night and the next morning, and our TV ads were running within minutes of that story without any response from Bob. A political coroner could have described it as unrecoverable blunt-force trauma to my predecessor's campaign.

We couldn't have asked for a better on-air closing message. On the ground, our entire campaign shifted to the field for the last weekend of Get Out the Vote (GOTV). We had so many volunteers show up that we sent them to canvass every priority area in the entire district. I personally spent the entire day before the election until 8:30 P.M.—my personal cutoff time for knocking on doors—hitting every door I could in Sudley precinct.

That night, my team assembled our yard signs to distribute at all eighteen polling locations, I gave a pep talk caught on camera by a documentary crew from *Vice*, and we all left to get a couple of hours of sleep before closing out the campaign that Tuesday in the rain. I started the day in Gainesville at the precinct most likely to have the highest voter turnout and where I was likely to do my poorest (Heritage Hunt), trying to win over any voters I could since we couldn't knock on doors in that gated community, and one of my volunteers was kind enough to give me a rain jacket as the afternoon storm came in.

I drove home to vote and cracked a smile seeing my name on the general election ballot, as the reality of the moment set in that it was going to be a very, very good day. I changed clothes, and because I was personally broke as hell and didn't own any boots other than some mangled high-lift ones left over from college eleven years ago, I slipped my feet into plastic shopping bags, slipped those into my Mary Jane shoes, and headed back out the door, stopping by a few precincts before ending the campaign in the pouring rain and wind at Tyler Elementary School in Gainesville.

"Where do you stand on the tolls?" one man asked me as he walked up the stairs to enter the school.

I told him I was opposed to adding tolls to Interstate 66 because it's a public road our tax dollars already paid for, so we shouldn't have to pay twice to use it, and that we shouldn't sell our public roadways for private profit. He nodded, then headed inside, and when he came back out, he told me he voted for a straight Republican ticket "until I got to you."

You never know how those conversations are going to go—and, even at that point, in the era of Donald Trump, some split-ticket, swing voters still very much existed. People just need to be present for the conversation, to connect with them. Sure, they're like finding a needle in a haystack or an actual bottle of Myers's in a rum cake, but that doesn't mean their vote is worth any less than a committed partisan.

For those of you campaigning: Any time that you can get on broadcast television for reasons that don't involve your own personal scandals, take it. You're able to introduce yourself and your message to a lot of people for free, and quickly. Then make yourself present and accessible, not just to reporters but to the public, so everyone who wants to talk to you has that opportunity. It puts a personality to the character someone just saw as a bunch of animated pixels on a television in their living room.

For everyone else: Someone attacking you for being you doesn't have to be the last word. There are lots of ways to flip the script; find a way to make that negativity work for you. What is the flaw or weakness in what someone's doing to you? How do you exploit that to turn the argument around and come out better for it, if still bruised and scarred? You may not get that opportunity often, and sometimes the hurt is real and there's nothing much in the moment you can do to make it better, because punching someone in the face or burying them under a pile of bricks is, generally speaking, frowned upon. But how it governs your day-to-day actions afterward is, to an extent, up to you, through how you choose to process that information. Will you let it break you down? Or will you never let the bastards grind ya down?

I chose not to let it personally affect me. I chose to be functionally dead inside when it came to attacks on my gender, which my career in journalism absolutely made possible from spending more than a decade writing about tragedies and being able to detach and disassociate myself from the horror of what I was covering so I could process it, turn it into a news story, and get that information out to the public while still being able to either sleep that night or go to band rehearsal or yoga practice or . . . whatever other outlet worked for me.

It's your choice to make.

SHOWTIME

**DOES DANICA ROEM WANT A STAR ON THE
HOLLYWOOD WALK OF FAME?**

Danica Roem promised to work for US, but is too busy
being famous.

*—Mail advertisement, paid for by the Republican Party of
Virginia, authorized by Kelly McGinn, candidate for
Delegate, 2019*

Okay, I have a pretty good idea why you bought, borrowed, and/or stole this book. I'm sure the self-help reflections, policy dives on Route 28, stories about now-president Joe Biden, all my coming-out shit, and seeing a book written by a politician with a lot of cuss words in it are all endearing and nice touches—the cherry on top of your politics sundae. And hell, if you're an opposition researcher digging up dirt on me, I've made your job the easiest ten thousand you'll ever make.

But now, I'll finally address *the* question, the one you've flipped through chapter after chapter to get to with bated breath since I alluded to it earlier.

So—finally—here it is:

"What's Demi Lovato like in person?!"

::*exhales*::

Well . . .

Actually, they're pretty chill. Demi invited me to be their guest at the American Music Awards less than two weeks after my election in 2017 in order to highlight the anti-bullying messaging they were promoting in their song "Sorry Not Sorry." I literally didn't know who Demi Lovato was and came to learn quickly that their videos on YouTube have been viewed *billions* of times—plural with a *b*. The heavy metal rock I live under is quite cozy, I must say. Anyway, because I didn't know who they were, I had no desire to fly out to Los Angeles for some television show I've never watched, but their management staff persisted anyway and I relented because what they were asking for was clearly a good thing: promoting an anti-bullying message to millions upon millions of people across the country who rarely, if ever, see trans people positively represented in their day-to-day lives. So out I flew to Los Angeles.

When Demi stopped by my hotel room, we just talked about metal bands for a bit—they like deathcore, I like melodic death—and I showed them my campaign's "Inspire" video with the three LGBTQ teens and me taking my hormones. They thought it was powerful, which I'm sure my TV guy, Scott Kozar, is loving as he reads this right now. Congrats, Scott. You won.

Other than that, the coolest thing about Demi was that their presence instantly made me stop feeling like a fish out of water who absolutely didn't belong on a red carpet, let alone with a hair and makeup team and a guy asking me which gown I wanted to wear for the evening. When Demi walked in, the part of my brain that had shadowed politicians for day-in-the-life stories took over and I thought, "If this is how I feel now, imagine how Demi must feel all the time under the constant spotlight. If Demi can do this, so can you." Surely my D-list celebrity self could keep up with just an ounce of the pressure they're under day in and day out on the A list, where every time you set foot in public, someone's taking a photo or has something to say about your weight, sexuality, or whatever else makes them feel better about themselves.

All of that said, I didn't run for office to rub shoulders with famous people, have my photo taken a bajillion times, or to be asked "who" I'm wearing.* When I was on the red carpet, I said on camera, "I just want to be a good delegate. I just want to fix Route 28." Of course, I ran for office to fix a road that I can't stand and to unseat someone who didn't get the job done because he was too busy filing bathroom bills and other discriminatory legislation. At the same time, if having a national profile means I can use it to elevate issues in the district or inspire other people to use their voice, run for office, or just see that someone like them cares, then, yeah, I'm going to use it. It's not every day that a transgender metalhead reporter stepmom gets to set the tone for the day.

The rush of visibility that ensued was just awkward. I didn't like being in front of paparazzi at all. I much preferred to talk to the techs and crew in black shirts—the people who are meant to make things happen without being seen or seen as little as possible. I had no interest in soaking up anything and felt super self-conscious when I had to flash a plastic smile for dozens of photographers, having no idea how much my transness would stick out like a sore thumb next to someone as unbelievably gorgeous, professional, and stoic as Demi Lovato. I could handle the job; after all, no matter how famous or what occupation someone may have, at the end of the day events like that are still just a collection of people and it's not (entirely) hard to just be nice to people for a night.

I saw a ton of people writing about Demi and me later that night on Twitter and Facebook and a few news articles to go along with it. I also called one of our local reporters back home from the red carpet—the only press I talked to beyond E! and the AMA hosts in separate interviews—just to make sure our Prince William County

---

*There is only one good answer: "The last person who asked me that."

journalists always knew that no matter where in the community or even the country I would be, they could always talk to me, and that the reporters who serve my constituents always come first for press.

I had also been invited to go on Comedy Central's *The Opposition with Jordan Klepper* the same night as the first day of orientation. I've been watching *The Daily Show* since I was in middle school, so there was no way I was going to pass up that chance. The host, who satirized right-wing conspiracy theorist Alex Jones, made his name as a correspondent for *The Daily Show* and now had the show that directly followed it.

I flew from Richmond to New York and I can't lie: *The* most fun I had in 2017 outside of skipping out to see Metallica one night during my primary was being at the taping of that show. Not only was Jordan super gracious, funny, and kind, but so were his staff. In fact, in the greenroom, *I* was the one making *them* laugh. I felt so at home so quickly that I knew Jordan could take a joke. Typically, during comedy shows like this one, the host is the one who makes most of the jokes because, I mean, that's literally their job. But I couldn't resist. It was too fun. When he said on-camera that we both had something in common in that we had a beef with *The New York Times* because they ran a column that labeled me as "boring" (it was meant to be a compliment), I responded, "I don't know at what point in American culture a transgender, metalhead, journalist, stepmom, vegetarian became boring, but guilty as charged . . ." to a round of laughs and cheers from the audience, who had greeted me with such ferocity when Jordan introduced me that I turned to him and said, "I think you just lost your job."

After my interview with Jordan—which various heavy metal news outlets shared immediately because I name-dropped Richmond thrash band Municipal Waste repeatedly—we both ended up telling jokes to the crowd and playing off each other's banter.

Jordan rolled with the punches and was just so much fun to be around. After the show, he even took photos with everyone who attended—including a big group shot with staffers from the LGBTQ group GLAAD. I later visited the people in the Comedy Central control room who actually did the online editing and got the show ready to go up on the web, since a friend of mine from St. Bonaventure—who loaded me up on so much Earl Grey tea that night that, nearly 3.5 years later, I'm *still* drinking it as I write this—worked there at the time. (Cheers, Justina. A highly caffeinated "good morning" to you as well.)

After the show, I made a horrible decision to take an overnight Greyhound bus from New York City to Richmond since I couldn't catch a return flight. I can't sleep while seated upright and was up the entire night, all eight or ten hours or however the hell long it was. I think I ended up missing like an hour or so of orientation, but it wasn't a big deal. At least I had tea. Lots and lots of it.

After all the pressure of the previous ten months, I was in my element and sincerely felt like I could actually show people a side of myself that doesn't always come out during interviews. I could just have fun and make people laugh while also talking about important policy issues. Try as the Republicans have for the last three campaigns to brand me as a conceited celebrity—the 2019 mailer that had my face on the Hollywood Walk of Fame was really a nice touch—I really just like being around people and living out an authentic experience.

Returning from Jordan's show, I was ready to get to work. I ran for office because I cared deeply about my community, understood the challenges people faced, and knew how to make things better. It was time to jump in.

As of this writing, I've been elected to my third term in office, and I'm entering my fifth General Assembly session since I was sworn in on January 10, 2018. I've been elected, reelected, and re-reelected. I've attended more than thirty local town halls and earned enough respect from my colleagues for them to pass—and the governor to sign—twenty-three of my bills into law, and that doesn't include resolutions and budget amendments. Also, I'm good at constituent service, especially with my constituents who have a little bit of flair.

Behind the scenes, any success I could possibly have made came because my chief of staff, Gigi Slais, was as determined as I was, if not even more so, to make me present with my best foot forward. Whereas hiring Ethan Damon to manage my first two campaigns was the best decision I made on the politics side, hiring Gigi to run my legislative office was the best decision I could have ever made on the policy side. She had volunteered extensively on my 2017 campaign from our first canvass launch in January until the end of election night in November. She also had worked in two congressional offices and on a couple campaigns, so she could think about the facts and text of a bill in terms of its policy impact while also understanding the politics of it, both in Richmond and in greater Prince William County.

For all of the dozens of bills I've had to present in front of subcommittees, committees, the House and Senate floors, and back home to constituents in the district, Gigi worked around the clock from the end of 2017 through early 2021 to make sure that I was prepared while also ensuring that our office kicked ass at constituent service. When a woman along Maplewood Drive in Yorkshire asked me in her living room if I'd like blueberry-flavored Earl Grey tea, I accepted. She had reached out to me on Facebook, asking to meet me to discuss the difficulty she has making a left turn from her house when going toward work. My favorite Queen song shortly thereafter cued up on her sound system as we discussed Route 28 over a bowl of fruit and caffeinated happiness in her decades-old, two-story house in an area where time seemed to have stood still. We chitchatted for a bit—about Freddie Mercury, her dogs—before getting down to what else: Route 28. "You have to do something about people blocking traffic!" she told me. One of the things I've learned about myself since being in office is that I don't put forth different character traits to different people as some expression of disingenuity and trying to be all things to all people. It's about recognizing that I'm a multifaceted person who wants to meet others where they are.

That is something we seem to have forgotten about as a population: It's possible to be several things at the same time. You can think different thoughts and hold different identities and be fascinated by different things all at once. It doesn't make you weak or distracted; it makes you human.

Long before I was elected, I tried to be the person I thought others wanted me to be, regardless of whether it was genuine. I finally had enough and transitioned. But that doesn't mean that the part of me that in the moment viscerally enjoyed the spotlight and attention for making people laugh has died. It's just . . . evolved into a different role, starring a thirty-seven-year-old middle-class stepmom who still likes to put on a show, as long as she can still make time for striking a Warrior II pose between sips of kombucha.

That was the attitude I took to my first term in the Virginia General Assembly. As you might know, freshmen legislators and mistakes go together like peanut butter and mayonnaise, or metal forks and electrical outlets. There's going to be a mess; the question is just to what extent. My first two years in power were like that, and I'll tell you the highlights here: good (expanding Medicaid to six hundred thousand people!); bad (I didn't get a single bill passed my first session—turns out it's hard to pass a bill with a Republican majority when you represent a swing seat); and ugly (remind me to tell you about the time an older Republican colleague tried to save my soul outside the state capitol . . .).

Anyway, just because I got elected doesn't mean my flaws, weaknesses, and eccentricities have gone away. I'm still me, just with a nice, shiny member pin on my shirt and a reputation for being a lady beast (beastess?) at constituent service.

AS A MEMBER of the House Democratic Caucus for two years when we were in the minority for the 2018 and 2019 sessions, I learned a lot of lessons from the more senior members about how to make a presentation and how to interact with Republican members in the majority.

Del. Sam Rasoul told me a story about how during his first bill presentation in subcommittee, he was so nervous he fainted at the microphone. He made some self-deprecating joke the next time he presented in order to save face.

Four weeks into my first session, I had watched Del. Eileen Filler-Corn, the future Speaker of the House, present a bill in subcommittee about offering tax credits for people who purchase gun safes. You would figure combining the two things Virginia Republicans love the most—tax breaks and guns—would be a gimme for the five-to-three Republican majority on that subcommittee but nope: it died, five to three. That showed me that being a Democrat, let alone one from diverse Northern Virginia, automatically bred suspicion. As one Republican member said to Democrats on the House floor about gun policy: "We don't trust you."

I realized quickly that getting things done would not be so easy in a Republican-held statehouse. I found out from two of my colleagues—including one Republican—that I was on something called the "kill list," which the Republicans made of Democratic freshmen from swing districts whose bills they would try to "kill," or defeat, no matter what.

It wasn't hard to figure out why I made the cut for their list: sure, I defeated one of their members who annoyed their caucus so much with his homophobic antics that some of the members actually thanked me in private for winning. But killing my bills was also the easiest way to ensure that I wasn't going to come home with policy victories that I could use during my reelection campaign.

One Republican, who wasn't a member of the legislature but had been elected a few times to municipal government, told me to watch out for the telltale signs that then-delegate Greg Habeeb was going to kill my bill in subcommittee. When Habeeb particularly hated a bill, he would rub his hands over his head, talk to whoever was around him, and then stand up and walk somewhere—assuming he wouldn't just jump in to annihilate it outright. During one particular rough patch when I was in front of the Rules Committee, I watched that play out on my resolutions for fixing Route 28 and reevaluating an extension of the Virginia Railway Express commuter train's Manassas Line.

I was totally unprepared for being so stonewalled. Not only was I not getting things done, but even worse, I had constituents crying in my arms—people who had driven hours to advocate for things important to them. Those moments will stick with me forever, and will be among the most difficult to experience—and they will also serve as motivation throughout my career.

The most heartbreaking one was a resolution I brought requesting all school staff be trained to recognize the signs of suicidal ideation in students. It wasn't even a mandate: it didn't require funding and schools didn't have to do it. It was just something important to one of my Manassas constituents, Kim Fleming, who had outlived her son, David J. Cobb. She brought a picture of him to the committee room for her testimony so that the members would have to look at his image as they decided the fate of the resolution in his honor. It didn't matter: they murmured their sympathies to her, then voted it down on a party-line vote, four to three, leaving my constituent crying in my arms outside of the meeting room.

This part of my job is particularly wrenching. During my first session, I presented six pieces of legislation that my constituents had driven nearly two hours to Richmond to support, only to see them go down in flames. Each time I had to watch it occur to my constituents that the thing they were advocating for just wasn't going to happen—that their hopes were in the process of being dashed. Each time I watched as tears welled up in their eyes and their voices cracked, and all I could do was be present with them.

One was when my first bill to eliminate school-meal debt shaming went down on a party line and my constituent from Gainesville, who had spent six hours writing the bill, watched it evaporate before her eyes. As I hugged her, she said she felt like she had failed all those kids. (That story has a happy ending, though: over the next three years, we broke it down piece by piece and passed most of it as individual bills among the eight total school-meals bills of mine that the governor signed into law from 2019 to 2021. If at first you don't succeed . . . make it bite-sized.)

Another constituent from Manassas, who had lost her dominant right arm below the elbow to an amputation, shed similar tears when my bill to mandate that health insurers cover the cost of mechanical prosthetic devices went down in front of her on a party-line five-to-three vote. Even though the bill wouldn't have guaranteed outright that she would get the technological equivalent of a new arm, it would have at least increased her chances. That's a tough one to watch die once, let alone three sessions in a row.

Finally, there was the one bill that died such a brutal death that it was the only one I lost a Democratic member on during my freshman term. It was a bill to allow people who sue regulated monopolies to tap into a special fund to help cover their legal costs. That was meant to even the playing field for citizens who don't have bottomless pockets against multibillion-dollar corporations that can afford armies of high-priced attorneys. During the hearing for the bill, one of my witnesses was so upset because of the questioning from one of the Republican members—who happened to sit directly next to Greg Habeeb—that she bolted out the door as I was presenting it. I, of course, had been focusing on the committee members and not who was entering or exiting, so when I later turned around to motion to her as part of my testimony . . . she was gone. I later found her outside in the hall and, for the fourth time, I held someone whose tears ended up drying on my dress.

Some lessons, the veteran members teach you through their own experiences. Other lessons, you find out on your own. They didn't teach you how to handle constituents crying in your arms during freshman orientation. Of all the training programs I had gone through since November 2016, none of them started with "You're in for an exciting treat because today we're going to talk about . . . real-time emotional devastation! Here's what to do when the people who put their faith and trust in you to carry their legislation have their hearts ripped out of their chests because you're a swing-seat freshman who's new to the job and the majority doesn't want to give you any wins! Really, you're going to want to learn the cradle hug technique. . . ."

Being a reporter covering the gruesome deaths of children—among others—taught me how to "let the robot take over" so I could separate my feelings from the job and look at it much more methodically than emotionally. Being a legislator is different, though, because doing the job well means you aren't a neutral, dispassionate, third-party observer. You are fighting for things you believe in, and you actually emotionally invest yourself in it. So when I was just completely dour after my sixth bill in a row went down during my 0 for 15 first session, whatever semblance of a poker face I had was gone by the time Del. Kathleen Murphy spotted me pouting on the second floor of the Pocahontas Building near the elevators.*

She quite literally pulled me aside and, ever the mother of adult children, looked me dead in the eye and told me, "Don't you *ever* let them see you like this! They'll eat you alive!"

I learned real quick: buck up, freshman. Welcome to Richmond.

That said, the first lesson legislators in Richmond tell you is "Don't fall in love with your bills." That one is universal from the veteran members, who know from experience how easy it is to get emotionally crushed when some (or all) of what you're carrying ends up on the cutting-room floor. The second most important lesson I learned came from Del. Lashrecse Aird, a Democrat from Peters-

---

*Kathleen also once saw me walking in the same hallway while wearing a sweater with holes down my arm. She tugged on that and snapped, "No!" before giving me a lesson in the aesthetics of power: how a blazer, even though I hated wearing them, conveyed seriousness while whatever the fuck I was wearing conveyed, "It's okay to talk down to me." She's as real as anyone you'll ever meet.

burg (south of Richmond) who had been the youngest member of the
House of Delegates but had years of experience serving as the legislative assistant for a now-former state senator.

She told my freshman class that if the first time she hears us talk
about our bill is in committee, then it's basically dead on arrival. You
have to network; you have to approach the legislators on the committee before your bill comes up to work out any concerns they might
have *before* your presentation. If you wait until you're in front of them
and you're a member of the minority party, all it takes is one person
to speak against your bill for the majority to have a reason to kill
it—and sometimes they'll kill it no matter who speaks in favor of it
or against it.

During my first session, a photo circulated of a Republican committee member who didn't guard his papers at the dais. Before the
hearing had even started, he had already written down which bills
would be allowed to pass and which he would kill, specifically marking a bill by a red-to-blue freshman, Del. Debra Rodman, for death
before she even presented it. That was the first bit of evidence that
the kill list was really a thing and not just something people who
don't get their bills passed say to make themselves feel better.

When you're in the legislature, your training mainly involves
procedure, written and unwritten rules about the General Assembly,
and where stuff is located. Really, though, it's just a chance to bond
with your fellow freshmen-elect. It's one of the few times where all
of you as freshmen, regardless of party, are in the same room at the
same time and are the center of attention instead of the veteran
members. Go figure that the first person I clicked with was a Republican woman elected on the same day I was who was just four
months older than me. My initial worry about whether Republican
women would flip out at me for using the women's room dissipated

when we ended up chatting, going to the restroom at the same time, and keeping up the conversation . . . twice. (Extroverts: we will find a way!)

If you're a member of the minority, you're expected to criticize the majority. But if you go too far, they will let you know in a heartbeat the error of your ways with full force. That's one of the lessons I learned from Del. Marcus Simon. Before my election, when the Republicans still had a two-to-one majority, he had managed to piss off the majority so much that they passed by every Democratic bill on the docket for the day as a warning not to mess with them like that again. Likewise, when we took over the majority in 2020 and one of the Republican members talked a bunch of shit online, his bills went down one after the next after the next.

Being in the minority caucus will teach you quickly what to do and not do. After the Republicans killed all my bills my first year, I genuinely tried to turn things around the following session by talking to Republican members about my bills in their home districts. It's hard to make the "we're killing your bills because we want to win back your seat" argument when someone drives 3.5 hours to meet up with you. And, as I learned in my career in journalism and on the campaign trail, when you personally connect with someone and explain why the issue you're talking about matters to them, you can change minds.

So that's what I did, stopping by two delegates' offices in one morning in Virginia Beach during the 2018 midterms right before the election, to work on my shield law bill to protect reporters and on another bill to make it easier for parents to apply for free and reduced-price school meals for their kids online. I then drove to Suffolk to spend time with a third Republican colleague—the one who I'd bonded with when we were elected on the same day—which was not only enjoyable but key in one other way: when you get along with someone, you're more likely to give them the benefit of the doubt on a bill you're fifty-fifty on. In time, the delegate who voted against my shield law (before helping me add one sentence to it) became the biggest Republican proponent of it in 2019 before we finally passed it in 2020, simply because we gave each other the chance to actually listen.

The delegate who helped me with my school-meals bill also helped me to pass it in 2019, marking the first of my eight school-meals bills to be signed into law and the only successful one from when I was in the minority. And the delegate who just hung out with me at her wine shop until after closing was the only Republican to vote for my bill to allow restaurants to participate in the federal Restaurant Meals Program, which basically just allows SNAP recipients to use their benefits to purchase hot, prepared meals. Every single interaction with someone whose support I was trying to earn taught me—over and over again—that it's the personal connection that changes minds.

As it turned out, that advice from Lashrecse was the one thing missing in 2018, and that's because I, ever the weird combination of extroverted loner, didn't take the time to get to know members of the majority on a personal level. While part of the job is reviewing legislation on the merits, it's absolutely true that you're more likely to be given the benefit of the doubt when someone's undecided about whether to advance your legislation if that legislator actually knows you well enough to trust you.

My team did everything they possibly could to make sure I had sound, structured arguments for my legislation and a ton of support from constituents and advocates for my bills. Gigi had worked so hard all four sessions that she spent running the ship for me in Richmond and back in the district, making sure I was prepared to answer every question for every bill in committee. We had enough staffers to field a basketball team when most delegates had only one or two, with my scheduler Maria Salgado—who had joined the policy team from my 2017 campaign team—taking on the excruciating task of making sure I actually arrived where I needed to be as a consummate late person. In Richmond, if you're five minutes late for a committee meeting, then you've already missed roll call and perhaps presentations of a bill or two as well, so there's little room for error. In fact, Maria did a solid enough job that Del. Paul Krizek ended up hiring her as his chief of staff.

So while my team was working on hyperdrive to keep me focused, what I didn't appreciate at the time was that the best thing I could have done to help my own cause was just to talk to my colleagues on the House floor beyond those seated in my immediate vicinity. Members would walk from one side of the chamber to the other to talk—literally across the aisle!—until the Speaker smacked his gavel to get them to shut up when they were too loud. I, however, mostly stayed in my seat. No one was seeking out the freshman in the middle of the second row for a chat by the windows in the back, and whether I wanted to believe it or not, I was too nervous to start those conversations myself during my first year.

By my second year, that changed. I was ready to come out of my shell.

During my childhood, I loved playing chess and memorizing the statistics on the back of baseball cards. I wasn't actually good at playing sports, but I at least had a sharp mind for the rules of the games, looking a couple moves ahead, and learning about the subject, if for no other reason than to compensate for my lack of ability. Growing up as my New York Italian mother's child, I spent my whole life debating before I was elected. I never doubted my ability to hold my own against a Republican in a campaign because . . . who was going to come at me harder than my mother? I had learned to be prepared to argue or debate from childhood because not only did my mother enjoy it, she wanted me to formulate my arguments and have thought through everything before I challenged someone. As much as our politics differ, I love my ma dearly for that lesson, let alone everything else she's ever done for me in my life, because she absolutely prepared me for life in the General Assembly, where the kind of story you tell needs to be the one that can win an argument.

When my second session started, I was prepared to bring my arguments to the table, not wait for someone else to ask me first. There's a photo of me in the *Richmond Times-Dispatch* on opening day of my second session taking a knee next to now–former delegate Chris Peace, going over the text of my bill to create a Freedom of Information Act ombudsman, which he seemed to be interested in as chairman of the committee where the bill was headed. I also learned that lobbyists love gossiping with one another—surprise!— so when some of them saw me in a House Counties, Cities and Towns Committee asking questions and grilling people about the policy minutiae of land-use issues that I learned from a decade of covering local governments, word got around that I knew my shit. The one problem was that I was a little too eager to put that on display and the subcommittee chair at my first meeting told me, "Don't cross-examine the witnesses. Everything goes through the chair."

That freshman folly aside, the reputation I earned in subcommittee was that I wasn't a reflexive partisan and I clearly enjoyed the work, even if I talked too much. That played out in my favor in 2019 when I scored what was possibly my most consequential victory on an otherwise benign bill.

To begin, it was "crossover" day: the day the House and the Senate had to complete their work on their own legislation before the House bills "crossed over" to the Senate and the Senate bills "crossed over" to the House. I had a bill that the Department of Social Services asked me to carry and, suffice it to say, the bill was vetted. Gigi and I had worked out every single detail possible with that bill in advance with DSS, and it passed through two different committees before making it to the House floor, so it was vetted as all hell. Just when I thought the bill was in the clear, I was told that the Republicans were planning to send it back to committee, which would have essentially killed it. When the clerk of the House called up my bill, I saw one Republican, Del. Lee Ware, start to rise in order to make his motion to send the bill back, and I jolted up, grabbed my mic, and said, "Mr. Speaker!" He called on me and I asked for the bill to go by temporarily. The move caught the other members off guard, but they agreed by voice vote to allow it.

What follows here takes a dive into procedural stuff, but it has a larger point that goes beyond the legislature: Learn the rules to whatever it is that you're doing. Knowing the rules allows you to exercise power without tripping up. In this case, Marcus Simon and I made the case that my bill had been vetted by two different committees. Eileen Filler-Corn privately mentioned to the other side's leadership that if they wanted Democratic support for one of their bills that was in trouble, they needed to work with me in good faith on mine.

The majority leader explained that his caucus had spent a long time debating the bill. When he referred to me, though, he first said "her" before quickly cutting himself off and saying "the delegate's . . ."

as a subtle reminder that my presence as a transgender woman on the floor of the House of Delegates still made some members uneasy.

Still, he called for the vote, saying he would be voting no but that other members could vote as they pleased. They did, and it passed, 58 to 40, with Lee Ware, chairman of the Finance Committee, voting yea.

The bill then did fine in committee, except that a couple of Republican senators weren't too happy with it. I worked out a deal for an amendment with one of them, but the amendment that appeared wasn't what we agreed to and that was the version that passed the Senate.

I had a choice: Reject the amendment and put the bill into conference or pass it and ask for the governor to send down an amendment to fix it. The former would have surely resulted in the death of the bill, so I reluctantly accepted the amendment, sent it to the governor, and eventually we voted on the governor's amendment and it died, 46 to 51.

I moved to reconsider the vote, this time trying all sorts of legislative maneuvering that most of my colleagues didn't even follow. We voted again and this time, everyone was seated . . . except for one Republican.

The vote went up. My side all voted green . . . but the numbers on the scoreboard just . . . weren't . . . adding . . . up . . .

"The clerk will close the roll," said the Speaker.

"Ayes forty-nine, nays forty-nine. The governor's recommendation is rejected."

Damn it.

As I found out, you can only win in the minority so many times. Goodwill and good deeds will only carry you so far when the majority has decided you've had enough. Still, I had demonstrated to myself, if to no one else, that I had a veteran's understanding of procedure despite being a freshman.

After two years of walking on eggshells in the minority, I didn't have to do that anymore when we were in the majority. At 55 to 45, it became much easier to set the agenda for those outside my caucus. Inside, we of course still had a power structure and you still had to earn votes for your bills from your caucus mates.

Outside, however, I was now in a power position to negotiate with various groups, inside and outside the legislature. It helped me pass a bill to ban aboveground transmission lines through the western part of my district for ten years, after a similar bill had died a year earlier, since I now could more reliably count on the votes needed to pass it.

One thing I also hadn't done as a member of the minority was speak often on LGBTQ issues on the House floor. Frankly, only one LGBTQ bill even made it to the House floor, to allow for gender-neutral surrogacy laws. The floor fight was epic and passionate to say the least, especially because a Republican former governor and former senator's chief of staff was pushing for it on behalf of his husband and children after a traumatic event they went through together as a family. Still, I was asked not to speak on that bill, to defer to the veteran Democratic members, as the Republicans fought among themselves. Standing up to speak as a trans woman on an issue that absolutely affects trans women could scare them away from backing it because, well, Richmond. What else can I say?

The only LGBTQ speech I gave on the House floor was for Black History Month, when I introduced a number of Black trans women in the gallery and spoke about the contributions one of them made to the greater Richmond community: Zakia McKensey. Republican members rolled their eyes and started talking to one another as I spoke, ignoring me when I told them that the average life expectancy of a Black trans woman in some cities was thirty-four—which happened to be my age at the time I spoke. The only differences: I'm not Black and I don't live in a city. I wanted to highlight that discrepancy, but it didn't seem to resonate on the other side of the aisle beyond a Republican staffer stopping me near an elevator to compliment me for it.

Then in the majority, I didn't have to give a shit about whether other members were going to get pissy or dismissive because I wanted to protect my LGBTQ constituents. In fact, we had twenty years' worth of LGBTQ equality bills that had always died when we were in the minority and now finally could get passed, so we had lots of debates on LGBTQ issues from 2020 to 2021 before losing the majority again.

Or, well, actually—we had very few debates on the House floor. It was more like Democrats introduced bills, most Republicans voted against them, and they passed without a word from the other side. Simply put, LGBTQ equality had become a losing issue for Republicans statewide, so there was no point in engaging—except for one member: Del. Dave LaRock.

During my first session, he had asked me to step outside of the capitol to catch a "breath of fresh air" with him. Knowing he was super close with my predecessor and had said horrendously transphobic comments repeatedly, the anthropological side of my brain took him up on it, if for no other reason than to find out what he really wanted.

Sure enough, he asked me about my relationship with God and told me to remember that "God is listening."

I stopped him and told him there was nothing he was going to tell me that I hadn't heard in thirteen years of Catholic schools. He admitted he forgot that part of my biography and I just reamed him for his transphobia, like telling a newspaper that transgender people shouldn't be allowed to teach kindergarten because we could confuse children. I mentioned how comments like his lead to trans kids trying to kill themselves because they don't feel welcomed or understood by adults in positions of power, then headed back inside.

In 2020, with a Democratic majority and a major equality bill up from now former delegate Mark Levine, who's the third out gay man to serve in the House of Delegates—the second who was out before being elected—Dave LaRock decided to launch another transphobic tirade, trying to make a martyr out of a teacher who lost his job after he refused to acknowledge a transgender boy in his class as the boy who he is, despite his school board's LGBTQ-inclusive nondiscrimination policy.

I'd had enough. I looked over my right shoulder, turned my head to one of our co-whips, and told him, "Mike, I'm going in."

"It's unfortunate that those who demand tolerance the loudest want to push anyone who does not conform," said LaRock.

I knew that boy who the teacher wouldn't refer to by his proper pronouns. He didn't need to be vilified yet again. I pressed the yellow "Request to Speak" button. "Keep it short," Del. Mike Mullin instructed me as I grabbed the microphone on my desk, jacking my left elbow behind my shoulder as if to pull a lawnmower cord. Before I spoke, I looked at a picture of two transgender teenagers standing at my sides during Equality Virginia's Commonwealth Gala in 2019: Morgan and James.

Morgan was the girl who had been left by herself with a panic attack in a hallway during a lockdown drill when school officials refused to let her enter any locker room. James was the boy singled out by the teacher now being lionized on the House floor.

Now given time to speak, I flipped my hair back over my right shoulder and told the stories of both teenagers. "And if you believe in a deity, then you have to understand that that deity made James who he is and made Morgan who she is," I said. I could have stopped there, but I knew no one else in that chamber knew what it was like to be transgender like Morgan or James . . . except for me.

"I was too afraid to be them," I told the members, my voice cracking with emotion. "I was too afraid to tell anyone who I was because that stigma and that fear is so real." My voice boomed. "You have no idea what it's like to be Morgan or what it's like to be James. You don't know until you have lived it, until you have cried yourself to sleep over it. No child in the commonwealth of Virginia and no person in the commonwealth of Virginia should ever be afraid to be who they are and be that well and to thrive because of who they are, not despite it and not for what discriminatory politicians tell them they're supposed to be."

I breathed and looked down at my microphone to close my speech. "Let's pass this bill." The Democratic members stood for twelve seconds to applaud, just as I had seen for Morgan and James ten months earlier. Then we finally voted, the clerk called the vote, and the Speaker of the House confirmed it:

"Ayes fifty-nine, nays thirty-nine. The bill passes."

Finding your voice in politics can be intimidating when you're new and you're not the person in power. The same goes when you're new to a cause, a job, or whatever else you're passionate about. There are often people who have been around longer than you, who know the ropes. And some of them want to be helpful . . . but others either can't or simply won't be helpful. Some will even be malicious: they want you to fail because you're getting in their way.

For all of that, your most honest internal default setting, in which you don't trip over yourself and stumble over how you think people want you to be, is to just be authentic. You don't have to keep track of who you are to some people and who you are to others. I say this as someone who inherently wants to be liked: If they don't respect you, they're not worth your time. If they do, though, let 'em know who you *are*, not who you think they want you to be.

EPILOGUE

DANICA ROEM WANTS A BOOK DEAL

—Mail advertisement, paid for by the Republican Party of
Virginia, authorized by Bob Marshall, candidate for
Delegate, 2017

R ight as I was finishing the first draft of this book, one of my cousins posted a transphobic political cartoon that's been making the rounds for years now. In it, a horseshoe-haired bald guy with a nineteenth-century western mustache is standing over a toilet, presumably peeing while yelling at a girl, "Whats [*sic*] your problem [*sic*] you little bigot? Havent [*sic*] you seen a lady pee before?"

Never mind the lack of a stall around the toilet or, apparently, a lock on the door marked WOMEN. The girl clutches the leg of her mom and says, "Mommy [*sic*] thats [*sic*] not a lady!!" only to hear, "Shhhhh . . . We arent [*sic*] allowed to speak the truth anymore . . ." in response. The caption: "Where we'll end up if you don't act soon."

Now, this raises a few questions: what action is this calling for? Perhaps a ban on waxing olde-timey mustaches? Understandable, though it'll never make it through committee unamended in the legislature. Perhaps installing locks on doors instead of the metal plate meant for pushing it open even though it's a one-toilet restroom? Also possible, though I'm not sure if government intervention is warranted. Or maybe, it's the use of two apostrophes in the caption when four are missing from the quote boxes? I mean, the same people who want to instate English as the official language of the United States sure do have a way of butchering the written word, so I'm not sure how laws written in text will help here.

All of that is to say that, even today, transphobia still very, very much exists. It's a reminder to those of us in progressive and Democratic bubbles that what we may consider a 101 course in understanding trans identities (which was soooo 2015) is still a conversation we need to have. The same goes for whatever you find in your life that makes you different or misunderstood: every time you share your own story, you do something to counteract another narrative that sometimes lurks in the shadows and other times is not so subtle.

I can't reach everyone, though Viking is at least rolling the dice enough to give little ol' me the opportunity to expand the number of people I can open up to. Regardless of whether you have the opportunity to write a book, telling your own story matters. You can challenge conventional wisdom or reinforce it in your own circles. Every civil rights struggle and social movement has only been successful because enough people gave enough of a shit to talk about it and do something about it. Word of mouth—or, in the modern era, pixel—still matters. Being vulnerable enough to be visible gives you a platform to tell someone, who you may not have even known needed to hear a relatable or inspiring story like yours, the opportunity to connect, either with you personally or with the message that you put out into your own corner of the world or web.

Your story can also tell other people who've been stuck in a rigid line of thinking to maybe, just maybe, consider that the whole world isn't binary; that their worldview may just be challenged from time to time by someone who has different lived experiences, or even similar experiences with alternate endings. We've seen that conversation happen a lot when police brutality makes the news and random, regular people share stories about their interactions with the police and quickly learn that two different people being pulled over or stopped for the same thing can have extraordinarily different outcomes, depending on where they live, their gender, and the color of their skin.

Social media, and the ability to stay in touch with a lot of people who would otherwise be long-lost memories, means your ability to influence a large number of people—and to be influenced by those same people—is the greatest it's ever been. That creates an interconnectedness and interdependency, as well as a feedback loop, from which people you may very well never see again in person can raise you up or bring you down—and vice versa. That will only increase in the future. And, because our species is prone to groupthink, our push for inclusivity may very well mean we'll inevitably weed out those we see causing us pain or discomfort in favor of those who amplify our echo chamber. This is reinforced even more through self-selective redlining and segregation, where we move toward people who are like us. I would argue that while no one needs to have trolls in their lives (sorry, 1980s spiky pink-haired dolls . . .), there is value in challenging someone's worldview when what they're saying just doesn't align with your lived experiences and the reality you've witnessed. That inevitably means you'll need to share your story, because someone else may just learn from it.

When my cousin wrote a number of problematic things about trans people making "choices" about who we are and how we should all use unisex stalls, I didn't take that as a moment to bash him or unfriend him and vaguebook some shit about getting rid of bigots in my life. My family's experienced enough death, loss, and trauma that I know you don't throw someone away just because they say or

do something frustrating. That's really reserved only for when someone's truly toxic. Sometimes it's just a learning moment.

I chose to believe the latter and shared a story one of my mentors
once wrote about me as a trans woman and a friend of hers who's a
trans guy with a beard and neck tattoos, explaining that when you
target trans women with bathroom laws, you're targeting trans men,
too. It's truly incredible how the very existence of trans men is so
often overlooked in this equation and that, when confronted with
the idea that, yes, trans men exist, you can, in slow motion, watch
someone's mind melt into cheese as they realize, "You mean . . . that
guy . . . is . . . TRANSGENDER?! Whaaaaat?!"

I added that the problem with telling a woman who's trans to just
use the unisex room is telling her that she doesn't belong. In my case,
every official document I have (driver's license, passport, etc.) identi-
fies me as a woman who, when she really has to pee, then uses the
women's room—though trans people don't always have the luxury of
having our documents match our gender expression or identity.

As for the prevalence of unisex restrooms, here's a take, just from
Manassas: My favorite place to get breakfast is Yorkshire Restaurant. It's a small little diner right off, of course, Route 28. For lunch,
I might stop at Tony's NY Pizza in Manassas, which moved in 2020
from its original Mathis Avenue location to Manassas Junction. For
dinner, the best spot in town is Bella Vita, an Italian restaurant with
Rat Pack tunes and decor. My family's been eating there since it
opened.

Every one of those spots have two restrooms and, as of this writing, neither are unisex. Our non-chain, local coffeeshops are the
same. Same at the places where I get my hair done and even the
concert halls where I see my favorite heavy metal bands. It may seem
like a lot of places are changing by having unisex restrooms, but the

reality is that they're still few and far between. Even if you don't know any nonbinary people who would be happy to use one, just think: whatever cuts down the line is always a good thing.

Anyway, I also explained to my cousin that my life isn't the product of a "Ya know, I think I'm going to be trans today" moment. I have the same feeling today at thirty-seven that I did when I was ten and scared to death to tell anyone because I knew I would get my ass kicked at school and disappoint my family at home. I didn't want to hurt anyone by coming out . . . all while internally suffocating myself until I was absolutely done, and by the time I was twenty-eight, my heart was dying inside.

I have always sworn I would never, ever contemplate suicide, because I know how it wrecks a family. But about two out of every five trans people do attempt suicide at some point in their lives—we're constantly told our existence is wrong by people who've never walked a mile in our shoes, and we learn to internalize that instead of just being ourselves. That's reality.

So instead of that happening to me, when I couldn't take it anymore, I saw a psychologist. She affirmed that I had/have gender dysphoria in adolescents and adults (ICD-10; F-64.1*) and the best treatment for me was to transition—and *all* that would come with it. That's not me saying, "I choose . . . this!" That's three different doctors (psychologist, endocrinologist, and voice therapist) evaluating me, reviewing my options, and working together on a treatment plan—transition—that helps so my exterior matches my interior as close as can be after three decades of it not. That's not what every trans person will go through and you don't have to have gatekeepers

---

*The International Statistical Classification of Diseases and Related Health Problems diagnostic manual.

to tell you who you are; but if you find someone who you connect with, who specializes in taking care of someone like you, whether or not you're trans, and you can afford to see that person, it certainly doesn't hurt to talk out how you're feeling about life and where you want to go from there.

I can't describe what living with that is like to someone who hasn't lived it. If there is a choice to be made about being transgender, it's in accepting who you are or letting it hurt you until you reach a breaking point. Nearly 9.5 years since my first therapy session, I'm now in a place where I'm me, full time, all day, every day. Because I transitioned, I met my partner and stepdaughter. I also have what, to me, is the best job in Virginia, public service, and the people I serve seem to think I'm doing a pretty good job, or at least they did when they renewed my contract for another two years in 2019 and again in 2021.

Because I came out, I'm now recognized for being the woman I've always known I was since I was a kid, even if I'm different from cisgender women. And, for years now, I've exclusively used the women's room, because it's there for women like me, just like every other woman who really, really has to pee.

For all of my identifiers, "legislator" and "candidate" are what give me an outsized platform to serve and tell stories; "metalhead" is what expresses my personality; "trans woman" is who I've known myself to be and fought so hard to present; and "girlfriend" and "stepmom" are those constant reminders that there is hope, compared to what's been and what could be. As of the publication of this book, I'll be the same age my dad was when, to paraphrase a letter from his brother I found in my childhood closet, his demons finally stopped haunting him as he exited the world by his own hand. "Child of sui-cide" doesn't typically go into the bio section of a social media account or on a résumé under the name and address or next to the high school GPA, but it is still something that informs your worldview about trauma, empathy, and how quickly what's around us can permanently change—even when you seem like you have it made.

That moment more than thirty-four years ago could have up-ended my family, but my mother, the grittiest person I'll ever know, refused to let it destroy her, her children, or the world she was making for all three of us. She taught me that you don't give up on some-thing you've started until you've accomplished what you set out to do in the first place. The world can really, truly seem like a boiling-hot mess because, well, it is. At the same time, we can figure out how to make it through times like these, sharing stories as we go that blaze the trail for the people who come after us to follow.

Rightfully so (says the politician) that elections and power struc-tures drive the macro narrative about where our communities, coun-tries, and world are headed. Just because people in power seem detached from the reality of what it means to struggle, that doesn't mean that elections, power, and our future should be left as spectator sports. *We* are in charge of saying what power looks like—even if it comes with a rainbow headscarf inside of a $324 '92 Dodge Shadow rust bucket. *We* decide who is and isn't electable, even if she made out with a guy wearing sweatpants sitting shotgun in said Dirty Dodge before she physically transitioned, let alone ran for office.

When someone tells you that no one's going to support your kind of leadership, they're forgetting that we no longer live in a world where people can tell you what they want. They have to show you. Now it's time to stop reading someone else's story and go tell your own.

Acknowledgments

First, there's no way I would have made my (extended) deadlines for this book without the help of Lindsay Bubar keeping me on track, spending hours on the phone extracting stories from me, and molding together something that's actually presentable to the public.

Next, endless thank-yous to senior editor Emily Wunderlich at Viking for your absolute restraint/patience as I dawdled and screamed my way over the finish line. Thank you for taking the deep dives over days' worth of video conferences and prodding my brain for the funny and good stuff, and especially for keeping your wonderful sense of humor intact. Also, lots of love to the whole Viking team who pitched in, including Nidhi Pugalia.

Now, everyone who contributed to this book worked really hard on it and, in a way, you're all winners. But, in another more *Simpsons*-esque way, my agent Anna Sproul-Latimer of Neon Literary is *the* winner. If anyone else ever approaches me with a business card with the handwritten scrawl "I hope you'll choo-choo-choose me" on it next to a bee, I'll scream, "No! That seat's taken!" Thank you so much for never giving up in the ::*deep breath*:: nearly 4.5 years of labor it took to finally give birth to this book. For all you've done for me, I like to think I've given you something back: mainly, the time you told me, "You've made me a worse person." <3

Okay, away from book-world but also linked to this, my story as a public servant is only possible because of my campaign team, who made it possible for me to earn election to office, and my policy team, who made it possible to do the people's business while in office.

At the forefront of all of that, there are no two people I trust more in politics, and in pretty much most of my life, than Ethan Damon and Gigi Slais, who will always have my endless gratitude for changing what's possible in politics with me: Ethan for leading the way twice, in 2017 and 2019, and for continuing to help me out in Richmond and giving guidance to Stephanie Medina and team for 2021; and Gigi for not only volunteering time and hustle on the campaign trail but steering the ship in Richmond to twenty-three House bill signings and leading the best constituent service team on the planet in the district in 2018, 2019, 2020, and 2021. Thank you also to everyone who trained me in how to run for office: the Victory Institute, Emerge Virginia, the Virginia House Democratic Caucus, Atif Qarni, and Don Shaw.

Now, for my campaign teams:

2017 & beyond: Thank you to my finance director, Rohan, and my field team of Chris, Maria, Brad, Jamie, Quinn, Gordon, Kyle, and Hannah; my consultants Alan Moore and Moore Campaigns; Scott Kozar and The New Media Firm, Joshua Ulibarri and Meryl O'Bryan and Lake Research, the folks at Grindstone Research and the Virginia House Democratic Caucus—specifically Trent, Trevor, Katie, and Jessica—and the coordinated campaign.

2019 & beyond: Thank you to my finance consultant Matthew "Money" McClellan, Courtney and Phil at Asana, field director Terence Stovall, and our field team of Myles, Rose, and Natalia, as well as our researchers, Alan Reger and Reger Research, and the team at Sena | Kozar Strategies.

2021: Thank you to Stephanie Medina for taking over the ship, Izzy from the coordinated campaign, Chartu and Jordan from our finance team, deputy campaign manager Ethan Gardner, and our field fellows Silas, Jacob, Luke, and Ethan (cubed), and our friends Sean Meloy at the Victory Fund and Sara Forman, Andrew Whalen, and Shawn Werner at EMILY's List. Thank you also to Pete Gibson at Gibson Print, ASAP Printing, and Tom Faraci for making us quite literally look good!

For all three campaigns, thank you so, so, so much to our legions of volunteers, donors, advocacy organizations/partners, and, of course, our voters. You make it all worthwhile. Thank you also to my kitchen cabinet of advice dispensers: Jeanette "Walk in the park" Hunsberger, Neil "Yup, it's dead" Linderman, Chris "The woooorst" Peleo-Lazar, and Donald "Diagram this sentence" Gilliland.

From my policy team, thank you to Maria, Jessie, Ethan G., Bailey, Gordon, Hannah, Philomenia, all of our administrative assistants, and the scores of constituents and advocates who often drove two hours to Richmond to testify for thirty seconds for our bills, showed up to our town halls, and made the case for change. I'm grateful.

From my journalism career, I'm especially grateful for the nine years and two months that I had the privilege to call Tara "Where's my story?!" Courtland my boss and for the six years since then that I've been able to call you and your family my friends/session roommates. Thank you for making this life possible. Also, special thanks to Brian "Shield Law" Karem, the funniest person I've ever worked with at any job and a genuine mentor. Thank you also to all the editors and staff writers at *The Hotline* who provided me the best political education I ever could have had, especially Amy, John, and Quinn for opening the door to D.C. politics for a weekly newspaper reporter from Manassas in December 2009. Thanks also to Laura,

Heather, and the Yoga Alliance team who were so kind and so cool to work with. I truly miss y'all.

To my TUH goon squad, SBU Champs and professors ("Stump the Lawyer," anyone?), my CRH bandmates, and the whole D/M/V metal scene—especially all of our Jaxx and Ball's Bluff alumni: You've been the backbone of my social life for twenty years now. So much love also to the remarkable women in my life who gave me permission to be me, especially Lauren, Kristina, Toni, Nora, Connie, Rachel, and so, so many of you who gave me a second family. My heart's in debt to you for all my days.

And, of course, thank you to my ma for choosing Manassas for this life I live and being the best debate partner I'll ever have, bar none. "Of course I can handle Richmond—my mother's from the Bronx!" Thank you to my sister, Katie, for letting me raid your CD collection for those Metallica CDs and introducing me to the world of music that's been my passion and joy for twenty-four years and counting. It's led me to where I am now and it was all under your influence. Thank you to Scott for being a rock for my ma and for all your kindness to our family for more than two decades. And, of course, to Tal, Ellu, and my Finnish family of choice (okay, okay: you too, LK)—Minä rakastan sinua. <3

Finally, to the people of the 13th District of the Virginia House of Delegates: Manassas. Manassas Park. Gainesville. Haymarket. No matter how the district lines change or whatever I do in public life, you're what makes our community my lifelong home. I'm grateful to the point of tears. No one could have imagined giving someone like me a chance in this line of work. You did, and we've changed our little part of Northern Virginia together. From the top, middle, and bottom of my heart, thank you.